THE
ESSENCE
OF
SOCIAL RESEARCH

A Copernican Revolution

The Free Press–New York
Collier-Macmillan Publishers–London

Charles W. Lachenmeyer

THE
ESSENCE
OF
SOCIAL RESEARCH

A Copernican Revolution

The Free Press
A Division of Macmillan Publishing Co., Inc.
866 Third Avenue, New York, New York 10022

Collier-Macmillan Canada Ltd., Toronto, Ontario

Library of Congress Catalog Card Number: 72-87692

1   2   3   4   5   6   7   8   9   10

CONTENTS

PREFACE

At present, social science does not look like natural science. If one assumes the desirability of the natural science model, this failure of resemblance can be interpreted as a deficiency. This familiar argument has an equally familiar rebuttal: "Perhaps social science should not look like natural science. Perhaps it will develop in quite different directions." This rebuttal is not answerable, nor is it demonstrable. What social science *will* look like is an open question. On the other hand, as the natural-science model has proven tremendously successful, it is reasonable to predict equal success for social science if it approximates that model. More correctly, it is more reasonable to advocate this position than to lay one's bets on a future form that has no empirical reference.

The real question is, "How well has social science approximated the natural-science model?" This question is preferable in two senses. First, it is fully answerable: A model of natural science must be developed, and the necessary comparisons can then be made to judge relative success of social science. Second, this question is preferable because in seeking its answer an important illusion is dispelled.

There is a movement coalescing among social scientists that damns the positivist-empiricist tradition. In brief, it maintains that this tradition has caused more harm than good and has impeded the acquisition of meaningful knowledge about man's behavior. "Dehumanization" is the key slogan of this movement. Contemporary examples are abundantly cited. The ones I have heard over and over refer to Project Camelot and the Rand Institute Vietnam war games.

The illusion to be dispelled is that this movement has merit because the idea of a social science is morally corrupt. The real issue is that social science has been an imperfect science. One important secondary gain to be had from attempting to compare social science to natural science is the demonstration of how imperfect a science social science has really been. As a social scientist I have come to accept methodological procedures that are sadly inadequate in the name of Science, when I really did not know what Science was all about.

This book will attempt to assess the scientific adequacy of social science to answer the questions I have posed. It is my understanding that social science has evolved in the right direction, but not quite far enough. I hope to convey my reasoning to the reader.

Acknowledgments must be extended to my family. My wife Julie has contributed greatly in thought and insight both as companion and fellow professional. My son, Nathaniel, is too young to understand fully, but he knows that "Daddy write a book." He has contributed several important insights, given his perspective as a newcomer to the world of language-games. Finally, George (my dog) has exercised me to the point of exemplary stamina and physical conditioning.

Again, Mrs. Elizabeth Beck has done an exemplary typing job in terms of accuracy and speed.

THE
ESSENCE
OF
SOCIAL RESEARCH

A Copernican Revolution

Introduction

Why another book about social research? How is this book different? Given the sheer bulk of the literature in research methodology, these questions must be answered.

Social research methodologists have developed elaborate and sophisticated treatments of methodology. For example, Kerlinger's popular text treats topics ranging from set theory to questionnaire design; Phillip's from science as communication to mathematical models; Simon's from practical precepts of research to the logic of inductive statistics.[1] However, these presentations cannot properly be called theories of research methodology. Principles of research are formulated, but they are not expressed as, nor do they generate, testable hypotheses. Further, no relations between principles are established.

1

Hence, there is no mention of what the use of inductive statistics implies for replication or what the use of certain data types implies for procedural design.

This strange lack of theoretical integration by theorists of theory and research is common to all texts on the subject. However, there have been scattered attempts at integration in the more esoteric literature. Pittinger *et al.*[2] wrote about the relationship between the interviewer's "first five minutes" with the respondent and the subsequent responding of each to the other as the interview progresses. Similarly, there has been some research on the reactions of respondents to different attributes of interviewers and of questionnaire design. There is also much research that constructs or tests hypotheses relating the interview or questionnaire instrument or its mode of use to the validity and reliability of the subject's responses.[3] Rosenthal's experiments[4] and Friedman's extensive analysis[5] having to do with experimental methodology extend these metatheoretic attempts to this domain: both endeavors relate explicit differences in experimenter behavior or experimental setting to differential subject behavior.

Although this metatheoretical literature does exist (and is far more extensive than my synopsis implies), it does not pretend to form a coherent theory of research; the universe of discourse in each case is usually restricted to specific social-research procedures that are problematic. It is instructive to note that, even within these segmented confines, a sharply critical theme emerges. These scattered attempts at metatheory construction usually work backwards: particular sources of methodological error are assumed and hypotheses are formulated to predict them. In any event, the effect is the same: a critical evaluation of social research. A metatheory of research apparently would generate a critical perspective.

Thus, textbooks about social-research methodology tend to be atheoretical and uncritical. Where metatheories of research methodology exist, they are duly critical but restricted and fragmented. Such is the state of affairs in research about social research by social scientists.

There is another approach to this subject that has received wide attention among philosophers and historians and to a more limited extent among sociologists. The procedures, methodologies, and behavior of scientists are analyzed. Principles are derived that seek to describe and explain "science." These principles are codified and refined and evaluated. Then the product is critically applied to social-science theory and methodology. This is the domain of the philosophy and the history of science.

Any attempted cataloguing of these disciplines would require an encyclopedic treatise. Among the many books on these subjects, the ones most familiar to social scientists include those by Hempel, Kaplan, Kemeny, Kuhn, Nagel, and Popper.[6] There are also several journals specifically designed for this purpose; including *The International Journal of the Philosophy of Social Science* and *Theory and Decision*. And this is not to mention those books and journals in these areas whose expressed purpose is the analysis of science and not specifically social science, but from which social scientists freely borrow in their labors toward a metatheory of social research.

Despite this diversity of output, this approach has proven to be of limited utility because of the equivocation of the derivable metatheoretic principles. The speculations of the philosophers and historians of science have not been codified or used as the base to derive testable hypotheses. Furthermore, they are not meant to be such. Popper's extensive arguments against "psychologizing" his logic of scientific inquiry[7] are meant as a clear indication that his descriptive devices should not be confused with predictive ones. Likewise, Hempel's famous (and much abused) concepts of "meaning analysis" and "empirical analysis"[8] are meant to be descriptive of part of the theory and research development process, not as predictors of the requisite action of scientists in developing sound theories. Dumont and Wilson's paper[9] applying these concepts to sociological research is illustrative of this confusion: in codifying what most researchers do anyway (define their terms and measure their events), they sound as if they have developed a program for improving sociological research.

However, social scientists cannot be completely blamed for this confusion, for philosophers and historians of science have often behaved as if their speculations were theories of theory construction without putting up a red flag and most certainly without rigorously testing the hypotheses they put forth. So Kaplan, Kemeny, and Nagel[10] can all offer favorable evaluations of social science, while hardcore social-science researchers like Sidman[11] can be highly critical. The difference is the predictable consequence of the difference between men who theorize about theory construction and men who construct theories. The former bring a formidable conceptual apparatus to bear, but with limited direct *experience* with the referents of the concepts. Their knowledge is of the finished product of the research or reports about how the research was conducted and not of the doing of the research. The latter usually labor without that conceptual apparatus, but with extensive knowledge of the practicalities of research. Their knowledge is experientially based. To put it simply, paraphrasing Einstein, the crucial difference between theorists of theory construction and those who construct theories is the difference between studying what scientists (or others) say they do and what scientists do.

This schism can be bridged by treating the speculations about theory construction as theories about theory construction and at some point testing them. As the philosophers and historians have not done so, although their endeavors are exhaustive, social scientists are left with principles of theory construction that they cannot wield critically.

This book will attempt to bridge the gap between the exhaustive but uncritical approach of philosophers and historians of science and the segmented but critical approach of meta-theoretical social scientists. A critical evaluation of social research will be preceded by a model of scientific research that is assumed to be exhaustive. As the book will not catalogue the procedural choices available to the social researcher, it is not to be confused with a traditional research-methods textbook. It is meant as a reintroduction to research methodology and a critical reanalysis of existing social research.

SCIENCE AS COMMUNICATION

Any act of communication is describable as the transmission of information between actors. In the prototypic case, two actors exchange information in one-way or two-way communication. In the first case, one actor is the source, the other the receiver; in the second, one actor is source, the other is receiver, and the roles are reversed according to the sequence of the information transfer. Where the communication is about events in the world, a second information transfer can be postulated between the events and both actors. Diagrammatically, this can be illustrated:

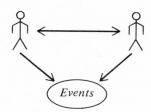

The double-headed arrows represent reciprocal information transfers between the stick-men actors and between the stick-men actors and the real world "events." Note that the question of sequence is concealed by the double-headed arrows. This added complexity is acknowledged but assumed away for the moment.

Events in the domain may be present or absent. When they are present either actor can utilize pointing as an aid to communication, thereby relieving himself of many burdensome linguistic problems. In fact, the effect of pointing simplifies the process of communication by reducing the number of linguistic units needed to convey a message. Most notably, any feedback devices like "questions" about meaning are largely unnecessary. In considering the prototypic communicative act the simplification resulting from assuming events to be present makes the model nonrepresentative because much communication is not denotative. Conversely, assuming the events to be absent complicates the model (possibly) to the point of nonrepresentativeness. If the analyst can assume the events to be absent, there are no constraints on him: nonmeaningful words can have their meaning assumed; different types of meaning can be posited endlessly with no confirmation of their existence; the meaning of words can be debated through many levels of meta-analyses with no terminus; and so on.

The optimal model of communication will include provision for analysis based on the presence *or* the absence of the events in the domain. This is easily accomplished by emphasizing the developmental aspect of any communicative sequence. That is, the actors can be said to construct messages that adequately refer to (in whatever sense) the events in their domain, and the test of the adequacy of these messages is the degree to which they can be said to be representative under the restriction of the events being absent. The crucial test for any message, in this sense, is how well it can be said to designate the events given their absence.

By adding an assumption that further restricts the model, the requisite *empirical conditions* for this test can be specified. The assumption is that a predictable set of actions is contingent on the communicative sequence. To put it differently, the communicative sequence is assumed to have a terminus and a purpose. The purpose is the performance of a limited, specifiable action or set of actions. Testable hypotheses of the following form are thereby derivable: "If messages X and Y that are supposed to designate events X^1 and Y^1, and events X^1 and Y^1 are not present, then actions A, B by the actors," assuming these actions to be contingent outcomes of messages X and Y. The test of these hypotheses is also a test of the adequacy of the messages.

A test of the *goodness of fit* of a message can be made without this assumption. One can record the percentage of agreement among users of certain messages that the messages do designate certain specified events. The percentage becomes a measure of the adequacy of the messages. This measure would presumably apply to the messages *qua* messages in the presence or absence of the appropriate events. All that is required is some way of independently designating the events in question. The hypotheses in this type test will be of the form: "If events X^1 and Y^1 (designated independently by messages U, V), then messages X and Y will be confirmed Z times as designators of these events."

This prototypic model of communication with its implied tests of communicative adequacy suggests further complications for its complete specification. One can specify the attributes of the actors, their verbal and nonverbal message-linked actions, the time and place of the actions, and the number, types, and actions of any others present who influence the communication sequence. Further, one can draw boundaries around the communicating actors and specify values for each of these parameters that demarcate the intrinsic and extrinsic context of the communication.

The relevant *attributes of the actor* can include labels he assigns to himself or labels assigned to him by others. Thus an actor may label himself by profession or training: "I'm a doctor" or "I've been through graduate school"; or by behavior patterns or emotional states he assigns to himself: "I'm hostile" or "I'm good-natured"; or by any other means. Or an actor may be labeled these things by others. The important *actor actions* include anything he does or says that can be construed as a message or as influencing a message. Communication theory[12] analyzes all behavior as message or potential message, so that a person's posture is a message just as much as his words; it may also be a message that frames his linguistic messages. In fact, *double-bind theory*[13] is a communication theory that analyzes the behavioral outcomes contingent on communication sequences in which messages and metamessages of all types conflict. Such is the possible complexity represented by an analysis of actor actions.

The *place* of the communication can be described as the physical dimensions of the room, building, field, or whatever in which the communication occurs; as any properties of the setting, like the number of doors or windows; as the distance between actors; or as the labels attached to the setting according to its designated use, like "classroom," "corridor," "bank," and the like. The *time* of the communication can be a temporal unit of any length: second, minute, hour, day, week, month, year, decade, century. Finally, *presence of others* can be analyzed according to actor labels, numbers, spatial arrangements, or actions of the audience or observers of the communication sequence.

The boundaries separating the intrinsic and extrinsic context of communication can be affixed according to these parameters in any fashion deemed appropriate. An actor may be said to have a past learning-history that affects his communications or a particular status that he brings to the communication. Actions may be said to be behavior patterns established prior to the communication. The place of the communication can be specified as the physical location of the actors or as the extrinsic setting of this physical location. The latter can influence the communication directly through the actions of the actors: e.g., actors in offices within courthouses act differently than actors in offices within hospitals. Or it can influence the communication through the actor's awareness that he is in a place within a larger setting: e.g., the same actor in the same office will act differently if he knows that that office is in a courthouse than if he knows it to be in a hospital. Likewise, one can embed the time of the communication sequence within a larger extrinsic time interval: a given communication sequence may last five minutes but the fact that it occurs on a certain day of the week may be significant. Finally, the others present during the sequence can be specified as the immediate observers of the sequence or as (purely) nonparticipants: a quarrel in Grand Central Station may be overheard by fewer than ten people but it occurs within a flood of humans.

This summary presentation is meant to be nothing more than suggestive of the possible components of any acts of communication. It obviously does not exhaust the innumerable complications such an analysis will entail. These complications are expressed by the concept of *umwelt*. This popular term in communication research has no exact English translation but is used generally to designate the entire or total context of any act of communication.[14] The question arises, "Do these components sufficiently exhaust the *umwelt* of any act of communication?" And the answer is "No," because there are as many components interacting in as many ways as the imaginative communication theorist can discover. Yet, the presentation is complete enough to initiate an analysis of science by suggesting certain directions such an inquiry should and should not pursue.

The scientific enterprise can be analyzed as a prototypic act of communication. Referring back to the diagram, the stickmen are labeled scientists, the events are the events in their domain of inquiry, and the dual information transfer is the process of research and theory construction. The test of the adequacy of this process is the same as that of the adequacy of any message in any information transfer: do the theory and codified research procedures designate the absent events in the domain in such a way that the contingent actions of those actors who utilize the information can be precisely predicted? Or, using the other criterion of message adequacy, do the scientist actors or metatheoreticians analyzing the communication of the scientist actors agree a significant percentage of the time that the theory and codified research procedures designate the events they are supposed to designate? The first question can specify many different contingent actions of several types of actors: e.g., can scientists replicate tests on the basis of the theory and research procedure information, or can applied researchers do what they are supposed to be able to do on the basis of the theory and research procedure information? The second question can specify two different levels of agreement about the information: do scientists agree (to specified percentage levels) about the designative accuracy of their theory and research procedure information, or do metatheoreticians analyzing scientific communication agree (to specified percentage levels) about the designative accuracy of this scientific accuracy? This distinction has important implications that will be discussed in the next chapter.

Further, the analysis can be extended according to the components of the communication sequence. The actors are scientists with specifiable characteristics: age, sex, race, religion, professional status including affiliation in professional organizations, prestige ranking, and the like. The actor-scientists do certain things: they employ the scientific method (what this term means will be left unspecified for the moment); they collaborate with colleagues; they do research; they write articles, books, and research proposals; and so on. The actor-scientists do these things at certain times (their work schedule) and in certain places (laboratories, libraries, offices). Finally, they do these things at these times and places in the presence of specific others, such as professional colleagues, grant administrators, or governmental or nongovernmental bureaucrats.

Similarly, the boundaries separating the intrinsic and extrinsic context of science as communication can be affixed. The scientist-actor characteristics can be distinguished from the "scientist-actor-as-man" characteristics. The educational level of the scientist may be analytically important, for example. The actions of the scientist as a citizen may be introduced into the model: e.g., how a scientist votes may be important in determining what position on a political issue his research and theory support. The laboratory or library or seminar room as place may be embedded in the larger place of the institution in which they are located: whether a scientist's lab is in a university or the Department of Defense can make a difference in the scientific communicative enterprise. Likewise, whether the scientist acts as scientist for twelve hours on Sunday as opposed to Monday can say something about the other components of the scientific enterprise for him: he may be labeled as "committed" or "professional," for example. Finally, the social influences on the scientist as scientist can differ greatly, depending on whether his scientific communicative sequence occurs in the presence of other colleagues in a research seminar or in the presence of his family and friends.

So the analysis of science as communication is practicable. Further, it can provide genuine insights into science. Kuhn's famous analysis of science[15] is instructive. It can be interpreted (in part) as an attempted specification of the relation between the *umwelt* of scientific communication and the content of that communication. His basic thesis is, first, that scientific methodology is only a component of the process of theory construction and, second, that it is not all-determining. In fact, he maintains that the historical context of science is a more important determinant: as "paradigms" of science and theory come and go, so do theories. Competing paradigms result in competing theories, and one theory becomes dominant because the paradigm becomes dominant. This thesis is interpretable within an analysis of science as communication. The concept of "paradigm" is roughly analogous to the concept *"umwelt,"* where the latter is taken to mean the extrinsic and intrinsic components of science, including both those we have mentioned and any others that can be formulated. His thesis can be roughly translated as follows: scientific methodology as a type of scientist action incompletely influences scientific theory and research information. A complete specification of this influence would require a complete analysis of the components of the scientific *"umwelt"* and the differential effects of these components. (This alters Kuhm's analysis only insofar as it provides greater potential specification than his historical analysis intended.)

Although Watson's less general, more popularized, and more controversial analysis[16] of one particular scientific discovery does not share the global, explanatory intent of Kuhn's analysis, it too is interpretable within an analysis of science as communication. Watson journalistically catalogues the influences on the scientific enterprise of factors that are usually presupposed to be external to it. He notes the competitiveness and professional rivalry involved in the discovery of the double helix as the model of DNA. Even more significantly, he notes the guesswork involved in a process that is supposed to be rigidly constrained by the canons of scientific methodology. His personal antecdotes, in effect, specify the interplay between the extrinsic components and the intrinsic components of a particular scientific communication sequence, i.e., that scientists behave as men rather than scientists.

These illustrations superficially evidence the insights into science that a communication analysis can have. Science becomes a particular form of social behavior and is analyzable as such. The major limitation of such an approach is its ambiguity arising from its complexity. For example, Kuhn's analysis has been faulted because he does not precisely define the concept of "paradigm".[17] Without a precise definition no definite principles or testable metahypotheses can be formulated with which to confirm or deny his arguments. This type of critique is equally applicable to the use of a concept like *"umwelt."*

Because of its ambiguity this analysis when applied to social science still suffers from the equivocation of the philosophy of science. For example, Fredericks[18] relies heavily on Kuhn to map the ideational changes in sociology in the twentieth century. He also acknowledges that his use of Kuhn's arguments violates the basic premise that the science so analyzed has a substantial amount of predictive worth. So, in effect, he is admitting that his analysis is historical and not metatheoretical. He generates no metahypotheses to guide the scientific (as opposed to humanistic) sociologist in his quest for sound predictions. Similarly, Gouldner[19] emphasizes the political influences that have operated on sociologist's theorizing. To interpret this congruently with science as communication, he is noting the effect of extrinsic actor characteristics (e.g., political persuasion), actions (e.g., politically oriented or not), place (e.g., free university vs. university heavily subsidized by Federal funds), time (e.g., pre- vs. post-World War II), and others (e.g., political persuasion of research benefactors) on the intrinsic components of sociology *qua* science. His analysis, like Fredericks', does not generate sufficient information so that one can use it to find out how to improve the predictive strength of sociological hypotheses. Or, finally, Henshel[20] poses a significant question; "(1) If sociology can create significant prediction in the manner of the physical sciences, why has this not been accomplished?" His arguments deal with the "historically critical" difference between constructing theoretical systems and utilizing natural theoretical systems in science, the political persuasion and source and amount of financing of the sociologist *qua* scientist, and the role sociology has played in negating certain world-views of society held by sociologists as well as others. Yet, this implicit communicative analysis provides no direction for the sociologist-scientist in pursuing his goal. Henshel concludes by way of addressing his original question: "Of course [this] question[s] [has] not been answered here. . . ." An analysis with apparently clearly stated goals actually is an apologia-rationalization for the weakness of one particular social science.[21]

Clearly, then, the most useful communicative analysis is one that limits its domain by focusing on precisely delimited sets of components. Only then can a limited number of metahypotheses about science be constructed. The present analysis will focus on the actions of scientists that can be said to be intrinsic to the communication sequence. This book will analyze the scientific method as a process of communication. The purpose of the analysis will be to posit the minimal number of principles or metahypotheses necessary to describe the actions of scientists. To put it differently, the purpose will be to specify the requisite number of rules of the game of scientific communication.

The effort can be represented diagrammatically (see page 14). The first two stick-men are metatheoreticians whose domain consists of science as communication and whose purpose is to develop the minimal number of principles or metahypotheses necessary to describe the actions of scientists. This is the domain and purpose of the present book. The task requires several buttressing assumptions. First, the scientist actions are assumed to be stable, predictable, and describable. Any attempt at theory construction invokes this assumption about the events in its domain. Second, the influence of any of the other intrinsic or extrinsic parameters of the other components is

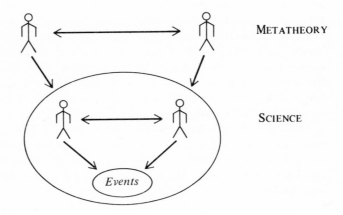

assumed not to negate this predictability. This is not to say that they will have no influence, which would be a much more stringent type of assumption (as Blalock notes[22]). It simply means that one can legitimately isolate and metatheorize about scientist actions as one component separate from the others. Further, the possible major disruptive influences of the other components will be duly noted and explicated in the analysis. Minimally, they will be given their proper place in the model; maximally they will be embedded as values in the appropriate metahypotheses.

This analysis of science will be the medium for the critical analysis of social research. Immediately, a cautionary note is needed. I have tended to use the phrase "theory construction" synonymously with research and theory development. I have also freely interchanged the terms "theory," "research," "research methodology," and "methodology." I have not drawn hard and fast distinctions because, in reality, none exist, and the belief that they do has done irreparable damage to social science. Appropriate logico-mathematical and semantic considerations about hypothetical relationships are inextricably bound to methodological considerations. The analysis to follow has as one secondary gain the demonstration of this fact. One point of nonoverlap must be noted. It is correct under certain conditions to treat as separate the relations between theoretical statements expressing hypothetical relationships. This is certainly true when these theoretical statements and relations are mathematically expressed. It is also true when considering deductive relations between theoretical statements however symbolically expressed: e.g., words vs. mathematical or logical notation. The present analysis of science, except for one brief passage, will have little to say about the necessary prerequisites for deductive theory or mathematicized theory. It will have much to say critically about social science's mathematicizing. This will be based on certain simple principles derived from the analysis which require no premises about mathematics or deductive logic.

SUMMARY, CONCLUSIONS, AND OVERVIEW

Part I of the book will utilize the communication model of science briefly introduced above. Chapter 1 will deal with questions about the events in the scientific domain (not to be confused with the metatheoretic domain of the first two stick-men). Specifically, language and reality will be discussed and related; the statement components of the action of scientists will be schematized; and the core requirement of science as communication will be introduced and defined. Chapter 2 will analyze the statement form of problems, questions, identity, and measurement and their interrelationships in the communication scheme. Chapter 3 will discuss the auxiliary hypotheses needed to attain the scientific goals of prediction and control of the events. The issue of control will be carefully analyzed. Hypotheses will be defined, and the logic of their tests also will be considered. All the statement types will be interrelated by way of presenting a coherent analysis of scientific action within the context of science as communication.

Part II of the book will deal with the inadequacies of social science given the model of science presented in Part I. In Chapter 4, social science identification and measurement will be considered. The discussion will deal at length with the single greatest failure of social science: the slighting of the identification cycle, with all that it implies for measurement. It will also be shown that social scientists have paid scant attention to the adequacy of their problems and questions. The significance of this finding lies in the demonstration that positivism-empiricism as a philosophical orientation has much to offer beyond the stereotyped modes of gathering and analyzing data. Logical-semantic considerations are equally important. For example, the imprecision of social science can be effectively analyzed and solutions suggested on the basis of these "nonempirical" criteria alone.

Chapter 5 will have to do with the weaknesses in social-scientific hypotheses of all types. Most of these weaknesses are directly implied by the failure of identification and measurement and by the general lack of precision of social science theory. Much of the chapter will be devoted to examining familiar metatheoretical solutions to the inadequacies of social science. This subsection is important because many familiar methodological edicts are open to question. Significant among these are the use of indicators and the sophisticated mathematical procedures implied; the current emphasis on conjoint and fundamental measurement in psychology; the use of multiple measures in psychology, sociology, and economics; and the extensive logic of control employed by most social scientists. The critique that emerges has the benefit of emphasizing continuities and consistencies among social researchers of different methodological persuasions. For example, experimenters and survey researchers are shown to not be as disparate in orientation as is frequently maintained.

To summarize, then, this book will depart substantially from typical social research methods texts. It will try to be exhaustive enough in content to create a cogent theory of research methodology. This metatheory of theory construction will be critically applied to social science. In so doing, new directions will be indicated, and old, problematic practices will be duly spurned. It is hoped that these criterial differences from typical methods texts will answer the question: Why another book on social research?

PART ONE

1

Science, Reality, and Words

Users of language in everyday discourse are amazingly free in the range of expressions available to them. Theoretically, there is a finite but very large number of linguistic expressions that can be formed by combining and recombining the basic linguistic elements of phonemes, morphemes, or words (depending on the level of analyses). Of course, the number of expressions is in reality restricted by context components. Does the listener-receiver understand the words of the speaker-source? Are the words appropriate for the place and time of the transmission? Even if some expressions are grammatically and semantically correct, they would be inappropriate if uttered in certain times and places: the familiar ethic of "curse with the boys, not with the family" is a good example. Are the words appropriate for the actor type who utters them? Clear discrepancies arise when certain expressions are uttered by certain actors: doctors can tell patients to get undressed, train conductors *qua* train conductors (as contrasted to husbands or lovers) cannot. Do the others present constrain the choice of expressions? Passionate avowals of love are not expected between students in classrooms.

Even within the *umwelt* of these constraints, everyday discourse is characterized by fantastic creativity. The primary action constraint is *understanding*: messages must be transmitted and received with understanding. It is a generalized constraint that is operative irrespective of the influence of other context components; as long as it is satisfied communication is possible above and beyond other constraints. And it is so easily satisfied that linguists have had a difficult time developing a theory of grammar that includes the semigrammatical expressions of conventional discourse.[1] People can make themselves understood with nonsentences or blatantly ungrammatical sentences. In fact, they can often achieve understanding without words by changes in facial expression, posture, and gesture.[2]

This freedom is severely curtailed with scientific discourse because the satisfaction of understanding is not enough and the importance of nonverbal communicative devices (such as facial expression) is downgraded. The language of scientists is restricted by necessary and strictly enforced relations with events. Minimally, that language must have some expressions that are designative of the events in the domain, and this designative relationship must itself be codified in independent expressions. The meteorologist must know when it is appropriate to utter "I have observed a low pressure system," and this determination requires linguistically codified procedures for making such observations. Maximally, the designative expressions are embedded in metaexpressions that refer to aspects of their use: definitions, mathematic or symbolic logic notation, or explicit rules of deduction. "Low pressure system" not only designates appropriate events and is embedded in expressions that detail the procedures necessary to observe these events but also optimally has its use in meteorologic theory specified by metaexpressions: e.g., "The following predictions are deducible from the following expressions in which 'low pressure system' is embedded . . ." or " 'Low pressure system' is defined as . . ." or "If X stands for 'low pressure system' and Y for . . ., the following equation expresses the relation between X and Y. . . ."

Nonverbal communication between scientists never receives consideration by scientists or by metatheorists of science. It is dismissed to the point of absolute denial. Such total negation of its possible influences on scientists' actions is the result of the pervasive strain in science that moves to symbolically codify all communicative action. Science is a symbolic endeavor and is taken for granted as being such.

Both the empirical restriction and the negation of the importance of nonverbal communication in scientific discourse greatly simplify its communicative analysis. As a consequence the range of inquiry about science as event is limited to the specification of expression type and the rules of use of expression type. This simplification is most obvious within the domain of semantic theory. "Meaning" is a problematic concept. Because it has been defined in several ways, it is common in semantics to speak of types of meaning and different definitions of types of meaning. For example, the "intensional" meaning of a word has been used as a synonym for "connotative" meaning and the "extensional" meaning as a synonym for "denotative" meaning. Moreover, "connotative" meaning has been defined differently as the stimulus-response associates of a word, the feeling states produced by a word, or the potential meanings a word may have. Similarly, "denotative" meaning has been defined as the "things" a word designates, the actual (as opposed to potential) meanings of a word, or the behavioral correlates of a word.[3] The analysis of science as communication with the implied restrictions limits questions about meaning to "referential" meaning. Furthermore, this "type" of meaning is specifically limited to definitional relations between words and designated events or words and words that designate events, or words and expressions whose components are words and words that designate events, and so on. Or more formally, a communicative analysis of science defines meaning according to a series of recursive definitions whose terminus is the designation of events in the domain of inquiry.

"Meaning," then, is given precise meaning because of the conceptual restrictions imposed by a communicative analysis of science. This is not to say that such an analysis is not complicated. But it is more precisely delimited as the events in the domain of inquiry than a comparable analysis of any conceivable communicative sequence in conventional discourse.

REALITY

What is reality? This question must be posed and must be answered, given the interface between scientific discourse and empirical events. It might appear that the metaphysical dilemmas posed by this question negate the advantages that the empirical limitations have for an analysis of science. After all, this question has been around for centuries and has been answered and reanswered innumerable times. Actually the answer is straightforward and initiates and guides the communicative analysis of science.

The first approximation to an answer is to rephrase the question by putting it in context. Let us now return to the two sets of stick-men (see the diagram at the top of page 23). Whether or not this represents scientific communication, the metalanguage must be distinguished from the object language. The object language is the language used by the men discussing the events. It is so called because it is object to the language used by the men discussing the events. The second language has expressions referring to this object language. Accordingly, the second language is called the metalanguage.

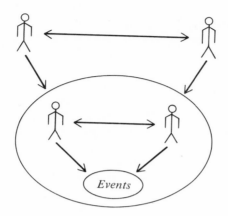

Quotation marks or brackets conventionally are used to maintain the distinction: expressions from the object language referred to in the metalanguage are contained in quotation marks or brackets; expressions understood to be in the object language are not. This usage will be modified somewhat herein. Brackets will enclose those expressions that are understood to be designative of events. These expressions will be called "metaexpressions." Nonbracketed expressions will be understood to be events and will be called "object expressions." By "expressions" will be meant any terms or linguistically whole statements of sentence or less-than-sentence length but consisting of one or more terms.

This simple distinction is the cornerstone of Tarski's famous correspondence theory of truth.[4] In answer to the question, "What is truth?" he offers a definition based on this distinction. It can be said, "[All birds have wings] is true if and only if all birds have wings." "[All birds have wings] is false if and only if not all birds have wings." The bracketed expression is from the object language and is embedded in the compound metaexpression from the metalanguage. Other general requirements must be met before this definition is complete: e.g., the metalanguage must be more extensive than the object language and every expression in the object language must be an expression in the metalanguage; the semantic and syntactical relations in the object language must be fully codified, and so on. The specifics of these conditions are not important here.

This theory of truth is in essence an attempt to grapple with the problem of the correspondence between expressions and events by recasting the question, "What is reality?" into a linguistic mold. In the example just given, reality is the expression "All birds have wings" in the definition "[All birds have wings] is true if and only if all birds have wings." That is, reality is an expression about events that stands in definitional relation with an expression. Formally, reality is the definiens and the bracketed expression is the definiendum. The resulting expression corresponds to Tarski's definition of truth given the satisfaction of certain conditions.

This conceptualization can be expanded beyond the confines of a definition of truth. Reality is any nonbracketed expression that is a definiens to a bracketed expression that is a definiendum in an expression that is a definition. One can say the definiens expression is "supposed to" or "is intended to" or "does" directly designate events. But this provision is irrelevant and reduces the elegance of the definition of reality by opening a Pandora's box of questions about the nature of the designative relationship. It is much simpler to define reality linguistically in this way. Questions about the appropriate specification of reality become questions about expressions: Should they be bracketed or not bracketed? Has the terminus of the definition been reached, or should the nonbracketed definiens be a bracketed definiendum to be eventually defined by a different nonbracketed definiens?

The utilization of this definition of reality beyond Tarski's definition of truth raises some important questions even though it avoids some problematic ones. Is this concept limited to definitional expressions of any particular type? In what sense can the nonbracketed expressions forming the definiens be said to be definitions of the "bracketed" expression that is the definiendum? What is the relation between the definiens and definiendum if more than one definiens is specified? Can different definiens be specified for one definiendum? These questions are important and must be dealt with by introducing additional definitions and provisions, as will be done in the final section of this chapter.

The important point here is not only that these questions are answerable, but that one great epistemological advantage mandates the use of this definition of reality irregardless of the additional questions raised. Any term that has no negative is suspect in logical inquiry (however broadly "logical inquiry" is conceived, as formal logic vs. an analysis of scientic method), because no rules can be specified that limit the use of such a term. The term that has no negative cannot be said to be used "incorrectly," "inappropriately," or the like because such labelling presumes rules of use that specify when the term can and cannot be used. The term has nondelimited meaning (however this is defined) and can be used universally given the satisfaction of certain (in this sense) trivial syntactical and contextual requirements. In other words, the term with no negative can never have its application falsified.

Reality[5] as construed beyond the scope of the definition just given has no negative. It is difficult to conceive of nonreality. An assertion falsifying reality is an absurdity. Or more carefully, such an assertion is a logical absurdity, for there are philosophical and religious systems built on analogous assertions: e.g., Berkeley's philosophy and Mary Baker Eddy's Christian Science (a rather interesting misuse of ["science"]). It is obvious that asserting an unreality or no reality violates intuition. Less clearly, it is confusing to say something is not real. How is such an assertion to be interpreted? To cite the familiar unicorn problem, if it is asserted that unicorns are unreal, a paradox ensues: how can uniforns be unreal and still be spoken of, for to speak of unicorns presumes their reality? As a term with no negative, [reality] has unbounded meaning: everything must be real if there is no nonreality. Logically, one can never know when the term [reality] is being used incorrectly, and the existence of things that obviously do not exist cannot be falsified.

This definition avoids such difficulties entirely by sharply distinguishing between object expressions and metaexpressions. Clearly, the expression "Unicorns do not exist" is permissible and precisely interpretable as distinct from "[Unicorns] exist." No paradox is implied. [Unicorns] as a term exists; unicorns as a class of events is irrevocably denied in the nonbracketed object language. Within this definition of reality, events can be falsified even if the existence of the requisite designative [terms] is implied in the falsification assertions(s). This advantage of this definition is crucial in scientific inquiry, as will be seen in what follows.

Avoidance of Confusing Word and Thing

It is instructive to recast slightly the preceding consideration of reality. Aside from the definition of reality that is facilitated, the "object vs. metalanguage" distinction has another important consequence. A notational convention is provided that precisely separates [word] and thing. The confusion of word with thing is one of the cardinal errors of mathematical and symbolic logic. Formally, it results in logical contradiction. Unicorns do not exist. Unicorns must exist to be named. Unicorns are called [unicorns], therefore unicorns exist. Unicorns exist and do not exist. This trite example has a more important analogy in logic, called the antinomy of the liar, that underlies the whole theory of truth and proof.[6] For our purposes the triteness of the example does not negate the important principle: word and thing must be distinguished to avoid logical contradiction. The use of bracketed and nonbracketed expressions avoids this: "[Unicorns] exist; unicorns do not."

Even though the confusion of word and thing formally results in logical contradiction, in human communication it has more sinister results, for the purge of logic does not always prevail. Human communication is to logic as human communication is to grammar: it can be so analyzed (presumably) by the metatheoretician but human communication at the level of the participants is notoriously illogical and ungrammatical. [Words] are not neatly separated from things by a vocal or nonvocal conventional notation. The rigors of logic are rarely applied so that logical contradictions are ferreted out and in some way disposed of. Confusions survive and have the potential for great damage.

Stuart Chase noted this with the brilliant title of his book, "The Tyranny of Words."[7] The use of the word ["power"] provides a contemporary example. It is used continually in expressions like "gain power," "dispose of power," "grab power," "use power," and "delegate power." It is used, in short, as if it were a thing to be acquired, dispensed, and stored like any other commodity or physical object. Yet, [power] designates a complex human exchange (that incidentally can be sufficiently described as a communication sequence). Its acquisition and use can be understood only as a complicated behavioral process that most often requires many acts over much time, in particular places.[8] Failure to recognize this complexity, because of the "tyranny" of [power] confused with power, results in the mistaken impression that the desired state of affairs can be produced rapidly and without much effort. For example, students trying to influence academe voice frustration, disappointment, and futility continually, largely because of this confusion. And theirs is only a microcosmic social arena.

Other popular examples could be presented. One that will be critical for this book is the term [change]. [Change] is frequently confused with change by communicating human actors. This is a devastating mistake when these actors are scientists. Anticipating the detailed discussion in Chapter 3, let us choose the rather benign example of historians debating the evolution of industrialized Western society. Consider an admittedly contrived but not misrepresentative assertion, one that recurs in different form again and again in historical theories of societal transition: "Agricultural society changed into industrial society." Assume adequate specification of agricultural society and industrial society, so that no ambiguities arise about these events. In this assertion, change should be written as [change], for it must always occur in the metalanguage. It is not a thing but a term that designates a process. And this process must be fully specified for the meaning of [change] to be clear.

To return to the example, let A = agricultural society and B = industrial society. The assertion "A changes to B" is ambiguous at the level of the object language. A can invariably and always change to B as a function of time. If $T_{1...n}$ is "time," then this relation can be expressed: B at $T_2 \equiv A$ at T_1 which reads "B at T_2 if and only if A at T_1." This can be interpreted as a stage theoretical assertion: "Agricultural society will always be a stage that precedes industrial society in the historical evolution of society." "A changes to B" can also mean that A is transformed into B because of the operation of other factors, such as economic factors. If $E_{1...n}$ = "economic factors" (whatever these are), then this relation can be expressed: B at $E_2 \equiv A$ at E_1. It is assumed E_2 follows E_1 because of empirical or logical necessity: there is good logical or empirical evidence for the sequence. (Without this assumption, the change of E_1 to E_2 would have to be specified and infinite regress would threaten.) The relation reads, "Agricultural society will always be transformed into industrial society given the operation of certain economic factors." As many other interpretations of the original assertion are available as there are possible factors that produce the change.

The important point is that the specification of change requires the isolation of factors that can be said to produce the change. In the example given, the first factor was time, the second economic conditions. Without these factors there can be no linkage between the events that are said to change. It is logically absurd to assert unconditionally "A changed to B", because some linkage is needed between A and B to show that B was once A: that caterpillars become butterflies can be known only with the added demonstration that butterflies were once caterpillars. Minimally, the demonstration is perceptually accomplished with the perceptions controlled by time of caterpillars that become butterflies; maximally, the demonstration is accomplished by isolating and manipulating the hormonal factors that produce the change. Every change, then, presumes the search for controlling factors. To speak of change as a reality conceals this needed specification. To speak of [change] and understand it to be a term, not an object, is to recognize the necessity of such specification. This confusion is not often recognized: e.g., "social change" is frequently treated by social scientists as if it were an object. [Change] will be more fully dealt with in Chapter 3.

Complications in Defining Reality

Reality as nonbracketed expressions is not a simple concept. Because language is recursive, object expressions, metaexpressions, meta-metaexpressions, meta-meta-metaexpressions, and so on can be constructed through many levels. For example, "Birds have wings"; "[Birds have wings] is true because birds have wings"; "[[Birds have wings] is true because birds have wings]] is true," and so on. Notationally this is easy to resolve by the use of more than one set of brackets.

It can now be noted that in Tarski's definition of truth the expression in which the bracketed metaexpression and non-bracketed object expression are juxtaposed is a meta-metaexpression and should be enclosed in double brackets. This violates traditional usage in which the definition would be nonbracketed and would be called the metaexpression rather than the meta-metaexpression. The definiendum would have one set of brackets and would be understood to be an expression from the object language referred to in the metalanguage metaexpression. The notation herein is heavily reliant on mathematical logic.

However, the situation becomes more complicated because the communicator or scientist is free to expand expressions to any meta-level. The scientist for example will assert "[Hypothesis A] is false" or even "[[Hypothesis A] is false]] is false".

Meta- and meta-metaexpressions of this form are the essence of scientific methodology. The metascientist or metatheoretician (hereafter just metatheoretician) can have any expressions of the scientist in his object language; therefore, he can have object expressions that are meta-metaexpressions: "Scientist A asserts '[[Hypothesis A] is false]] is false'". To illustrate the possible degree of complication: the metatheoretician can assert meta-metaexpressions about his own metaexpressions that are about object expressions that are meta-metaexpressions of communicators.

This situation is somewhat simplified by the fact that an analysis of science will not need to deal with such complicated expressions. Yet, it will be crucial to distinguish levels of expressions by levels of communication. So the following terminological convention will be amended. Object expressions, metaexpressions, and meta-metaexpressions will be distinguished with the appropriate notation. When the object expressions of the metatheoreticians are any one of these expression levels of scientists, it will be duly noted. This case will be distinguished from meta- and meta-metaexpressions of the metatheoretician (although this will be necessary only at the level of hypotheses of research). Furthermore, it will arise that there will be expressions of the metatheoretician that will not be expressions of scientists: e.g., there will be hypotheses of research that are extraneous to normal scientific inquiry. Also, there will be metaexpressions of the scientist that will not be needed by the metatheoretician to describe the communication process. When either of the latter situations arises, it will be duly noted.

Reality Reconsidered

One point deserves emphasis. Reality is nonbracketed object expressions. Frequently in metatheoretical inquiry it is implicitly assumed that object expressions form an arbitrary terminus to the inquiry. Object expressions are assumed to be refinable to expressions that are truly designative of reality.

Or more strictly, object expressions are assumed to be further analyzable by direct appeal to the events that they designate: Things are conceived to lie beyond the pale of words. The confirmation of words translates into the establishment of the appropriate linkage between word and thing. Reality, then, is all too frequently assumed to be the knowable event beyond the boundary of language. Reality must be specified to confirm language, but such confirmation is left to the scientist or to other metatheoreticians. Such an assumption, for example, is a cornerstone of Carnap's metatheories.[9] He distinguishes object from theory language and assumes the former to be a relatively stable correlate of real-world things that are specifiable but not specified.

Construing reality in this way is a logical absurdity. If Wittgenstein[10] teaches one thing, it is that reality is language. In the terms used herein, reality is not only expressible by nonbracketed expressions, it is nonbracketed expressions. The definition of reality just given is not to be misconstrued as an extension of Carnap's object language. It is meant to say that reality is equivalent to nonbracketed expressions. If it were interpreted in any other way, no real event could be falsified, as noted.

A perfectly legitimate question immediately arises. How can one know when terminal object expressions that are reality have been specified? Given freedom of language use, how can a set of object expressions be isolated that can be said to be reality? Doesn't the relative lability and variance of language over time, across users, and within contexts preclude the specification of a limited set of object expressions that can be said to be reality for any given set of scientist-communicators? Three answers exist for the metatheoretician. In order of ascending complexity: first, the assertion that reality is equivalent to object expressions is meant heuristically. That is, reality can be so construed to facilitate communication analysis, as any further specification would introduce largely irrelevant metaphysical arguments. This answer leaves the door open to other interpretations of reality and therefore assumes a definition of reality to be open-ended. It would seem that the equivalence between reality and object expressions is violated: this answer is a subtle variation on the theme that reality is something beyond language, albeit expressed in language.

The second answer to the question is that, within the bounds of a given scientific communication sequence, the metatheoretician can isolate a limited set of object expressions that scientists use as the events in their domain. That is, the metatheoretician can enumerate the object expressions that are the scientist's reality within a given *umwelt*. The metatheoretician, in effect, can catalogue reality by cataloguing the object expressions. Operationally, this would appear to be easy enough. The metatheoretician could poll the scientists about their object expressions and determine those most agreed upon as the limited set that is their reality. This procedure is analagous to the first general procedure specified in the introduction for evaluating the adequacy of a communication. Here the determining question is, "What object expressions can scientists agree with the highest percent levels are equivalent to the events in their domain—equivalent to their reality?"

Although this technique for isolating the object expression-reality of scientists appears to answer the question about the possibility of the full determination of reality conceived as object expressions, there is a serious objection. Practically, total agreement on a fully determined set of object expressions would seem to be impossible. Scientists do not codify and exhaustively list their object expressions. This task would be up to the metatheoretician. In other words, some object expressions of the metatheoretician that are supposed to be the object expressions of the scientist will not be so formulated by the scientist. Invariably, there will be error in the metatheoretician's codification of the scientist's object expressions. This will be coupled with the error that will result from an attempted determination of the set of scientist's object expressions; scientists will disagree over the set of object expressions even though they will totally agree on particular individual object expressions. Both of these sources of error will result in an indeterminant set of object expressions. This indeterminancy indicates one of two things: either reality is indeterminate or defining reality as object expressions is indeterminate. Hence, this answer also has its drawbacks.

The final answer to the question about the determinancy of reality conceived as equivalent to object expressions is a compound one. In essence, it is that reality must be so conceived because reality is communicable only in these terms. Reality as object expression is the only reality. Events can be spoken of only by the use of object expressions. This argument is akin to Wittengenstein's argument against the possibility of a private language.[11] Language to be known must be shared and language to be shared must be known; therefore language must be shared or, more strictly, language is only shared; any other interpretation is an absurd artifact of language. Because man can metacommunicate he can refer to private language. However, the fact that private languages can be spoken of only in metalanguage that must be shared is often overlooked, resulting in the mistaken impression that private languages exist independently of metalanguages that must be shared. Similarly, reality to be known must be shared via object expressions, and in order for reality to be shared it must be known, again via object expressions. Because object expressions can be referenced in metaexpressions or meta-metaexpressions, it is assumed that object expressions are not expressions but things designated by expressions; things that exist beyond the expressions. However, they are only knowable as shared object expressions.

This argument can be expanded. The limited set of object expressions can be specified through determining percent agreement of scientists *and* through developing and testing predictions that relate object and metaexpressions: those that are the events in the domain of inquiry of the scientist and those developed by the metatheoretician as designative of the actions of the scientist. This procedure is analogous to the second general procedure specified in the introduction for evaluating the adequacy of a communication. Predictions are tested that relate the actions of scientists and their use of specific metaexpressions: e.g., "if [measure X] then scientist A will do U, V, W" or "if scientist A does U, V, W, then he develops [measure X]". The "will do U, V, W" is an object expression for the scientist or metatheorist. The [measure X] is a metaexpression implicitly designating certain instruments or operations in the object language. Finally, "meaningful predictions" is to be understood as "confirmable predictions." Strictly speaking, these predictions are meta-metaexpressions. Again, congruently with mathematical logic, where the brackets become unnecessarily redundant they will be deleted, but will be understood to be implicit.

The full resolution of the dilemmas posed by conceptualizing reality as object expression will be approximated in the following two sections. The principle to be gleaned from the discussion up to this point is this: the initial task of a metatheory of science as communication consists of the categorization of the appropriate statement types, levels of statements, and levels of communication. The ultimate goal of that metatheory is to interrelate members of the three sets so that the object expressions that are the verbal and nonverbal behavior of scientists are placed in appropriate predictions. Short of this goal, the metatheory should provide rules of research which will be metaexpressions related to object expressions that are the verbal and nonverbal behavior of scientists.

The Paradigm of Science

The question of reality can be restated with the use of two dichotomies: shared and unshared experience, and experience that is or is not symbolically represented. These two dichotomies can be related in a fourfold table:

	SHARED	UNSHARED
Symbolic	3	2
Nonsymbolic	4	1

If reality is object expressions, what becomes of those aspects of reality that the scientist experiences personally but cannot formulate symbolically and cannot share or that the scientist experiences personally and can formulate symbolically, but cannot share? Strictly interpreted, the definition of reality presented would preclude categories 1 and 2 (and also 4).

Yet it would seem obviously mistaken to deny the importance of these real experiences, for they cannot be denied. Personal experience and interpretation is, of course, the cornerstone of science. It is a truism that scientists create and have varying degrees of genius and that much of the advance of modern science can be laid to the work of a handful of men (e.g., Aristotle, Galileo, Newton, Darwin, and Einstein). Genius and creativity are the realm of categories 1 and 2. Another term often used to describe an aspect of scientific inquiry that is crucial is "discovery." Assuming an adequate meaning for this term, it is again a truism that discovery has been overwhelmingly important to the advance of science. Discovery is also an event or process within categories 1 or 2. It would seem, then, that this conceptualization of reality rules out phenomena crucial to science.

A contradiction is apparent: creativity, genius, and discovery fall within categories of events in scientific inquiry that are precluded by a definition of the reality of science *qua* communication, and these phenomena are at the same time recognized as crucial to the process of science *qua* communication. The resolution of this contradiction is attainable within the distinction between metatheorist and scientist. The scientist can have unshared experiences that are and are not represented symbolically. But these experiences can be shared only at the level of metatheory by appropriate object expressions. The scientist may not formulate the object expressions, but the metatheorist must in order to deal with events in categories 1 and 2. Classes of scientist action vaguely denoted as genius, creativity, and discovery can be object expressions in the metatheory even if they are not object expressions used by the scientist. Reality again can only be object expressions.

A special cautionary note is needed in this case. The metatheorist must observe the scientific canon in his efforts. Specifically, if he asserts object expressions about a scientist's actions that the scientist does not assert, the metatheorist must make certain his superimposed object expressions are adequate. Specifically, he must apply one of the two procedures described above. Generally, he must be a good methodologist —what this involves will be the subject of the book.

It has happened in the discipline of metatheory construction that the object expressions shared by metatheorists but not by scientists have been declared unrepresentative. A reality was superimposed that generated principles and hypotheses which scientists or other metatheoreticians described as moot to the arena of scientific inquiry. Hanson[12] has contested the knowledge of philosophers of science about the development of the physics of elementary particles. Kuhn's aforementioned analysis[13] questions traditional metatheoretical formulations of science. Popper[14] has stated that inductive logic exists for the philosopher of science and not the scientist. Kaplan[15] distinguishes between a "reconstructed logic" and "logic-in-use" to underline the possible schism between metatheoretical and scientist object expressions. Even social scientists have questioned the philosophy of science formulations about what scientists do; Skinner's article is an excellent illustration, and there are others.[16] This type of argument can be avoided only by developing metatheories that are methodologically sound. The metatheoretician must be a good theoretician.

With this caution duly noted, a simple general principle can be presented which partially avoids this problem of the transposition of metatheoretical and science realities. The diagram of dichotomies will be interpreted as a process or sequence of actions, rather than as a twofold table. The arrow in the revised diagram which follows will indicate a progression of scientist action from one category to the next—a transition of scientist action through four stages:

	SHARED	UNSHARED
Symbolic	3	2
Not symbolic	4	1

The scientist can initiate the process of inquiry in category 1, but he must convert his nonsymbolic unshared experiences into symbolic unshared experiences. Category 2, in turn, must be converted to shared and symbolically formulated experiences. These experiences can be confirmed by reference to shared and not symbolically represented experiences. Whether or not the scientist engaged in inquiry starts at 1 or proceeds from 3 to 4 is contingent on several other things. In other words, for the moment, these aspects of the diagram can be considered optional. However, no matter what the contingencies, the scientist must always pass through category 3. Science is a communicative enterprise; symbolically formulating experience and sharing the resulting expressions is the essence of science.

This initial interpretation de-emphasizes the transposition of reality problem by positing that in science all experiences must be shared and symbolically formulated. Classes 1 and 2 are assumed to be important, but Class 3 provides the all-important constraint on the process, a constraint that is necessary for events in classes 1, 2, and 4. As indicated in the Introduction this constraint has both a hard and a soft interpretation according to whether the events are absent or present. The resolution is that class 3 is crucial to the process with the ultimate test of adequacy of any scientific expression being certain features of its symbolic representation and its shareability, whether the events in the scientific domain are present or absent. This constraint will be more fully elaborated in the final section of this chapter.

Even with this paradigm of science as process, the meta-theorist must posit object expressions for classes 1, 2, and 4.

So the transposition problem is not fully satisfied, for the risk exists that these metatheoretical object expressions may not have scientific counterparts, and the metatheorist may construct a scientific reality that does not exist for the scientist. This risk is fully minimized only by casting a metatheory of science with an eye to the criteria of communicative adequacy mentioned previously.

FIRST PRINCIPLES OF SCIENCE

The cardinal rule of science has been presented and will be greatly expanded on. The utility of this paradigm is demonstrated by the fact that after an admittedly vague first approximation, a principle of great import can be extrapolated. To reiterate the rule: What characterizes science as communication is that every experience must be both shared and symbolically represented. A second principle limiting the first is that there will always be some residue in the translation process. Or more affirmatively, unshared symbolic and not symbolic representations of experience will never be totally translatable into shared symbolic experience. There are two subprinciples to this principle derivable from the paradigm: the transition from unshared and not symbolically represented experience to unshared and symbolically represented experience must always be incomplete; the transition from unshared and symbolically represented to shared and symbolically represented experience must also be incomplete.

The scientist has perceptual experiences that must be formulated into words. Words can never totally represent these experiences according to the law that symbols are never the thing they symbolize. If symbols were the things they symbolize they would not be symbols but the errorlessly reconstructed things they represent; representations of reality cannot be that reality for if they were they would not be representations. If reality is construed as object expressions this law reads: bracketed metaexpressions are never synonymous with nonbracketed object expressions to which they have a definitional relation; they may be linguistically the same, having the same words and grammar, but they are not identical. The brackets are used to avoid this confusion. The scientist must always expect to lose information, then, in translating his perceptual experiences into words. Once understood, this principle should dispel the illusion that errorless science is possible. A false sense of satisfaction is not necessarily implied, only the recognition of the fallibility of knowledge and the resolution of several confusing arguments about problem and question formation that will be discussed in the opening sections of the next chapter.

Furthermore, the scientist must expect probable information loss when he shares his private symbolic representations of his experience. He is free to pick and choose his words or other symbols, but when these are transmitted to others he cannot assume complete understanding. All human experience is such that individuals are the product of multiple influences interrelated and acting in different ways. In communication parlance, the *umwelt* is never replicatable from person to person and specifically from scientist to scientist. To be sure there must be a communality or overlap for communication to occur. But, at minimum, the extrinsic components will be different, and probably significant aspects of the intrinsic ones as well. For example, scientists trained in different schools or different laboratories can expect significant differences in the *umwelt* of any communication sequence from their partners. Or, less obviously, because scientists have different physiological systems, they can expect differences in their perceptions, experiences, and thought, differences that may or may not have significant impact on communication. The differences in the *umwelt* for individual scientists can be of sufficient magnitude to produce information loss when scientists share their symbolically represented experiences. Admittedly, this problem is relative. It is significant in social science, less so in the more advanced sciences. But it is a problem that all scientists must deal with at one point or another. No scientist can assume perfect understanding when he communicates.

Interestingly, scientists reckon with this problem by formalizing techniques to handle it. Formalized definition is the most apparent device. It is a metalinguistic device that attempts to codify the meaning of expressions in order that discrepancies can be pinpointed and resolved and communication proceed unimpeded. However, even if a common base of meaning is established, information loss through the transition of unshared and not symbolically represented experience to unshared and symbolically represented experience can still disrupt communication. Definition is not sufficient. The same significance and limiting condition can be asserted about other metalinguistic devices like logic and mathematics. Measurement is the scientific device that most closely approximates a self-contained corrective for totally solving the problem of information loss during transitions from class 2 to class 3 and from class 1 to class 2 events. Hence, measurement assumes preeminence in the chapters to follow.

The dual information losses in these two transitions relate in unknown ways to produce invariable error as a limiting condition for science as communication. The metalinguistic devices just discussed do operate to limit the error, but the sharing of symbols is never error-free. The important point is that this error is estimable. It may limit communicative efficiency, but it does not impede communication because the degree of error can be specified and its influence estimated. Scientists can proceed to reformulate their expressions to approximate maximum communicability. The criterion providing the error estimation is precision.

INTERPRETATION

> To say that an expression U is an interpretation of a different expression T is the same as to say that there is at least one person P and a situation S such that U can express the same assertion as T for P in S.

Borrowing Naess' definition,[17] an "interpretation" is a meta-metaexpression asserting a definitional relationship between two metaexpressions. The definitional relationship is identity so that an interpretation reads: [[X] is [Y]] where [X] and [Y] are the two expressions. More intuitively, an interpretation can be taken to be a meta-metaexpression asserting a synonymic relation between two metaexpressions. Naess rightfully puts this definition in psycholinguistic context by specifying P, T, and S. For the present analysis the Person is actually two prototypic scientist-communicators and the Situation is science as communication sequence. In toto, then, his definition of interpretation can be recast for this analysis to read:

> An interpretation of a metaexpression [X] is a meta-metaexpression in which [Y] is said to be synonymous or identical with [X]. This meta-metaexpression may be asserted by scientists or by metatheoreticians about the expressions of scientists.

The first thing to notice is that metaexpressions, not object expressions, are being related. It is assumed that any given object expression is tautologous. No object expression will have an interpretation. As every object expression will be equivalent to itself, the only relationship that can be said to hold between object expressions is equivalence: "Birds have wings ≡ Birds have wings." Such an assertion is a tautology. This is also true for object expressions that are negations: "Lizards do not have wings ≡ lizards do not have wings."

It is important to distinguish tautology between object expressions from the truth relationship between object expression and metaexpression. "[Birds have wings] is true if and only if 'Birds have wings.'" An interpretation asserting an identity relation between the two expressions is clearly a fallacy. To ancitipate future arguments—to establish this truth relation requires other object expressions and metaexpressions in addition to the meta-metaexpression asserting the truth relationship, whereas the tautology "Birds have wings" or "Birds do not have wings" is an invariant empirical necessity.

However, meta-metaexpressions in which object expressions are embedded can be related in interpretations. For example,

[[[Electrons have a negative charge] $\equiv$ measuring instruments have readings X, Y, Z]] is synonymous with [[scientists $A_1 \ldots n$ apply and read measuring instruments X, Y, Z and assert [electrons have a negative charge]]]; this meta-meta-metaexpression is an interpretation. Even though object expressions are assumed to be tautologous, interpretations of expressions can be presented in which object expressions are embedded. This rule will be important in the subsequent chapters when considering so called "correspondence rules" between concepts and measurements.

To avoid the rapid proliferation of "meta" prefixes with these definitions, the term "expression" will suffice until such time as the "meta" distinction is crucial for a definition, hypothesis, or whatever other statement we wish to make.

Any expression (understood to exclude object expressions) can have more than one interpretation. In fact, most expressions will have more than one interpretation. To borrow an example from social science, the expression [Person X has high social status] will have multiple interpretations: [[Person X has high social status] is synonymous with [Person X is valued highly by his peers in group Y]]; [[Person X has high social status] is synonymous with [Person X has U occupation, W income, V education]]; [[Person X has high social status] is synonymous with [Person X has high prestige]], and the like. What is the relationship among multiple interpretations of an expression?

A terminological revamping is necessary to answer this question. Consider the following interpretation: [[X] is [Y]]; [[X] is [U]]; [[X] is [V]]. For the sake of parsimony let this reduce to: [[X] is [Y], [U], [V]]. And let the expression [is] or [is synonymous with] be replaced by the expression [means]. [Means] will be defined then as the identity relation between expressions. Implicit is that the expression following [means] in an interpretation will be substitutable for the expression that precedes [means]. The term [interpretation] will be retained as the label for the meta-meta-expression asserting the identity relation between expressions.

The expressions to the right of [means] will be called the [meanings] of the expression to the left of [means]. In the example, [[X] means [Y], [U], [V]], the [Y], [U], and [V] are [meanings] of [X]. The total meta-metaexpression will be said to be the multiple interpretations of [X]; if only one interpretation were specifiable then the meta-metaexpression would be called an [interpretation] of [X].

To relate this terminology to more standard ones, it should be obvious that [definitions] are [interpretations]. The following asymmetric relationship holds between definitions and interpretations: a definition can be a meaning because an interpretation and therefore a definition can be specified as the meaning of an expression. The resulting expression would be a meta-meta-metaexpression. Symbolically this would be represented: [[X] means [[Y] means [U], [V]]]. However, a meaning cannot be a definition, because it must always be an expression (to whatever metalevel) within a definition. It is the definiens. More significantly, if a definition is an interpretation and if the definitional relation [means] is identity, then the definiendum and the definiens will be substitutable for one another. In the "new" terminology this relation was expressed by saying that the related expressions would be substitutable for one another (see the preceding paragraph). This smacks of Aristotle, with all the accompanying counterarguments. For example, as Scriven[18] notes, it is never true in the history of science that definiendum is replaced by definiens: [temperature] is always used, never the terms that define it as a property of events. To avoid this difficulty, it can be said that this requirement is a formal one only. It is necessary to deal with the question of the specification of the interrelationships among multiple interpretations.

The original question can now be answered; what is the relationship among multiple interpretations? Each meaning of an expression is to be understood as formally substitutable for the expression. It may never be practicable to substitute meaning for expression; it must always appear in an interpretation in such a way that expression and meaning are juxtaposed and separately stated components of the interpretation; but each meaning should be understood to be a sufficient meaning of the expression. Each interpretation, then, can be discussed separately from every other interpretation when the issue of multiple interpretations arises. This implies that each interpretation can be evaluated separately from every other because the interpretations are independent. To anticipate future discussions, interpretations can be compared as to their communicative adequacy by formulating meta-meta-metaexpressions that relate the interpretations to other expressions; simply, metahypotheses can be formulated about the adequacy of an expression's meanings in the event of multiple meanings.

This relationship is crucially important. Part of its importance lies in the clarification of a possible confusion. It can happen that an expression has multiple meanings that are not independent. For example, [high social status] can mean [being valued highly] *and* [having a specified occupation, education, and income] *and* [having high prestige]. The meanings of an expression may be conjunctive with one another as in this example, or they may have more complicated nonindependent interrelationships. However, according to this analysis, when interpretations are not independent the expression is not said to have multiple interpretations. It has one interpretation with multiple nonindependent meanings that are interrelated conjunctively or in some other way. There is a distinction, then, between an expression with multiple interpretations and an expression with one interpretation specifying multiple, interrelated meanings. This distinction is analogous to the one in set theory between identity or class equivalence and class membership.[19] The ultimate utility and importance of the distinction relates directly to the concept of precision.

One further preliminary clarification is necessary to preface a definition of precision. The meanings of an expression can be interpreted in two ways; they can have two general types of meanings specified in their interpretations. The expressions in the definiens can be understood to be other expressions, as opposed to expressions that specify how the original expression is used. In the first case they will be identical in form, [[X] means [Y]]; in the second, the definiens will specify "use", [[X] means [X is used in circumstances U, V, W]]. Generally, then, meaning can be construed and specified as an attribute of expressions or meaning can be construed and specified as a function of the use of expressions. Tarski's correspondence notion of truth[20] is a metatheoretical system predicated on meaning (in this sense) as an attribute of words. Wittgenstein's (later) philosophical analysis[21] develops the notion of meaning as use. In social science, formal linguistic analysis can be discriminated from functional psycholinguistic analysis roughly according to these divergent ways of interpreting meaning.[22]

Although no formal theory of meaning-as-use exists (largely because no formal theory of human communication exists on which to predicate such a theory of meaning), such a conceptualization of meaning has a tremendous advantage for a metatheorist of science. Assertions about the adequacy of interpretations are testable within this framework. Metahypotheses about interpretations are falsifiable and therefore testable. (The relationship between falsifiability and testability is fully discussed in Chapter 3.) They are falsifiable according to the simple rule: A meaning-as-use can be said to be false if the expression that the meaning defines can be said to be used incorrectly. That is, interpreting the meaning of an expression as the use of the expression implies possible falsification of the application of the expression according to whether or not the expression is used correctly: If used incorrectly contingent on the meaning, the meaning is false. This favorable situation contrasts with meaning-as-attribute of words. No clear criteria exist in the latter case for the falsification of the meaning of a word. In what sense can an expression be said to have no meaning? By virtue of its existence as an expression, an expression must have a meaning. The limiting case of no meaning for an expression can only be an expression that is not an expression: i.e., a string of nonsense syllables that is said to be an expression, as in some psycholinguistic research.[23] Unfortunately, this analysis is in no position to take advantage of this benefit of the specification of meaning-as-use because no such formal theory of meaning (and human communication) exists.

PRECISION

An expression will be said to be unequivocally interpretable if and only if one interpretation of that expression can be formulated with the meaning being the expression itself.

In other words an expression that is tautologous is said to be unequivocally interpretable. Because, according to prior definitions, object expressions are tautologous, they are also unequivocably interpretable. It is now being asserted that every expression that is tautologous is unequivocally interpretable. So an interpretation that relates a metaexpression and an object expression will be said to be unequivocally interpretable if that interpretation has itself as an interpretation. Formally this would be written:

$[[[X] \text{ means } Y]] \text{ means } [[X] \text{ means } Y]]]$

or by way of substantive example the following expression is unequivocally interpretable: [[[Birds have wings] means Birds have wings]] means [[Birds have wings] means Birds have wings]]]. Any expression (to whatever metalevels), then, that is tautologous is unequivocally interpretable.

Unequivocal interpretability solves the falsification of meaning-as-attribute problem by providing an upper bound for a scale of precision of interpretations. Such a scale does not strictly provide for falsification of meaning, but it does permit assertions to the effect that certain expressions are less precise than others. Expressions can then be rejected as inadequate or retained as adequate on the basis of assertions about relative precision. This, of course, is weaker than being able to falsify meaning-as-use and the appropriateness of expressions. Specifically, such ability would provide the meta-theorist with an unequivocal zero-point of applicability and interpretation, while this scale of precision provides only comparative determinations of applicability and interpretation. Putting it simply, this scale is partially ordered. In the extreme, some interpretations can be said to be "best" because they are unequivocally interpretable, while, generally, others can be ordered according to degree of precision. However, there will be cases in which alternative interpretations will have the same level of precision even at the upper bound of unequivocal interpretability. In this case, as no clear determination of relative adequacy can be made, no interpretation can rightfully be rejected. That is, in the event that two interpretations are said to have the same precision, neither can be rejected, which can occur at all levels on the scale including the upper bound. This situation contrasts with the case where meaning can be unequivocally falsified so any interpretation can be unequivocally rejected as inadequate.

After the extreme of precision has been defined, a full definition is relatively straightforward. Again, Naess' definition for precision provides a useful take-off point.[24]

> Precision (which he calls "preciseness") dt = " 'a' is more precise than 'b' " is equipollent to "There is no interpretation of 'a' which is not also an interpretation of 'b' whereas there is at least one interpretation of 'b' which is not an interpretation of 'a' and there is at least one interpretation of 'a.' "

To translate into our teminology: expression [a] is more precise than expression [b] if they both have the same meanings but [b] has at least one additional meaning that is not shared with [a], and there is at least one meaning of [a]. The latter proviso should be understood to mean that [a] has a meaning different from itself, that [a] is not a tautology.

The latter restriction is the first point of departure for this analysis because tautology is the upper limit of preciseness. Since every expression can be the meaning of itself, every expression *will have* at least one meaning. In the limiting case, [a] is a tautology and [b] has a meaning discrepant with [a] but one shared with [a], so [a] must be a meaning of [b]: i.e., [[a] means [a]] and [[b] means [a]; [c]] because [a] is said to be more precise than [b]. This means generally that the meaning of any expression can be said to be more precise than the expression. What Naess' calls "preciseness" or "precization" is to be understood, then, in this analysis as a culmulative communication process. The expressions are interpreted and have their meanings specified; the meanings are interpreted and have their meanings specified; the meanings of the meanings are interpreted and have their meanings specified; and so on. The terminus of this communication process is tautology.

This process of "precization" (I shall borrow Naess' term) proceeds with questions about meaning. Although these questions may have differing contents, the basic form is [[What does [X] mean?]] They are meta-metaexpressions that are supposed to elicit responses that are interpretations of expressions. This core process of communication is especially important in science. Generally, the more advanced a science, the fewer the number of meaning-questions and interpretation-responses necessary to terminate the precization process at tautology. This general principle of metatheory will be evidenced continually as the analysis proceeds. It should be emphasized that precization is to be understood as a process fixed to one communicative level: i.e., metaexpressions are not transformed into tautologous object expressions. Such a transformation requires the statement of specific hypothetical relations between expressions at different levels. These explicit or implicit hypotheses play a crucial role in science and should not be downgraded by confusing them with definitions (see Chapter 3 especially).

Precision Redefined

Naess' definition is too restricted for a full-blown communicative analysis of science. Abstractly, it is possible to speak of expressions having synonymous meanings, but this condition rarely exists in reality. Expressions would be freely substitutable and, to the extent that this was true, redundancy would minimize information transmitted. Or in less technical terms, if large numbers of expressions can be construed to have at least some shared meanings (a necessary condition to speak of a scale of precision according to Naess' definition), then the discriminating function of language would be inhibited. The number of different things that a language could permit a user to say would be restricted. In the extreme, if synonymity was as common in a language as Naess' definition would presuppose, then the user of that language would either have a restricted base of different expressions or, if he had a nonrestricted base of different expressions, he would have a prohibitively large vocabulary of expressions because each expression would have synonymic alternatives. In either case, the existence of such a language is untenable.

To rephrase the argument slightly, Naess' definition of precision would restrict the use of precision as a scale of communicative adequacy to rather special cases. The history of change in meanings of expressions could be studied: e.g. $[[a]$ means $[b]$; $[c]$ at $T_1]$]; $[[a]$ means $[b]$; $[c]$; $[d]$ at $T_2]$] and therefore $[a]$ at T_1 is more precise than $[a]$ at T_2. Such diachronic studies could expand the applicability of precision analysis, but synchronic studies of precision would be severely restricted to those expressions at a point in time that could be said to share meaning. These cases, as noted above, are relatively rare in a language and are trivial. Of course, the generality of such synchronic studies could be expanded to cover the use of the same expression by different populations, but again such an analysis is hardly congruent with a communication analysis as previously defined.

The answer lies then in redefining "precision" to expand its application in a communication analysis of science:

> D_1: Expression $[a]$ will be said to be more precise than expression $[b]$ if $[a]$ has a known range of interpretations and $[b]$ does not.

According to this definition one expression will be more precise than another if it has a finite set of specified meanings and the second expression does not. Elsewhere, and with different emphasis, I have called expressions with limited and known meanings "ambiguous," and expressions with nonlimited but specifiable meanings "vague."[25] Ambiguous expressions, then, are more precise than vague expressions because the set of meanings is fully specified as opposed to specifiable. For example, if [[a] means [u]; [v]; [w]] and [u], [v], [w] exhaust the meanings of [a], then [a] is ambiguous; if [[b] means [x]; [y]; [z]; . . . ; [n]] with the [n] indicating specifiable but unspecified potential meanings of [b], then [b] is vague. Further, [a] is more precise than [b].

> D_2: Expression [a] will be said to be more precise than expression [b] if [a] and [b] have a known set of meanings—[a] and [b] are ambiguous—but [a] has fewer meanings than [b].

This second definition approaches Naess' with one crucial difference: there is no provision that the meanings of [a] and [b] be synonymous. This, of course, considerably widens the comparative base and broadens the applicability of the scale of precision. Any two terms that are ambiguous can be compared according to relative precision. It may seem that the definition will prove problematic because it permits all expressions to be compared. But this is not so.

It must be remembered that interpretations are independent of one another. Meanings can be compounded to any level of complexity (e.g. [[a] means [u] and [v] and [w] and . . . so on]], but each compound meaning will form a separate interpretation of the expression. Those expressions requiring multiple compound meanings in interpretation are comparable in precision to those expressions with multiple, simple (singular) interpretations. This means that complex and simple interpretations are comparable even though such comparison would violate intuition. For example, if [[a] means [u] and [v]; [x] and [y]] and [[b] means [L]; [M]; [N]], then [a] is more precise than [b].

A very important relationship is implied by this possible comparison of expressions with complex and simple meanings. The compounding of an expression's meanings can increase the precision of that expression if that compounding relates previously independent meanings into a complex meaning. In the above example if the interpretation of [b] could be made to read [[b] means [L] *and* [M] *and* [N]] then [b] would be more precise than [a] because [b] would then have only one meaning and one interpretation. It will be assumed that a communication mechanism for this type of transformation exists even though it has yet to be fully described. That these transformations do occur in science cannot be denied. They underlie the whole logic of control and are especially important in social science, as will be expounded in Chapter 3.

Finally, the second definition of precision is not problematic even though it relates all expressions on a scale of precision, because precision is a process. All expressions are treated as if they can be made more precise through successive interpretations. This follows from D_1 and the upper bound of unequivocal interpretability. Every expression has interpretations even if the sole meaning specified is the expression itself: tautology. Object expressions are of this type and are unequivocally interpretable. Further, those expressions that are not tautologies can be interpreted to the terminus of tautologies. True, these successive interpretations may produce multiple complex and simple meanings but the process will have a terminus when every meaning is interpreted to tautology. Accordingly, if meanings are specified to unequivocal interpretability, the precision of every expression can be assessed according to the limit of unequivocal interpretability (maximum precision) or D_2 (relative ambiguity). And those (vague) expressions that are not exhaustively interpreted can be said to be less precise than those that are exhaustively interpreted (ambiguous). In fact, every expression can be measured on a scale of precision.

Note that this rule is true of abstractions, even though it would not normally be thought so. This class of expressions is usually characterized by broad meaning in the sense of an attribute that adheres to expressions: simply, these expressions are said to mean a great deal. Yet, even if meaning is construed in this way, every abstract expression is interpretable, ultimately to tautology, more commonly to ambiguity *and* tautology. Interpretation of abstract expressions can proceed with meaning defined associationally or defined according to use; in either case, the two general mechanisms for determining communicational adequacy can be applied. No expression escapes this analysis.

PRECIZATION AND COMMUNICATIONAL ADEQUACY

Precization and communicational adequacy are interdependent. Precization of scientific expressions *can proceed without* systematic empirical confirmation via one or the other of the procedures for assessing communicational adequacy: agreement of usage or metahypothesizing about use. But in order to be empirically confirmed, precization must proceed according to one of these procedures. That is, the degree of precision of a term can be empirically assessed only through calculating percent agreement about meanings or by constructing and testing metahypotheses with the term of preassessed precision as antecedent and some aspect of use as consequence.

Percent agreement becomes a crucial index of precision. Whether a metaexpression is tautologous or an expression is an object expression (and therefore a tautology) can be determined by asking scientists and calculating percent agreement among respondents. Likewise, whether an expression is vague or ambiguous can be determined by polling scientists as users of the expression and calculating percent agreement as to range and degree of closure of range of interpretations. Finally, the members of the range of interpretations of an expression can be assessed by polling scientists and calculating percent agreement as to number and content of meanings; when this has been done for two expressions, they can be compared in degree of precision according to D_2.

The construction of metahypotheses about the use of expressions can also be used to assess level of precision, by the postulation of two intervening metahypotheses. Because these will recur repeatedly in subsequent arguments, they will be stated formally here:

> H_1: To the extent that an expression is precise, it will result in differing percentages of agreement among users as to its range and content of meanings; or, more strictly, degree of expression precision varies directly with percent agreement of meanings or interpretations of that expression.

The following corollaries are implied: object expressions and tautologous metaexpressions will produce the greatest percent agreement; ambiguous expressions will produce greater percent agreement than vague expressions but less than object expressions or tautologous metaexpressions; vague expressions will produce the least agreement; ambiguous expressions will produce percent agreement that varies inversely with the number of meanings interpreted for the expressions. Interestingly, the interpretation of the interpretation of an expression with one interpretation will be a tautology: e.g., $[[[a]$ means $[b]]$ means $[[a]$ means $[b]]]$. Therefore, minimal ambiguity (one interpretation) and maximal precision occur with tautology.

The logical elegance of H_1 is illustrated by the fact that according to it expressions will vary in percent agreement and precision between the traditional logical forms of tautology and contradiction. As just discussed, tautology will produce the upper limits of agreement and precision. It remains to be shown that contradiction will produce the lower limits of agreement and precision. Consider the following interpretation: $[[a]$ means $[b]$ and $[\sim b]]$. The compound meaning

$[[b]$ and $[\sim b]]$ is contradictory. This meaning is indeterminant in the sense that it has an unbounded number of interpretations: the meanings of $[[b]$ and $[\sim b]]$ are infinite. Given limitless interpretations any contradictory interpretation will produce the lowest levels of precision and agreement. These will approximate zero. Theoretically, they should be zero, but some interpretive chains may not be followed to the point of contradiction.

The latter fact is the result of the vagaries of communication: expressions with multiple meanings may not, in practice, be interpreted to the point of contradiction. Logic as a meta-communication control device in science, in fact, is supposed to function to guide communication to the limits of interpretation; if not generally conceived of in this way, logic at least can be so construed. Logical contradiction, in this formulation, is a crucial form of corrective feedback in the process of precization. Interpretations that are contradictory are immediately known to be inadequate. The interpreted expression can be rejected or can be interpretively reassessed so that the contradiction is resolved. As Popper and Tarksi[26] note, contradiction becomes a growth mechanism in logical inquiry. For Popper it is the logically implied take-off point for alternative hypothesis formation because all hypotheses are implied by contradictory hypotheses. For Tarski it is the boundary of applied (truth functional) logic beyond which premises and truth correspondences must be reformulated. Slightly different from either formulation, for this presentation contradiction is the lower limit of precision and along with tautology becomes a terminus for precization. When and if it is reached the metatheorist or scientist knows he must in some way reapply the process.

An apparent circularity in H_1 must be dealt with before one proceeds to H_2. In those cases in which percent agreement is the way of assessing level of precision, H_1 is indeed circular because level of precision and percent agreement must co-vary. So H_1 must imply a separate way of assessing relative precision if it is not to be circular. This requirement is easily fulfilled by an impressionistic analysis, formulating an independent object language that codifies relative precision according to object expressions about aspects of observable events, or by criteria for assessing change in use of expressions. The first technique is popular with logical semanticists, the second with certain psycholinguists, and the third with philosophers of science.[27] Whatever the technique, the important point is that H_1 should be used with the proviso that precision is defined and measured independently of percent agreement.

> H_2: To the extent that an expression is precise, action contingent on its use will be more or less equivocal.

The following corollaries are implied: object expressions and tautologous metaexpressions will produce the least equivocal action; ambiguous the next least according to the number of interpretations involved; levels of equivocal action would be predictable according to levels of ambiguity; and vague expressions will produce the most equivocal action.

The obvious problem with this hypothesis is the meaning of "equivocal action." Generally what is meant is that action contingent on tautologous expressions will be most predictable with action contingent on vague expressions being least predictable, and action contingent on ambiguous expressions being predictable according to the levels of ambiguity. Again, it is implied that contradictory expressions are the lower limit and that therefore action contingent on them will be unpredictable.

Conversely, any metahypotheses with expressions as antecedent and scientist action as consequence will have fixed levels of error according to the levels of precision of the expressions. Intuitively, this makes sense with vague expressions because if the range of meanings is not known and action is contingent on those meanings, the range of action cannot be known. Similarly, ambiguous expressions have a fixed range of multiple meanings and action contingent on those meanings should vary in content, the action type not being totally predictable because the particular meaning is not predictable. If those meanings were scaled in some way to assure predictability—weighted in probability of occurrence according to context of emission, for instance—then the contingent action would not have preassessed, determinant levels of error. It could be predicted with levels of error that presumably would diminish with appropriate refinements of testing methodology. However, in this case, by definition, the ambiguous expressions would no longer be ambiguous because the independent interpretations would be compounded to produce an interpretation with a complex meaning: in this way the expression would be made more precise and presumably tautologous. For example, $[[a]$ means $[b]$; $[c]$; $[d]]$ would be transformed into $[[a]$ means $[b]$ in X context *and* $[c]$ in Y context *and* $[d]$ in Z context$]$. Finally, because tautologies have only one meaning and contradictions have unbounded meanings, action contingent on the former should be predictable with minimal error and action contingent on the latter should be unpredictable.

Besides such intuitive appeal there is some empirical evidence that indicates this is the case. Lachenmeyer[28] found that latency of response in a simple task could be ordinally scaled according to tautology, ambiguity, vagueness, and contradiction. Subsequently an elaborate apparatus has been designed which allows more precise testing of the effects of differential precision on action.[29]

It must be cautioned that, because error is empirically determined, this logically sound relationship could be false. For the moment it is sufficient to wave a red flag. The complexities involved will be fully discussed in the section on "Proof" in Chapter 3.

The key to empirical validation of H_2 lies in determining what contingent actions to predict. The research just referred to dealt with a dimension of action—reaction time—that is trivial for a metatheory of scientific research. Two general classes of action that are less trivial can be specified. If precization is the core requirement of science, then the effects on this process might be studied. Communicational adequacy as measured by number of requests for clarification, length of communicational sequence as measured by time and number of expressions necessary to terminate the process, levels of confusion in communication as measured by discrepancies in recording and replication of the message content by the same or different communicators, and other such aspects of precization might be predicted according to H_2. Circularity may be implied in such predictions if precization is not measured independently of precision or, more correctly, if the stage in the precization process is not measured differently from the level of precision achieved. Circularity is easily avoided, as will be seen, when the type of verbal action to be predicted and the type of antecedent expression are fully specified: e.g., meta-hypotheses of the form, "if questions, hypotheses, etc. of X precision level then questions, hypotheses, etc. predictable to Y level of error."

The second general class of significant scientist action that can be predicted according to H_2 is quite frequently mentioned as being crucial to science. It is labeled reproduction or replication. These terms will be distinguished in the following way: reproduction includes all acts necessary to reconstruct a given scientific communication sequence; replication all acts necessary to retest a hypothesis with or without modification. Reproduction is broader in definitional scope than replication, and replication can be defined as a subset of reproduction. Congruently with what follows, any scientific communication sequence can be said to consist of a set of expression types and an ordering of these. The ordering is not yet important; the types include questions as expressions of problems; hypotheses as answers to questions; questions about meaning; expressions about measurement and identity; object expressions about scientist action (e.g., "reading of measuring instruments"); interpretations of questions, hypotheses, identities, and measures; expressions about obtained results; falsification expressions that may or may not be any of the preceding expression types in the negative; metaexpressions that are not interpretations but relate any of the preceding expressions with object expressions about the behavior of scientists (e.g., explicit and implicit hypotheses that can be developed at the level of metacommunication to predict certain aspects of scientist "test and inference" behavior). Reproduction includes all these metaexpressions and object expressions that must be utilized by the scientist in reconstructing a given communication sequence. Generally, such reconstruction will include every expression type or must be metadescribed as including all these. More traditionally, this can be interpreted as saying that reproduction involves any scientist redoing the research of another scientist or of himself, starting the process "from scratch."

Replication, on the other hand, includes all the given expressions necessary to repeat the test of a hypothesis, most notably expressions of hypothesis, identity, measurement, results, and implicit and explicit hypotheses having to do with procedure. In replication, questions, problems, interpretations, and certain classes of compound expressions are excluded. Following Sidman's distinction,[30] "direct replication" will refer to the test of a hypothesis while "systematic replication" will refer to the test of a hypothesis that has been modified slightly either in the phraseology of the hypothesis or the deletion or rephrasing of some of the other expressions or the introduction of new expressions of the requisite types with the exception of a new hypothesis. With replication, then, any scientist is retesting a test of a hypothesis with or without modification. (Interestingly, Galtung[31] does not recognize direct replication as a form of replication.)

Reproduction or replication is contingent on precision and can be predicted according to H_2. There are important classes of scientist action that can be so predicted, thereby avoiding circularity in H_2. Precision is necessary to restate any expression type with the same consequences for replication or reproduction. Intraexpression comparison with replication and reproduction is implied and two questions are suggested: Can the expression be repeated with minimal error, and does repeating the expression alter the content of any of the other expressions in the reproduction or replication? How these questions are answered will differ according to the type of expression (which will be dealt with subsequently), but, generally, the level of precision of an expression can predict differences in the success of repetition of an expression. Success is measured by the number of alternative interpretations of the expression and interpretations of the meanings of the expression with repetition as well as the number of changes in and alternative interpretations of the other expressions involved in reproduction or replication.

In other words, the very process of precization of an expression and other contingent expressions will produce quantitatively different results depending on the level of precision of that expression when that expression is necessarily repeated for reproduction and replication. A hypothesis that is vague, for example, cannot be repeatedly tested because every repetition can and will generate different interpretations to be tested. Or a measurement expression that is ambiguous (e.g., has X meanings about the application of the referenced measuring instrument) will produce differing known interpretations with repetition. Or a measurement expression that is ambiguous may produce a change in object expressions referencing the action of the scientist with each repetition: if a measurement reading means different things on each application, the scientist must change his actions in the application and reading to accommodate such changes.

H_2 is a metahypothesis, then, that permits noncircular assessment of precization. By this is meant that H_2 allows the prediction of specific behavioral outcomes of scientists contingent on level of precision. These outcomes along with those specified in H_1 can be used to determine the level of precision of an expression. More importantly, they along with D_1 and D_2 demonstrate the consequences of level of precision for the scientific enterprise. They spell out the sense in which precision can be conceived of as the core requirement of science as communication: minimally, scientists must agree on the use of their expressions and must be able to replicate and reproduce sequences in order to proceed.

THE COMMUNICATION SEQUENCE SPECIFIED

Within the shared-unshared, symbolic-not symbolic progression of inquiry different classes of expressions can be specified. The requirement of precision implies different consequences according to class of expressions. The remaining chapters of Part I will deal with each expression type and the implications of precision for it. This chapter will conclude with a brief introduction of expression types. These are not to be conceived of as exhaustive, but as the minimal number and types necessary in a description of science as communication. As such they are sufficient to document how the prototypic research endeavor proceeds. Further, they do generate rules for scientific research that are proscriptively and prescriptively useful as guides to how research is to be done.

The types of expressions can be conveniently summarized by elaborating the diagram of the progression of inquiry, as in Figure 1.

At quadrant 1 perception of events occurs and is referenced by object expressions. Perception is oriented by problems that are referenced by several types of expressions but that are codified by questions. These are extraneous to the particular scientific sequence. The arrow from 1 to 2 indicates the codification of perception object expressions by appropriate meta-expressions about identities, relations, and observational modes. Quadrant 2 progresses to shared symbolic representations via measurement expressions, refined identity expressions, and compound hypotheses that relate object expressions referencing the action of scientists and other metaexpressions that can be measurements, identities, relations, or compound hypotheses. These hypotheses can be implicit or explicit according to the stage of development of the science. At quadrant 3 hypotheses to be falsified are formulated. Quadrant 3 progresses to 4, which is the test of the hypothesis. The media

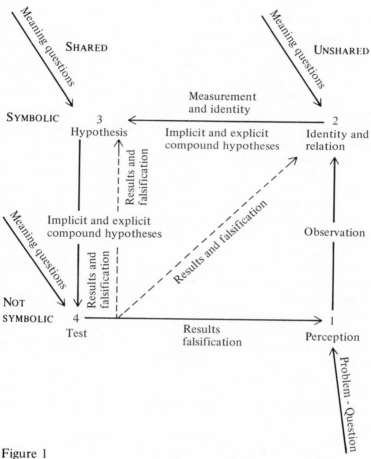

Figure 1

for this progression are implicit and explicit compound hypotheses that relate scientist action, measurements, identities, other compound hypotheses, relations, observations, or object expressions about perception. Control hypotheses are an important subset of implicit or explicit compound hypotheses necessary for the progression from 3 to 4.

Expressions about results and hypothesis falsification can

close the process by providing progression from 4 to 1, 4 to 2, 4 to 3 where the cycle begins anew. If progression is from 4 to 1 via falsification, the whole cycle is reformulated, from 4 to 2 the cycle repeats with identities, relations, observations, or from 4 to 3, the hypothesis is retested. Reproduction is closure from 4 to 1 according to results or falsification. Falsification can also produce a *complete change* rather than repetition of the whole cycle. Replication is closure from 4 to 2 or 4 to 3 according to results or falsification. Either can produce a change in 2 or the nonhypothesis components beween 3 and 4, in which case replication has been called "systematic" as opposed to "direct." The important point is that results that are nonfalsifying can still produce replication or reproduction, but that falsification can produce "shocks" in the cycle that completely alter its component expressions and may transform it into a "new" cycle. Finally, questions about meaning, the prime mechanism of precization, occur at 2, 3, or 4 with the general effect of reversing the tangent arrow. Such questions at 2 reverse the direction of progression so that 1 is repeated, at 3 so that 2 is repeated, at 4 so that 3 is repeated. These questions cannot function as feedback mechanisms at 1 because object expressions, by definition, have no interpretations. Meaning questions, via precization, can transform the expression components to which they apply and those that contingently precede them. Further, they can transform the cycle in the sense of systematic replication. But they are not sufficient to produce reproduction or change in the whole cycle.

This synoptic presentation will be elaborated in the following chapters of Part I. Although expressions will be treated separately, this brief overview is sufficient to demonstrate the interdependencies involved. In Chapter 3 the interdependencies will be emphasized again in more elaborate fashion. It will be shown that this relatively simple description is a sufficient description of science that permits the application of several important rules to social science.

2

Problems, Questions, Identity, and Measurement

An important "discovery" of the philosophy of science is that perception is always determined for the scientist by extraperceptual events. Perception is considered purposeful according to thought; it is structured and determined by cognitive processes that are not perceptual. This analysis accepts this rule with modifications appropriate for a communicative analysis.

PERCEPTION

Perception for the scientist occurs in the realm of non-symbolic and unshared experience. As an act it is largely un-codified. However, the metatheorist codifies perception in object expressions referencing the behavior of the scientist. The extent of this codification is determined by the purposes of the analysis. Conceivably a fullblown metatheory of science will be contingent on a theory of perception, as all of science is predicated on the perceptual experience of the scientist. Such a theory would specify the processes of perception and generate hypotheses relating these processes and their contingent codification in the brain. Current work in perception theory is split between psychological physiologists studying perception as a neurological event and psychologists studying the relation between perception and reports about perception.[1] Unfortunately, the former tend to restrict their research by excluding the extraperceptual mechanisms for selecting, codifying, and storing perceptual experience, while the latter treat the subjects' reports about their perceptual experience as synonymous with that experience. This schism is quite artificial and easily bridged by the recognition that perceptual-neurological experience and perceptual-reportoral experience are interrelated according to this rule: if neurological experience contingent on perception, then reports about perception contingent on the codifying and storing mechanisms of this neurological experience. Hypotheses of this general form would seem to be the logical business of perception theory. Such hypotheses are certainly needed for a metatheory of science.

Given that such a theory is lacking, statements about perception as a quadrant 1 event must be restricted to general object expressions referencing the perceptual behavior of the scientist. In these, perception will be treated as a given. Immediate complications arise because scientists will self-reference their perceptual experience as they progress to quadrant 2: perception will be referred to in object expressions when converted from unshared nonsymbolic experience to unshared symbolic experience. These object expressions of the scientist should not be confused with the object expressions of the metatheorist that reference the perceptions of the scientist; the scientist may not perceive that he is perceiving in the sense that the metatheorist says he is. This, of course, is a caution against the transposition of reality problem mentioned in Chapter 1. Even though perception must be a given for the metatheorist because of a lack of knowledge, this caution is well heeded. The generalizations to follow cannot be falsified on the basis of intuition, but must be treated as hypotheses to be tested.

PROBLEMS AND QUESTIONS

The scientist, then, begins his inquiry by perceiving the events in his domain. What events are to be in his domain are determined by nonperceptual phenomena. These phenomena are expressions that are labeled problems and questions. This is the communicative interpretation of the rule that perception is purposeful according to thought. Yet it is more specific, for "thought" is interpreted as problems and questions as expression types.

Problems are any metaexpression that self-references itself as a problem. Within quadrant 1 they focus perception and can themselves be experientially based. Again, the metatheorist can speculate about the types of experience upon which problem formation is contingent. Generally, the scientist's problems can be said to be formulated on the basis of two drives, curiosity or pain. "Drives" is meant as an object expression, and no intent to base a theory of science on drive theory or motivation theory is implied. Neither are curiosity and pain the only precursors of problems. Yet, the process of problem formation does seem to be best described as initiating in curiosity and pain. Given the speculative nature of these initial remarks, it is also plausible to state that curiosity and pain are the experiential correlates of problems for the scientist. A system is suggested: problems arise from curiosity or pain and give rise to curiosity or pain. Again a lack of knowledge hampers further generalization, although much psychological research on curiosity and exploration is quite suggestive of the salience of these cursory comments.[2]

Problems imply solutions; more strongly, problems that

exist without solutions are a logical absurdity. Problems are not things, i.e., they are not object expressions. They are metaexpressions that reference object expressions or events. As such, they are communicationally intended to direct attention to states of affairs asserted in object expressions that must be transformed in some way. This transformation is called a "solution" and is expressed by different object expressions or metaexpressions referencing the change in object expressions. At the meta-level every problem implies this change and together with the change produces the meta-metaexpression, [[The problem has been solved]]. No communication sequence involving a problem expression is terminated until this meta-metaexpression is asserted; more formally, the ["solution"] references the change in object expressions. The problem initiates the derivation of the [solution] and "primes" the communication sequence until sufficient information is formulated to assert [[The problem has been solved]], which is sufficient to terminate the sequence. In this sense, problems are formed to be solved: their purpose is in the derivation of solutions.

Problems are expressed by questions. Other forms of expression may be used to describe problems and may combine in different ways to be labeled as descriptions of problems. But questions are the prototypic expression type that asserts problems. To put it differently, problems can be expressed in numerous ways, but every problem can be sufficiently expressed by a question or series of questions. For it is questions that permit the derivation of solutions via communication sequences, because questions imply answers, and solutions are answers. The following relation, then, exists between problems and their solutions and questions and their answers: problems must be expressed in questions even though they can be described by different expressions; solutions are answers even though they may be described by different expressions.

Questions have the same relation to answers as problems to solutions. Every question implies an answer (and those which do not are specially labeled as question-like nonquestions, i.e., "rhetorical questions"). More strongly, questions that do not imply answers—with the exception of "rhetorical questions"—are a logical absurdity. In effect, questions are asked to be answered. They are expressions which immediately imply other expressions. Answers as the other class of expressions are sufficient to terminate the questions. In fact, they can be evaluated only according to their success in terminating questions.[3] The meta-metaquestion [[Is this answer sufficient?]] is answerable according to the extent that the [answer] deletes the question as an expression component of the scientific communication sequence. This is so because of the inseparability of questions and answers, which demands a joint evaluation, and the inherent vagueness of any other criteria of answer success. Questions, then, are expressions that reference object expressions. Answers are implied by questions and reference different object expressions or changes in object expressions. Questions maintain the communication sequence until sufficient information is formed to assert, [[This is the answer]]. Answers strike out the questions as viable components of the sequence, in effect terminating their occurrence. (The history of science is to a large extent the history of questions recurring until they are terminated by answers.)

Questions as metaexpressions are interpretable and subject to precization. Every question can undergo the transformation involved. The mechanism for this process is meaning questions, which should be distinguished from the substantive questions of science just discussed. The answers to meaning questions are other questions because meaning questions applied to questions produce interpretations of those questions. The interpretation of [X?] is [[X?] means [Y?] and this is the answer to [[What does [X?] mean?]]. This interpretation will not of itself terminate the meaning question. The meaning question will be applied and reapplied until precization is terminated. Any particular instance of it will be fully answered, but the interpretation that is the answer can have the same question asked of it. This chain of successive answers that become successive questions is the precization process; and even though a particular meaning question will be terminated, the same question frame reapplies until the process is terminated. The adequacy of answers of meaning questions, therefore, cannot be evaluated according to their success in terminating such questions: other criteria must be introduced, and these criteria are the same as those that terminate precization. Meaning questions applied to substantive questions are sufficiently answered when that answer is a tautologous interpretation of the original substantive question: e.g., [[What does [X?] mean?]]; [[X?] means [X?]].

There are forms of questions in science that are tautologous. This is different from saying that there are tautologous questions in science. Generally, there are specific tautologous questions and these form the substantive base of much of science: e.g., "How is DNA operative in the transfer of genetic information?"; "What are the types of elementary particles?"; "What are the constituents of the cell?". A specification of these would require a catalogue. Forms of questions can be specified, however, that tend to be tautologous: the question frames tend to have a tautologous interpretation even if the terms filling the frame do not. Questions about cause and effect are usually tautologous: e.g., [["What causes X?]] means [What causes X?]]. [Why?] and [How?] questions are also usually tautologous as are questions about occurrence or relationships: e.g., [Does X occur?]; [Is X related to Y?]. These cannot unequivocally be asserted to be tautologies, however. This is true irrespective of the extent to which the components of the frame—the [X] and [Y]—are not tautologous. [Cause], for example, has (to some) a range of meanings[4] while [Why?] is the basis for much of the debate in the philosophy of science about what explanations and laws are.[5] Again, however, the transposition of reality problem is suggested: just because these questions have problematic interpretations for philosophers of science does not mean they do for scientists. Scientists search for causes and generate explanations and laws without the hindrance of examining the possible interpretations of Why-questions and Cause-questions.

Therefore, these question frames tend to be tautologous for the scientist because they are immediately suggestive of answers. The answers are hypotheses. To anticipate much that is to follow, all hypotheses are expressible in implication form: "If A then B". The question [Is X related to Y?] will have an answer that is a hypothesis: e.g., [If X then Y]. The resulting hypothesis must not be falsified to be a sufficient answer, but the answer will be a hypothesis that, if not falsified, will terminate the question. This is the simplest case because the question directly implies the hypothesis and the component antecedents and consequences. The other questions also will be answered by hypotheses but the interconnections are not so obvious.

Cause-questions are answerable when causes have been determined. If all hypotheses can be stated in implication form, then the search for causes translates into the search for antecedents. This is not to say [cause] is equivalent to [antecedent], only that [cause] is interpretable as [antecedent]. There are other possible interpretations, as many as there are forms of hypotheses. Chapter 3 will deal extensively with this subject. For the moment it is sufficient to note by fiat that cause and effect statements must be interpreted into some logical form in order to be testable. The form being advocated here is implication; the answer to any cause-question will be an "if . . . then . . ." hypothesis. Again, to be sufficient to terminate the question in the communication sequence, the hypothesis must not be falsified. Moreover, the hypothesis may have multiple antecedents. In fact, any search for [cause] will most likely yield multiple antecedents, for the world is not neatly packaged causes and corresponding effects. Any one [cause] may be suggestive of multiple antecedents simply because reality corresponds more closely to a probabilistic model than a deterministic one (see Chapter 3). For example, [What causes the diversity of species of living things?] was answered by Darwin by the hypotheses of evolution: e.g., [If natural selection then evolution] with [natural selection] having several interpretations like [genetic mutation] and [adaptability]. The same question was answered by Lamarck by hypotheses that include: [If adaptation through certain phenotypic characteristics, then corresponding genotypic alterations]. And in present biochemical research, hypotheses of the following form are beginning to emerge: [[If [if adaptive demands X, Y, Z by the physical environment then alteration of DNA by RNA] then genetic modifications with resulting phenotypic alterations]]. It is still too soon to specify these hypotheses exactly.

The latter example suggests an added complexity when formulating answers to Why-questions. If the immediate interpretation of a why-question is that question (tautology), then it can be answered by one hypothesis, albeit one with multiple antecedents. For example, [Why does genetic mutation occur] may be answerable by [If X, Y, Z interactions between RNA and DNA, then U, V, W mutant genetic alterations]. Again, a not-falsified hypothesis with antecedents to whatever level of complexity will be sufficient to terminate a tautologous why-question. However, why-questions may be tautologously interpretable, but may be reapplied to the hypothesis that is the answer to the original why-question. [Why C?] may be answered by [If B then C] and [Why B?] may be asked and answered by [If A then B]. It should be obvious that these two hypotheses are the base of the simplest form of deductive reasoning, the categorical syllogism: [[If [If A then B] and [If B then C], then [If A then C]]]. From answers to two why-questions, a third hypothesis may be deduced. This whole deductive chain initially can be taken to be a sufficient answer to [Why C?]. That is, a why-question can be treated as insufficiently answered until a deductive chain of hypotheses is derived. This is often the case in science. Part of the confusion among philosophers of science over the sufficiency of scientific explanation has to do with the ambiguity of intent in asking why-questions: are they to be treated as sufficiently answered by one hypothesis or by deductive chains of hypotheses? The answer, of course, is contingent on multiple components of the communication sequence: e.g., are the scientists trained to generate deductive chains, are these hypotheses sets the purpose of the scientists, are they considered feasible given constraints imposed by the events in the domain of inquiry, and so on. Two things are certain. First, most scientists do not consider their why-questions sufficiently answered until they have formulated deductive theories: in other words, they actively pursue deductive theory as a goal and terminate why-questions only contingent on nonfalsified, deductively related hypotheses. Second, deduction seems to be a process inherent in the human mind with thought processes continuing until its realization.[6] For the purposes herein, it is sufficient to note that, in either case, why-questions are answerable by hypotheses.

This is also true of [How?] questions. The difficulty with a demonstration of this fact is the multiple ways in which [How] can be interpolated into question form: e.g., [How is X caused?] is an interpretation of [What causes X?]. The class of questions being dealt with must be restricted beyond labeling them [How-questions]. This class of questions will include members that are intended to uncover the mechanisms for the production or elimination of certain events. Although the distinction is admittedly vague, there is a difference in the questions, [What causes an automobile engine to produce movement in a car?] and [How does an automobile engine produce movement in a car?]. The difference is that any how-question of this type will have multiple cause-questions or why-questions as interpretations. This question type does not presume the sufficiency of any one interpretation. For example, the second question can be interpreted sufficiently into any number of cause or why-questions: e.g., [What causes the electrical system to burn the fuel so that the car engine will produce the necessary r.p.m.'s?] or [What causes the fuel to be injected into the piston chamber?] or [Why does the lubricant system prevent the car engine from "freezing up?"] or [Why does the constellation of gears produce forward motion?]. Given these multiple interpretations of the original how-question, the number and types of the hypotheses to answer it can vary. There are no *a priori* criteria for judging the sufficiency of any one hypothesis, for they are all equally permissible. This, of course, is not true of why- or cause-questions that immediately presume a limited range of sufficient hypotheses.

[How can *B* be eliminated?] as a class of how-questions is perhaps more illustrative of this point. The corresponding hypothesis answer will be of the form: $A \supset \sim B$; (if A then not B). In order to define "not-B", B must be defined: the original how-question presumes this definition. The range of not-B's is unlimited. Phrased differently, any affirmative will be not-many things: cats are not dogs, or goats, or elephants. A limited definition of what B is not is clearly impossible. This is one reason that the use of negatives in definitions traditionally has been frowned upon.[7] It follows that the range of antecedents that result in not-B will be potentially unlimited. Hence any hypothesis set in answer to [How can B be eliminated?] will be theoretically unlimited. Of course, this logical possibility is constrained empirically by the lawfulness of nature: the elimination of B is ultimately an empirical question that will be answered by a limited number of related A's. The important point is that all how-questions are answerable by hypotheses.

The final question form that tends to be tautologous may be called the identity-question. There is one main form: [What is X?]. Derivatives of this question may refer to measures of X or to the certification of the occurrence or existence of X. In any case the problem is to establish X as an interpretation of science relating a metaexpression and an object expression. An important epistemological issue can be settled in considering such questions.

For the scientist, questions about existence are replaced by questions about occurrence. Not that questions of existence are not posed: witness the current debate in nuclear physics over the existence of quarks[8] and gravity waves.[9] But such questions are treated as if they are questions of occurrence. In other words, questions of existence are legitimate in science but are either translated into questions of occurrence or viewed as necessarily confirmable and only confirmable by such translation. The search for quarks and gravity waves goes on within the context of rigid experimentation and measurement procedure. This is one of the clearest demarcations of science from philosophy and metaphysics in which questions of existence are treated as directly answerable. The systematic empirical confirmation that questions of occurrence suggest is avoided in favor of rigid logical and semantic debate. To put it succinctly, questions of existence do not presume the systematic criteria of empirical confirmation that questions of occurrence do, and when the former are posited in the absence of the latter, one is in the realm of philosophy or metaphysics. This distinction has its parallel in questions about identity and questions about measurement. These will be discussed exhaustively in the remaining sections of this chapter.

All questions of this general form are answerable by hypotheses, remembering that existence is equivalent to occurrence for the scientist. These hypotheses are rather special. They usually have some aspect of the scientist's actions as antecedent and the identification interpretation as consequence. These actions can be simple object expressions having to do with the scientist's perception or observation behavior. Or they can be more complicated object expressions having to do with certain sequences of scientist actions aimed at manipulating the objects of his concern. Intuitively, in the first case, the scientist can answer identity-questions by direct perception or observation. In the second case, the scientist can answer such questions through systematic alteration of events in his domain: i.e., measurement, application and reading of instruments, experiment, and so on. The latter case is even more complicated when the events the scientist is trying to certify are said to be not directly observable or perceivable: atoms and molecules used to be the favorite examples in the philosophy of science. However, as will be seen shortly, an even more important complexity for this analysis arises when these hypotheses are implicit for the scientist: in effect, his action is so routinized that the hypotheses that are necessary to answer his identity-questions need not be stated. This will tend to occur more when the necessary action is perception and less when the necessary action is an elaborate sequence. But it can occur developmentally in either case. Despite these complications, the important point is that identity-questions are sufficiently answerable by this rather special class of hypotheses. These hypotheses will form a crucial component of the following discussion of measurement and identity.

To summarize, problems are codified in questions. Questions are subject to precization. In science there are several types of questions that appear to be tautologous: why-questions, how-questions, cause-questions, relation-questions, identity-questions. All of these questions are answerable by hypotheses. They can be terminated or deleted from the scientific communication sequence when the requisite hypotheses are formulated and not falsified through testing. In the sequence of events of the process of science, precization of questions precedes hypothesis formation and has its terminus in tautologous questions that are answerable by hypotheses. This is not intended to imply that these question types are the sufficient ones for any science, only that as tautologies they do have this important relation with hypotheses. In science every question implies an answer and that answer will be a hypothesis or set of hypotheses. The question and corresponding hypothesis-answer, of course, can be treated as a whole compound expression. If so, this expression will be tautologous; and this result is the ultimate in scientific achievement.

IDENTITY

It is a truism that scientists deal with things or object expressions. The problem of identification of these object expressions would seem to be straightforward. It is not.

The traditional conceptualization of identity has been one in which metaexpressions are mapped onto object expressions or words onto things. The linkage between these expression types has usually been treated as some form of correspondence. Tarski's previously cited formula for truth is illustrative: [[birds have wings] is true if and only if birds have wings]]. Carnap's object-versus-theory language and the notion of "rules of correspondence" are also attempts to specify the relationship.[10] A slightly more complex idea is the linkage between metaexpressions and corresponding object expressions via the medium of measurement and auxiliary hypotheses.[11] Two intervening constructs are added to bridge the gap; but the idea that the relationship is one of correspondence is basically unaltered.

The problem with the identification of phenomena in science lies not with the phenomena, but with the metaexpression labels used to identify the phenomena. As metaexpressions these labels can be used independently of their corresponding object expressions. I am not referring here to the possible confusion of word with thing dealt with in the last chapter. Rather, the very fact that identity-expressions can exist assertionally independent of their corresponding object expressions is problem enough.

Wittgenstein's discovery that words of themselves do not have meaning[12] can be interpreted as a consequence of this problem. Because words exist assertionally as words it is assumed that they function linguistically as words. As Wittgenstein demonstrates, this is empirically absurd. Words are used, and it is in the context of their use that they can be said to have meaning. The same thing is true of identity expressions. Even though as expressions they can be spoken of independently of their corresponding object expressions, they are not interpretable independently. The apparent schism between metaexpression and object expression is a result of the linguistic independence of each. However, this separate usage implies nothing about their development, their co-variation, their joint use, or in fact, what they mean. In essence they are inseparable, and any analysis of identity must be based on this premise.

Identity and Perception

The simplest form of identity-expression is one that relates a metaexpression and an object expression about the scientist's perception. These might be called perceptual identities. Every philosopher of science usually talks about expressions that interface the events and the language the scientist uses to describe these events. Carnap calls them the object language and Nagel calls them observation statements.[13] In this analysis this interface consists of expressions in which metaexpressions (usually terms) are juxtaposed with object expressions. Perceptual identities are meta-metaexpressions in which the object expressions are the scientist's perception. It is such identities that are usually referred to by traditional statements like "behavior is directly observable" or "chromosomal damage is directly observable." Yet, upon close inspection even the simplest case of identity is really quite complex. This can be seen by reconstructing the developmental process of identification. The basics of the diagram at the end of Chapter 1 can be used for this purpose, for identification is a communicative process in the same sense that science is. This cycle or sequence of events will be called the "identification cycle" and is to be understood as separate *or* as a component of the cycle of inquiry at the end of Chapter 1.

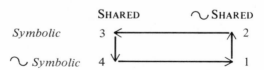

If identification is conceived of as in this diagram, its general purpose in science is to convert the unshared and non-symbolically represented experience of the scientist into shared and symbolically represented experience: to move the scientist from quadrant 1 to quadrant 3. Perceptual identity involves the labeling of the scientist's perception in quadrant 1 and relating the resulting object expression to an appropriate metaexpression in quadrant 2. If the events are present, the scientist can move the process to quadrant 3 by pointing: e.g., scientist A asserts "That is the chemical attractant of the gypsy moth," then points to a smear on a slide, and scientist B nods agreement. This subset of perceptual identity is so simple that it is unrepresentative of how science is practiced in the same way that the events-present evaluation of scientific communication was seen to be unrepresentative of science. (Interestingly, Tarski's rationale is similar for the necessary exclusion of demonstratives like "this" and "that" from his theory of truth and proof.[14]) However, even assuming this paradigm to be representative of science, the transition from quadrant 2 to quadrant 3 is at best incomplete when the sole medium for this transition is perceptual identity. The reason for this stems from the requirements this transition imposes on the communicator.

The scientist cannot progress from quadrant 1 to quadrant 3 on the basis of identity expressions alone. This is true in both a strict and a less strict sense depending upon the assumptions used in the illustration. To play a Wittgensteinian[15] language game: imagine conversing with a naïve communicative partner, one who has no idea whatsoever about the events in your domain or your perception of those events. The strict assumption is that you and he share a common language system but that none of the words in your identity expression are known to him: he understands the grammar you use but not your substantive terms. You utter, [a [telephone] is an object with X, Y, Z properties]] with the intention of permitting him to perceive a [telephone]. Obviously, if he does not understand "X, Y, Z," he cannot perceive a [telephone]. The argument need proceed no further given this strict assumption: perceptual identity expressions cannot of themselves translate the scientist's unshared symbolic experience to shared symbolic experience.

The objection can be raised that this assumption is too strict, that science never proceeds this way. However, the conclusion is the same even with the utilization of the less strict assumption that your partner understands all the words and the syntax of your perceptual identity expression with the exception of [telephone]. The information is not sufficient to tell him where and when he might perceive a telephone. Since he cannot locate the requisite events, he cannot confirm receipt of the message. Further, even if he has located and perceived a [telephone], he cannot confirm it because the necessary confirmation expression is not permissible in the game. The minimal necessary confirmation expression is an indication of receipt of the message. This feedback can be as complex as the receiver repeating the message or as simple as a gesture indicating receipt. In the example concerning the "gypsy moth sex attractant" demonstration, the head nod of scientist *B* is the necessary feedback. The maximal confirmation expression is feedback that the message was received and understood. Neither variant of a confirmation expression is permissible in the game. Consequently, the scientist can never know if he has shared his identity expression or if his message has succeeded in producing the perception of a [telephone]. Again, perceptual identity expressions cannot of themselves satisfy the requirements of quadrant 3.

There are profound consequences for the theory of science from this fact. It is a fallacy to speak of perceptual identities as the base of science as traditional theory has done. They cannot be treated as necessary or sufficient independent expressions, for they do not even satisfy the minimal criteria for science in any sense. So even these as the simplest form of identity expressions must be amended. Only the first shocks of this principle are being anticipated here; the significance of the argument will continue to unfold.

What supplements of perceptual identity expressions are necessary so that they can be shared? Basically they are the same as the requirements of observation. Perception and observation can be distinguished according to the following rule: observation is confirmed perception. Perception is necessary for observation, and observation is sufficient for perception. Observation can be defined in accordance with traditional research methodology usage. Categories of events are established; rules of sorting events into the categories are presented; these events can be directly perceived; rules for perceiving the events (when and where) are provided; the events are categorized by two or more independent observers repeatedly; the "goodness" of the observation procedure is measured by calculating the reliability of the observations by finding the percent agreement in categorization by number of events categorized or number of observations made. Observation is necessary and sufficient to convert perception into shared symbolic experience.

A translation of this rule into the terminology of the current analysis keeps the requirements intact but alters their mode of formulation. The categories of events are perceptual identity expressions, as it is required that the "event can be directly perceived." The two independent observers are the communicators, and the calculated reliability of the observations is based on the process of confirmation. That is, feedback expressions must be provided to assure "agreement," and they are necessary and sufficient for confirmation.

Reliability as percent agreement of observations is related to agreement of usage as a measure of precision. Reliability is percent agreement of matching metaexpressions (terms for categories) and object expressions (terms or expressions that are the perceivable events) by communicators. Precision can be assessed according to H_1 in Chapter 1 as percent agreement of matching meta-metaexpressions and metaexpressions or metaexpressions and object expressions. In the second case, precision is equivalent to reliability. In the first case, precision is the reliability of sorting metaexpressions into categories that are meta-metaexpressions symbolizing the use of the metaexpressions: e.g., are certain metaexpressions defined as "defined" (derived) or "undefined" (primitive) terms by scientists and with what percent level of agreement! So observational reliability as traditionally conceived is a subset of precision as percent agreement of usage of expressions by communicators.

Finally, in terminology congruent with this analysis, rules of sorting and perceiving events are special classes of meta-metaexpressions. They are hypotheses relating the nonverbal action of the scientist and the perceptual identities he formulates. There are two crucial components to these hypotheses. First, they must specify not only the perceptual characteristics or properties of the events, they must also specify their location. Second, they must tell the scientist how to perceive the events. The former is crucial to all identification and measurement. It will be called the "Space-Time" rule or "ST-rule" for short. Basically, it states that a necessary condition for the identification of events so that they can be communicated or shared is their location in time and space. To anticipate future arguments, this means that measurement and identification are inseparable in science. This topic will be exhaustively treated in the section on measurement that follows.

The second component of these hypotheses assumes adequate ST specification. "How to perceive events" translates into instructions for the scientist about what actions he is to perform in order to perceive the events. Generally, he may be informed that he must in some way arrange the events in his domain, that he must isolate certain events, that he must select certain events, that he must change the position or transport certain events, or that he must alter his behavior in some way without altering the events (e.g., change the degree of displacement of his eyes from center position either vertically or horizontally). These, in fact, will be the object expressions that are scientist action throughout this metatheoretical analysis. As a component of the hypotheses necessary for perceptual identity they can assume either antecedent or consequence position, although most likely the latter: e.g., "if he is to confirm [[identity-expression X]] then scientist B must isolate events X', transport them and place them under his microscope, and look into the microscope lens."

Hypotheses that specify the requisite actions of the scientist in order for him to confirm or create confirmable perceptual identities assume the satisfaction of the ST rule, just as reliable observation consists in part of rules for perceiving and sorting events into appropriate categories. More formally, the ST rule is necessary for such action-hypotheses. Along with requisite identity-expressions and provision for confirmation (i.e., reliability or, generally, calculation of precision) both hypotheses are sufficient to permit the scientist-communicators to translate their unshared and not symbolic experience to unshared and symbolic experience to shared symbolic experience: to progress sufficiently from quadrant 1 to quadrant 3. This is the only way in which perceptual identities can be conceived of as scientifically sufficient.

Once the scientist has proceeded to quadrant 3 in the identification cycle, progression to quadrant 4 by way of formal confirmation is relatively straightforward. The requirements of this quadrant are that the originally naïve scientist-communicator can proceed to sufficiently identify the events identified by the knowledgeable scientist. Initial confirmation is necessary in quadrant 3; in quadrant 4 the naïve scientist can successfully repeat the identifications without any further information from the original source. This final step in the progression is a consequence implied by quadrant 3. This quadrant is the crucial one for science in the sense that once its requirements are met scientists can proceed to repeat identifications and if necessary to replicate or reproduce the original identification cycle.

The expression [perceptual identity] is to be understood in what follows as amended by all these considerations. Occasionally, this point will be reinforced by substituting for it the expression [observable identity].

Perceptual Identity and Precision

Identity-expressions *qua* expressions must satisfy the requirement of precision. If the identification cycle proceeds with its requirements satisfied, then the requirement of precision is also satisfied. Confirmed identity-expressions will be compound tautologies, i.e., the metaexpressions and tautologous object expression will form one meta-metaexpression that is a tautology. This fact follows from the equivalence between reliability and precision: if the observations are reliable then the identity expression observations are reliable then the identity expression is precise by definition. The obvious is not belabored here, for identification can be insufficient and not tautologous in science. Generally, the stage of development of a science can be assessed by the precision of its identities. Nuclear physics as the most advanced science is searching out new perceptual identities on the basis of communication sequences involving tautologous identities, i.e., the search for subatomic particles is the last frontier in physics according to some physicists. Social science, on the other hand, has burdensome identification problems at present. This point will be elaborated in Chapter 4.

It is possible to relate an important set of structurally (as opposed to semantically) tautologous questions previously discussed with the hypotheses needed to supplement perceptual identity expressions. Generally, [What is X?] or identity-questions are answerable by these hypotheses and the appropriate identity-expressions. This is a specification of the previous rule that this class of questions like all questions is answerable by hypotheses. Identity-questions in this sense can be interpreted as a class of meaning questions applied to object expressions and metaexpressions that are interrelated in identity-expressions. As such they are the mechanism of precization for identity-expressions and are sufficiently answerable when the hypotheses supplementing these expressions are confirmed. They are by definition structurally tautologous, but their component terms are not necessarily semantically precise. They can be reapplied to themselves. This internal precization will be terminated upon the derivation of tautologous and confirmed identity-expressions which imply tautologous and confirmed action-hypotheses. This subset of meaning questions is therefore quite special: its precization to tautology implies its termination by its answer. In other words, when questions of this subset are maximally precise they will be answered; conversely, when they are answered they are maximally precise. With all other question types in science their structural or semantic precision has no comparable relationship with their hypotheses-answers: even if the particular question is totally tautologous, its sufficient answer is not implied.

This important principle requires illustration. Suppose the question is [[What is the [sex attractant] of the gypsy moth?]]. "Gypsy moth" is treated as an object expression and is tautologous. Assume the metaexpressions [sex attractant] to imply a sufficient identity-expression; then it too will be tautologous by definition. As an identity-question it is tautologous. So the question is maximally precise. However, [sex attractant] as a sufficient identity-expression implies all relevant action-hypotheses (including ST-specification): what to do to a gypsy moth to locate the attractant, how to isolate the attractant, how to perceive it, how to analyze it into its perceptual properties (that will be object expressions), and so on. On the basis of this question alone the naïve scientist would have sufficient information to proceed to answer it, given that the identity cycle has been completed sufficiently prior to the question. In other words, this question if maximally precise (unequivocally interpretable or tautologous) suggests its sufficient answer.

By way of contrast, suppose the question were [[How is the [sex attractant] of the gypsy moth operative?]]. Even if the component identity expression were tautologous, thereby making the question tautologous, a sufficient answer is not implied. The [sex attractant] may operate by activating hormonal changes in the male gypsy moth, by stimulating his olfactory sense, by transforming the pattern of nervous impulses in his brain, or by any combination thereof. There is, in fact, no limitation on the range of possible hypotheses that might sufficiently answer this question. As previously mentioned, this is true of all [[How?]] questions. No other question type implies the relationship between precision of questions and hypothesis-answer that identity-questions do.

Precision and Action Hypotheses

The special relationship entailed by identity questions is the result of the action hypotheses implicit in sufficient perceptual identities. That these hypotheses are implicit is of significance. First, because they are implicit, they are often overlooked as the basis of perceptual identification. They do not exist as hypotheses for the scientist. More correctly, they are not codified until such time as they are falsified. If for some reason the scientist is prevented from isolating, selecting, arranging, transporting, or altering his behavior so as to perceive the identified events, and thereby has his perception of them impeded, then he will try to discover [[Why?]]. And this question can be answered only by making the implicit hypotheses explicit. In effect, if he cannot perceive what he should be able to, then he will codify and test the hypotheses that should be necessary to permit the perception. Barring such falsification, these implicit hypotheses are not subject to test by scientists. However, the implicit hypotheses of the scientist are necessary metaexpressions for this theory of science. Carnap,[16] Hempel,[17] Popper,[18] and several measurement theorists[19] anticipate this importance but never systematically analyze it. Carnap, for example, implies that all observation is founded on laws of behavior. Hempel suggests the importance of laws for concept formation and measurement. Popper declares outright that all measurement is codifiable by Carnap's reduction sentences or other disposition concepts, that is, Popper implies that all measurement can be expressed by hypothesis sets. And most measurement theorists emphasize that measurement is based on laws. Yet, analysis rarely proceeds further. As this discussion proceeds, the analysis will be extended beyond these few preliminary remarks.

A more important consequence of the implicit nature of these action hypotheses is suggested by the question: "Why are these hypotheses implicit?," or by implication, "When do such hypotheses become implicit?" An answer requires a definition of [implicit]. Any expression will be said to be [implicit] in a communication sequence when it is not uttered by the communicators, is uttered by the metacommunicator, and has important consequences for the communication sequence. These action hypotheses fulfill all three definitional criteria. They are not codified by scientists, are codified by metatheorists, and have been shown to be crucial for the process of perceptual identification, a core component of science. As the scientist can play metatheorist, he can elect to explicitly codify hypotheses at any point. Saying that he will do so when they are falsified is tantamount to saying that he will do it when the consequences of the implicit hypotheses are disruptive, when they impede science by impeding perceptual identification. This is a converse answer to the original question: implicit hypotheses will be made explicit when they are falsified and the flow of scientific communication based on them is consequently disrupted.

The answer to the original question is the converse of the converse: hypotheses become implicit when they are never falsified. This is precisely the case with action-hypotheses as the basis of the scientist's perceptual behavior. They have permitted perception and identification with such unaltering success that they need not be codified. In other words, their test and confirmation flows from the constant success of scientists in perceiving and identifying events on their basis. So action hypotheses are implicit because they are so well confirmed that their codification introduces unnecessary redundancy into science. When they are falsified for whatever reason, thereby disrupting the communication sequence, they will be explicitly stated. For a metatheory of science they must be stated because they underlie much of the explicit communication of scientists. This general relationship applies not only to this special class of hypotheses but also to all scientific hypotheses, and it will be especially relevant for nonperceptual identification and measurement.

Nonperceptual Identification

Not all identities in science can be perceived directly. Atoms, molecules, and radioactivity are but a few oft-cited examples. These entities traditionally have posed problems for hard-nosed empiricists. Their existence for science has been the basis of the counterattack by those who deny the possibility of reducing theory to an observation-based language. Although attempts to develop such a language have been ingenious, they are recognized to have been unsuccessful.[20] Yet this class of events is not at all mystical. It is easily analyzed within the rubric of science as communication.

All identities must have observable consequences; their occurrence must produce observable effects. Perceptual identities encode those consequences as object expressions directly associated with metaexpressions. The prototypic meta-meta-expression for nonperceptual identities is more complex. In it, one or more expressions intervene between the original meta-expression and the object expression. These expressions may assert other identities or they may not. Invariably, however, they must be juxtaposed with measurements. Let us consider two cases by way of illustration.

First, a nonperceptual identity expression may be phrased: [[X] is [measured by Y]]. A metaexpression is therein juxtaposed directly with a measurement expression. Many of the crucial nonperceptual identities in science have this form. For example, [electron beams] and [x-rays] are equivalent to certain means for their production. A betatron utilizes certain electrical and magnetic measures (e.g., high-frequency oscillating voltage) to accelerate electrons and form electron beams as well as x-rays. Or, [alpha rays, beta rays, and gamma rays] as components of high-energy radiation can be identified by passing the radiation through a magnetic field. Or, [temperature] is identified by the relative expansion of mercury or alcohol in a capillary tube in one measuring instrument. It can also be measured by a thermocouple, a resistance thermometer, or a bimetallic thermometer.[21] Or, the [pheromone] (chemical attractant) of relevant organisms is known by its chemical analysis (i.e., by chromatographic procedures).[22]

A very special subset of nonperceptual identities includes the specification of the measurement dimensions of science. The [dimension] itself is juxtaposed with other measures. The identity expression in this case has the form of a mathematical equation. [Pressure], for example, is equal to [force acting per unit area]; [[Density] equals [mass per unit volume]]; [[Distance is the product of [rate and time] of movement]]. It is important to realize that although the identity dimensions are nonperceptual of themselves, they are translated into the appropriate perceptual object expressions via other measurement expressions. In a sense, all measurement dimensions are interpretable as nonperceptual identities, even those dimensions that are directly translatable into observable sets of scales and procedures, so-called "fundamental measures." [Depth], for example, is a nonperceptual identity characterized by its particular scales; in fact, it cannot be perceptually known. The dimensions of measures are artifacts of the communicative act, not properties of objects; like [depth], they cannot be perceptual identities.

A second class of nonperceptual identity expression has the form: [[X] produces [Y] which is observable and [Y is measured by Z]]. This form differs from the first in that a perceptual identity expression is inserted between the metaexpression to be identified and the measurement expression. [Pheromones] or chemical sex attractants are an excellent example. They are identified by appropriate chemical analysis, usually fragmentation, segmentation, and chromatography, and are an example of the first form of nonperceptual identity. But this is so only after a lengthy identification process involving this second form of identity. First, in order to be certified as occurring the pheromones must have an observable effect upon the movement of the organisms relative to each other. Second, the secretion itself must be located and the chemical isolated and transported. Then chemical analysis consisting of sophisticated measurement can be applied to the substance. The identification expressions of all pheromones will consist of expressions symbolizing each step in the process.

A more specific example of this type of nonperceptual identification comes from the biochemical research that isolated and identified the important hormonal attractant in the social amoebae.[23] The process included a number of steps: First, a careful description of the life cycle of the amoebae, which portrayed an aggregation stage before reproduction. Second, assertions of occurrence of the attractant by having diluted it in water near an aggregation center of the amoebae and re-applying the mixture to nonaggregated amoebae with the observation of their subsequent aggregation. Third, isolation of large quantities of the diluted attractant through special procedures. Fourth, quantification of the attraction of the substance by measuring the distance traveled by amoebae (or more precisely, the ability of amoebae to break out of a droplet of saline solution) as a function of quantity of attractant. Fifth, measurement of molecular weight of the attractant by spectral analysis. Sixth, application of other measures to the attractant, such as measurement of stability at varying temperatures. Seventh, comparison of the attractant with known biochemical substances. Eventually, this final step led to the identification of the attractant as [cyclic - 3′, 5′ - adenosine monophosphate]. The attractant has a formal identification expression that reads [[attractant] has X_n observable consequences, can be isolated in Y_n ways and can be measured by Z_n dimensions (i.e., amount, distance of contingent movement of amoebae, molecular weight, chemical stability)]].

This detailed example is a good illustration of what might be called compound nonperceptual identification. Structurally, this form of identification differs from simple nonperceptual identification in the number of requisite object and measurement expressions in the full identification expression.

In fact, all identification can be categorized according to the expression components. Perceptual identification relates a metaexpression with one or more object expressions. Simple nonperceptual identification relates a metaexpression with one or more measurement expressions. Compound nonperceptual identification relates a metaexpression with one or more object expressions and with one or more measurement expressions. The number of component expressions can vary freely in all types of identifications.

It is possible to specify different types of relationships between the identified and identifying expressions. For example, identifications are often incomplete in science in the sense that identifying expressions necessary for the identification are missing. The example of cyclic-AMP is a good one: the identification of the attractant was complete only with the establishment of its equivalence with cyclic-AMP. An important benefit is to be had with complete identifications for they are tautologies. Scientist action contingent on their use will be unequivocal, as noted by H_2 in the last chapter. On the other hand, incomplete identifications are vague, and any contingent action must always be equivocal. For example, such identifications cannot be used by the scientist to establish others: e.g., [distance] would not be identified by [rate] and [time] if these were not completely identified. Or, the scientist could not successfully isolate instances of the identified event without complete identification. This inhibition of definite action would apply to all classes of scientist action, transport, selection, and so on. It follows that the identity cycle could not be replicated or reproduced by other scientists. In short, the whole process of science would be hampered with incomplete identification. Scientists accordingly strive for completeness as they analogously strive for precision. Incompleteness exists only out of developmental necessity. Another important rule of science emerges: the identification cycle is applied and reproduced or replicated until identification is completed. This type of endeavor describes much of the process of scientific inquiry.

A much more salient relationship between identifying and identified expressions has to do with the sufficient falsification of the identification. First, every identification must be falsifiable no matter what its form. This apparent truism is not as obvious as it sounds. More attention has been paid to constructing identifications in the philosophy of science than to falsifying them. Popper's work is a well-known exception.[24] In order to be falsified, an identification must be complete. There has been an emphasis in the philosophy of science on incomplete identifications partially resulting from operationism as well as a reaction against Aristotelian dogma about complete definitions being the best definitions.[25] This emphasis has effectively caused the circumvention of this "obvious" necessity. That identifications are and must be falsifiable follows from the fact that the boundaries of occurrence of events must be known, and these boundaries imply nonoccurrence. Simply, the location and confirmation of identities presume the ability to discriminate when the identities do occur and this, in turn, presumes the ability to assess when they do not occur. Degree of confirmation as reliability or precision is computed as a percentage, which implies a specific number of nonoccurrences of the identifications.

More intuitively, scientists do say that something has not occurred or that it does not exist because it has not occurred. True, much of their work consists of establishing identifications, and these efforts may distract the metatheorist. But these efforts are always falsifiable for the scientist. Part of the confusion arises because questions of existence are mistakenly taken to be pure: is it not a paradox to conceive of science as the search for nonentities? Yes. But it is not a paradox to conceive of part of science as an attempt to identify entities that is always supplemented by the availability of the falsification of the resulting identifications. Remember that for the scientist pure questions of existence are expressible only as questions of occurrence. One can debate endlessly about when it is shown sufficiently that something does not exist, but for the scientist such debate is meaningful if and only if it ultimately turns on the falsification of identifications. Whether or not the falsification of identifications is the rule or exception in science is not the point; the fact remains that it is crucial that all identifications be falsifiable.

Although falsification is an empirical question, falsifiability as Popper[26] has shown is not. The necessary condition for the falsifiability of identifications is maximum precision. The rationale is the same as for the rule that identifications must be complete to be falsified. Basically, in order to know what something is not, one must know what something is. Incomplete identifications are not fully specified and therefore cannot be falsified; any falsification of incomplete identifications can be falsified by saying that the negated identifying expression was not the crucial component of the identification. The crucial component expression lies forever in the distance, to be discovered at some future date. The same possibility exists for vague identifications that are by definition incomplete ones: any falsification of the identification by negation of an expression component can be denied by asserting that the falsified component was really not crucial. Again, the crucial component would not have been falsified if only it were known.

Incompleteness of identifications implies vagueness and that vagueness implies nonfalsifiability. One can posit a scale of falsifiability of identifications that corresponds to a scale of precision. Vagueness has obvious results. Contradictory identifications are absurd because they cannot be falsified. The contradictory components imply all possible members of their ranges. For example, to say [[X] is measured by [Y] and [not-Y]] where Y is a measurement dimension and scale extends the possible range of relevant measures to infinity. Obviously, the identification cannot be falsified. More intuitively, a contradictory component expression is dually asserted as confirmed and falsified *a priori*, and the fact of its falsification can never be precisely determined. Ambiguous identifications are slightly more complex. They are identifications with multiple component expressions of the same type. They should not be confused with compound identifications that have multiple component expressions of different types. A compound identification might be [[X] is measured by [Y] and isolated by [Z]] and can be tautologous. In order for this expression to be ambiguous, it would have to have at least one paired identification understood to be independent but an identification of the same events: e.g., this additional identification could be [[X] is measured by [U] and isolated by [V]]. For any identification to be ambiguous it need have only one component with multiple interpretations: in the example either the [U] or [V] could be [Y] or [Z]. Presumably, a falsifiability scale could be constructed to match the scale of ambiguity: an identification with a component that has one alternative interpretation would be more easily falsifiable than an identification with a component with two alternative interpretations, and so on. It is an unanswered question whether falsifiability would be decreased multiplicatively or additively with an increase in the ambiguity and number of ambiguous components.

Generally, then, the degree of falsifiability of an identification varies directly with the level of precision of the component expressions. This is true independently of the completeness-incompleteness dimension and is a much more important relationship between component expressions of an identification. This principle will prove a valuable analytic tool. Scientists apply and reapply the identity cycle to the point of maximum precision. Vague, contradictory, and even ambiguous identifications are not tolerated. In fact, it is hard to think of an appropriate example. One criterion of good science is the precision and falsifiability of its identifications.

MEASUREMENT

Much of the definition of measurement has already been anticipated. Any measurement expression, if complete, will consist of four components: a scale with certain mathematical properties, a unit value on that scale which discriminates certain quantities, a numerical or symbolic assignment on the scale that corresponds to the units, and a dimension that is said to be the measurable or quantified property. Anyone familiar with the vast literature in measurement theory knows that this is only one possible definition. Stevens' definition[27] is quite popular: "measurement is the assignment of numerals to objects according to a rule." Savage has written an extensive critique of this definition.[28] And this critique has been criticized in turn.[29] However, the definition given here should be general enough to satisfy most of the criteria of a definition.

Specifically, for the moment at least, the scales of measurement will be identified as the traditional nominal, ordinal, interval, and ratio scales. The unit of the scale is the lowest quantity specified on the scale, the smallest demarcation width. Nominal and ordinal scales do not have units in the sense of demarcations or quantities. With nominal scales the unit can be defined as the reciprocal of each category to the total number of categories: e.g., the unit of a nominal scale with four categories is 1/4; the unit of a nominal scale with eight categories is 1/8. With ordinal scales the unit can be defined as the reciprocal of each ordered category to the total number of categories according to the scale position of the category. For example, if five categories were ordered according to the numbers 1, 2, 3, 4, and 5 with each number representing a category, the unit for category 1 would be 1/5, for 2, 2/5, and so on. Notice that the units for ordinal and nominal scales are reciprocals, not fractions. The unit for interval and ratio scales corresponds to the smallest unit on the scale: e.g., for temperature, $C°$ it is "one degree" centigrade; for distance the unit can be millimeter, centimeter, meter, foot, or inch, according to the dimension used. That is, the unit for interval and ratio scales is derivable directly from the scales; simply, it equals the name applied to the smallest difference recorded between intervals.

The unit on any scale discriminates quantities according to a numerical assignment. This discrimination is lawfully derived from the mathematical properties of the numerical assignment. In essence, the numbers or other symbols of the scale establish relationships between the units. At one extreme, with nominal scales, no relationships between units are specified. At the other extreme, with ratio scales, the relationship between two given units can be construed as a ratio of the particular numbers corresponding to the two units. In between, with ordinal scales, the relationship between two given units is their numerical ordering; and with interval scales, the relationship between any two units is expressible as an addition or subtraction of the appropriate assigned numbers. The precise mathematical transformations permissible with one scale or another is of no concern in what follows.

The dimension (or "quantity" according to Kaplan) is that which is measured.[30] It is that common aspect of events that is divisible into units and can have numerical scales mapped onto it. It is the comparative base against which unit and scale readings are taken. Common examples are length, breadth, width, temperature, time, distance, speed, rate, and velocity. The dimension, not the scale or unit, is crucial for science. The scale or unit are interpretable only with reference to the dimension. [[X is 3 cm. long]] and [[Y is 5 cm. long]] can be jointly interpreted as [[Y is 2 cm. longer than X]], because of the communality of length as the dimension of X and Y that is being measured. To say that the joint interpretation makes length at least an interval scale or to talk about "centimeters," is not insignificant. However, it is possible to assert these meta-metaexpressions about measurement because the dimension is the common component of each meta-expression. This is to say that statements about units and scales are contingent on dimensions. To predicate a measurement theory on a theory of scales is to miss the forest.

In other words, measurement is to be understood with respect to its communicative aspects.[31] It is a type of expression in science, and its effects can be assessed accordingly. The first principle of this analysis has to do with what measurement expressions permit the scientist to do or say. Dimensions are crucial because they permit comparative expressions.

Units and scales are important because they permit statements about differences according to dimensions. Units on nominal scales permit the expression [[X] is [Y] and [U] is [W] with a unit value of $\frac{1}{N}$]]. Units on ordinal scales permit the expression [[X] is more of [U] than [Y] with a difference in unit value of $\frac{1}{N}$]]. Units on interval scales permit the expression [[X] is [N + 1] more of [U] than [Y] with unit value N]]. Units on ratio scales permit the expression [[X] is [KN] more of [U] than [Y] with unit value N and where K is a constant]]. These difference statements can be understood as differences between different identities whose unique identifications are implicit or as differences in identifications of the same identity over time. In the latter case, repeated measures are being taken through time. The structure of the expressions changes somewhat. With nominal scales the expression would be read [[X] is [Y] at T_n and [Z] at T_{n+1}]]. With all the others the [Y] would be replaced by [[.... [X] at T_{n+1}]].

Difference expressions, therefore, can be construed as changes in identifications or comparisons of identifications. Interpreted in this way, difference expressions are the *sine qua non* of science, because they are the essence of hypothesis formation and testing. This point will be elaborated in Chapter 3.

Identification and Measurement

Again there is a danger that a familiar confusion will arise. Identities (analogous to the definiendum in definitions) are uninterpretable without their corresponding identifications (analogous to definitions or interpretations). A change in one component of any identification is sufficient to make it a different identification, even though the identity remains invariant. Difference expressions relate different identifications either in the sense of recording different measurement expressions for the same identity over time or comparing the measurement expressions of different identifications at one point in time. These two relationships are possible because of the invariance of the measurement dimension and the precise relationship between units and scales. A complication immediately arises with this simple but pervasive principle of science.

Dimensions can be identities. In fact, the most powerful laws of science relate dimensions that are identities in one of the two ways just given. Unit values of the same dimension may predictably change as a function of time, or different dimensions and units may be compared. Time is a dimension. The first type of relationship therefore reduces to the second type of relationship: unit values changing as a function of time are different dimensions and units being compared. Another important principle of science emerges: all difference expressions reduce to comparisons of dimensions and units. In the case of dimensions as identities this principle means that dimensions are related to dimensions in the fundamental laws of science. Einstein's famous equation, $E = MC^2$, is a perfect example. It states that energy is equivalent to mass times the square of the speed of light, and all these terms are dimensions.

This is a possible interpretation of all "derived measures". Derived measures are understood to be: "Ones which are carried out by making use of laws, logical or empirical, relating to fundamental measures."[32] Kaplan's example is [[density] = [mass per unit volume]], which is derived from the lawful relationship between mass and volume. Other examples of derived measures are [[pressure] = [force per unit area]] and [[distance] = [rate times time]]. All derived measures are interpretable as relationships between dimensions. To call them "measures or measurements" is misleading. They form much of the corpus of the laws of science and are better understood as laws. Their utility is comparative in two senses. First, they are themselves compound meta-metaexpressions that relate identity-dimensions. Second, they can be used to make further compounds comparing other dimensions. Density and pressure can be related, for example, in such a way that unit values of pressure are contingent on unit values of density with precise mathematical description. Again, the construction of such higher-level compound expressions is much of the work of science.

Dimensions that are identities raise an important epistemological issue. The resulting identifications cannot be perceptual identifications. Dimensions are not perceptual in the formal sense of being observationally confirmable. Intuitively speaking, one cannot perceive mass, volume, density, velocity, gravity, pressure, magnetism, and the like. Formally, this fact means that identifications of measurement dimensions must be nonperceptual, with all that that implies. They can be completely expressed only by the inclusion of measurement expressions. They can be falsified only by reference to measurements. They will include object expressions that refer to the scientist actions necessary for the appropriate application and reading of the measuring instruments: i.e., the location, isolation, selection, transport, or necessary change in scientists' behavior to apply or read the measures. Finally, their falsifiability. will be contingent on their precision: i.e., they must be complete and have maximally precise component expressions. Dimensions as identities therefore are not observable things; they are nonperceptual identifications that fulfill the criteria of such identifications.

An interesting relationship is derivable from this conceptualization of identity-dimensions. Measurement has traditionally been conceived abstractly as a mapping of symbols onto events. There are two rival interpretations of this process. The first is called the representational theory of measurement,[33] which interprets measurement as a process whereby the symbols represent the events. Given certain constraints that define good measurement, the symbols are substitutable for the events. The manipulation of the symbols is tantamount to manipulation of the events. On the other hand, the indicator theory of measurement interprets the symbols as indicators of the events. The significance of the measurement is the information it gives the scientist. The measurement is properly construed as a numerical index of the events. Symbols are no more substitutable for events in this formulation than words are for things. Accordingly, there are important empirical constraints on the appropriate manipulation of symbols. The representational theory of measurement after years of pre-eminence following Campbell's classic formulation[34] is now being questioned and (probably) gradually replaced by the indicator theory of measurement. Savage's book[35] (for example) attempts to coordinate and systematize the attack of the latter theory, with the expressed goal of replacing the former one.

Neither theory quite matches the concept of measurement being presented here. This concept is best expressed by the relationship suggested by the treatment of dimensions as identities previously presented. Symbols are mapped onto events. The events in this case serve as confirmation for the measurements. Briefly, events are neither replaced or indexed by measurements; they are the necessary prerequisities for the test and confirmation of the measurements. Generally, measurement does not exist in the service of events; events exist in the service of measurement. If dimensions are identities, they are identified by apppropriate measurement expressions including scale and unit value and object expressions about scientist action in the application and reading of the measurement devices. These identifying expressions are in turn predicated on other identifications. These identifications are of the events in question and can have component expressions of any form. The important point is that these identifications are necessary for measurement. Or to put it less formally, measurements can be taken only if the dimensions, units, and scales match the properties of events. If these dimensions are construed as identities and their identifications are used to formulate important scientific laws, and if these dimensions can be confirmed only on the basis of other identifications of events, then the events produce the confirmation of the measures and laws. The events do not exist to be measured, but rather the measures exist to be confirmed by the events.

Measurement is primary. Yet dimensions as identities form nonperceptual identifications, which is only one class of identification. Before turning to the relationship between perceptual identifications and measurement, it should be noted that the establishment of the primacy of measurement in this argument has pervasive consequences. If some of the laws of science are identifications relating measurement dimensions and if difference expressions form the basis of other identifications as another subset of scientific communication, then much of the scientific enterprise consists in dealing with identifications that are nonperceptual. It remains to be shown that perceptual identifications are uninterpretable without reference to measurement. The primacy of measurement will then be shown to be complete.

Nonperceptual Identification and Measurement

Much of the argument has already been presented in synoptic form. Perceptual identification, in order to be confirmed—to satisfy the demands of the identification cycle—must conform to the ST-rule. Minimally, all appropriate object expressions must be predicated on location of events; and such location requires the specification of space and time. Space and time are of course measurable by interval and ratio scales. This ST-rule may be implicit for the scientist according to the principle that well-confirmed action hypotheses (like location) as well as any hypotheses that are well confirmed may be unstated unless and until falsified. However, the ST-rule's being implicit for the scientist implies nothing about its viability or indeed necessity in a metatheory of science. This synoptic presentation will now be fleshed out in greater detail. It is first necessary to define the primitive components of measurement.

Measurement has already been defined, preserving much that is traditional. Attention will now be turned to the primitive components of measurement in general, using this definition. What transformations does measurement perform on the world? Or better, what assumptions about reality are entailed by measurement? How does measurement structure and organize perception? What are the nonfalsifiable prerequisites common to all measurement? Or finally, in conventional terminology, what are the fundamental properties of measurement?

All measurement imposes a geometric structuring on perception. The fundamental components of this structure are boundaries and positions. The boundaries of some measures are defined as other positions. Boundary in this sense is relative. Distance, direction, and patterns of movement are good examples. Boundary can also be conceived of as an absolute. In this sense it is specified by multiple positions that are contiguous. Space coordinates, measures of spatial dimensions like length, breadth, or width, and measures of shapes are all good examples of the use of continuous boundaries. "Relative" and "absolute" are to be understood as referring to the specific relationship between boundary and position. In the relative case, the boundary is other positions; the particular boundary position used as the reference point can be any position in the field. With absolute boundaries the reference point is fixed by the boundary, which can be construed as continuous positions. The boundaries are mapped onto events, forming invariant properties of the events. The distinction is best illustrated by the contrast between measures used to map the positions of the planets as opposed to those used to determine the position of a ship at sea, i.e., sets of longitudinal and latitudinal coordinates.

Time is an important boundary. As such it is interpretable as neither positional nor continuous. It is completely separate. All events can be said to occupy positions within time as boundary. The purest measurement example is any measure of duration of events. As such, time in effect is the boundary within which the events originate and terminate. Notice that these important abstractions for science, origination and termination, are expressible according to time as boundary.

Positions are interpreted relative to boundaries. Concretely, they can be scale values with the point of origin and the end point of the scale being the boundaries. More generally, they are points within the area delimited by the boundaries. If the boundary is another position, this position may be fixed or it may be changing. If it is a continual position, it is fixed. Where it is time, it can be fixed or changing. The important point is that one position is read and that this position can presumably vary freely. This free-varying position is analogous to the scale value that is read on the measure; it may be a pointer or it may be the events that change against the measure.

Boundaries impose closure on perceptions. They reference free-varying positions. However, boundaries may be construed as opened or closed. With open boundaries the free-varying positions are absolutely free in their variation. With closed boundaries the free-varying positions can vary only within the limits imposed by the boundaries. Measures that are predicated on open boundaries theoretically have no upper bound on scale values: for example, electrons can be accelerated to speeds limited by technical capacity, not by any upper bound on the scale of acceleration. Even the speed of light as a possible upper bound is open to question in modern physics.[36] Measures predicated on closed boundaries theoretically have an upper bound on scale values: for example, water is said to change states at the boiling-point scale value of temperature. Generally, science seeks closure, which usually implies closed boundaries, e.g., Einstein predicted that space would not be infinite for free-floating bodies. Closure does not *necessarily* imply closed boundaries if closure is construed generally as structure. It is in this sense that measurement structures perceptual experience.

The theory of relativity deals directly with these primitives of measurement. The idea that positions as boundary and free-floating value can both change is, of course, at the heart of relativity theory. Conceiving time as a boundary is another abstract derivative of the theory. Most important, however, is the idea that time and space are the primitive concepts of measurement. For the primitive concepts so far discussed are synonymous with time and space.

The ST-rule can be elaborated on the basis of these primitives. All identities in order to be identified must be located in time and space. That is, all identities must be given positions within boundaries, whatever the form of these boundaries. This is the weakest form of the ST-rule. It can also be asserted that in order for identifications to be falsifiable and therefore confirmable, they must reference positions within boundaries. Confirmation assumes position, falsification assumes negation of that position, and in order for a position to be assertable, it must be contrasted with the negation of that position. This comparison will be seen to be at the heart of all scientific expression types and of all of science.

Space and time can be interpreted as positions and boundaries, and hence we have both variations of the ST-rule. It is being asserted that location in space and time is the fundamental prerequisite of all identification. This is true whatever the particular measurement dimensions used in the identification, if any are required. However, these dimensions can also be intepreted with the use of these primitive notions. This is true in two senses. First, all measurement occurs in space and time. Boundaries and positions as the geometric-perceptual components of space and time are the context of the application of measures. This case is not trivial: it asserts that the ST-rule applies to the identifications of measurement. It also follows that measurement dimensions that are identities must satisfy the ST-rule. Second, all measurement dimensions, units, and scales in one way or another are deducible from these primitives of space and time. Certainly, there are other necessary components in the deductive chain, but these primitives are common to all deductive chains whose terminus is measurement.

The final point is easily proven. Minimally, for any measurement to be read it must discriminate positions and boundaries. In order to make the assertion [[X] has measured value [Y]], this value must correspond to a unit and be on a scale.

Units and scales must be segmented and discriminated, which presumes positions and boundaries.

One possible complication with this conceptualization of space and time centers on the flexibility possible in the use of the term "space." Wittgenstein speaks of a "logical space," Osgood, *et al.*, of a "semantic space," Inkeles of "social space."[37] The term therefore has almost as many interpretations as there are theorists willing to use it. Interestingly, all these interpretations employ the common interpretation of space as boundary and position. However, the drawback of these abstract primitives, and the corresponding complication with the concept, is that they can be employed to construct "spaces." The boundaries and positions can be artificially interpreted to fit the needs of the theorist. Three criteria are necessary to distinguish between such artificial constructions and "true" space. "True" space must have perceptual correlates. This is not to say that space is a perceivable entity. It most certainly is not. It is a construct imposed on perception that structures it, confirms or falsifies it, and makes it symbolically shareable. But space is perceptually bound in the sense that as a symbolic construct it permits movement to quandrant 4 and beyond to the replication or reproduction of identifications. That is, space is always subject to perceptual confirmation and is utilized as a construct to permit this type of confirmation. Second, "true" space must be expressed in measures. Measurement expressions must be derivable from "space." The "semantic space" of Osgood *et al.*, does not fulfill the first criterion, but it does fulfill the second because it is the basis for the derivation of the "semantic differential" as a measure of meaning.[38] However, both criteria must be fulfilled for "space" to be true space. A final tecchnical criterion must also be fulfilled. Precise mathematical relationships must be derivable from space. To put it grandiosely, the full power of higher mathematics must be applicable to and generated by space if it is "true space"; "true space" will generate rigorous mathematical deductions beyond its perceptual representations. These three criteria are sufficient to distinguish space as it is used as a primitive of science and space as it is constructed by the theoriest.

The ST-rule is all-pervasive. It applies to both perceptual and nonperceptual identifications. With the former, the rule applies because perceptions to be communicated must be located and represented in space and time. With the latter, the rule applies because all measures are deducible from or have as necessary components or are located as identifications in space and time, as herein broadly conceived.

This rule is equivalent to saying that all identifications must contain measurement expressions, for space and time are the fundamental measures. In effect, then, perceptual identifications as usually defined in the philosophy of science do not exist. That is, nowhere in any science do scientists speak of "observables" (the traditional term) without concomitant, eventual, or developmental reference to measurement. Part of the confusion arises from the implicit nature of the action hypotheses and space and time primitives that permits observables to be perceived as communicative observations. Because they are implicit for the scientist does not imply that they were not once explicit. In fact, they have become implicit because they need not be explicit any longer, if in fact they ever had to be explicit. At the level of metatheory, however, they are necessary for understanding science. Another source of confusion is that certain identities are explicitly related to measures and this type "gets all the play" in metatheories of science. Other identities are treated as unmeasured primitives almost as a second thought because they are needed in the analysis.

Yet, the practice is clear. Scientists may developmentally drop references to certain actions and primitive measures. Philosophers of science may write of "observables" that are perceptually realizable. However, measurement is the key; and the ST-rule and the primitives of measurement are the foundation of science.

Movement

In the argument that all identifications must be measured, action expressions were dealt with as if they themselves were not also subject to the principle of the primacy of measurement. Of course, if these expressions are identifications for the scientist—if he talks about his actions *qua* scientist engaged in measurement—then they too are subject to the ST-rule. But there is a more important way in which these expressions are subsumable under this principle. Again, a lengthy detour is necessary. This time the final primitive of measuurement will be elaborated.

All measurement is predicated on movement. Again, this primitive is a geometric-mathematical, not a perceptual construct. Movement is a change of positions with respect to a boundary. This change must be recorded in time. Time in this sense is not a boundary but a recording mechanism, a dimension extraneous to the space that must be mapped onto the space in order to assess whether change in position has occurred. Thus, time here is measurement, not primitive. Of course, time can also be the boundary within which the movement occurs. In this case there will be two times, because time as measurement is still necessary to record the change. For example, this situation arises for the behavioral scientist who records the reaction time of a subject (a change from no action to action) at different times of day (in which case time is measurement).

Movement also may be recorded as direction of change of position, but it still implies time. Minimally, change of position requires repeated recordings even if direction is the basal dimension. This repetition implies temporal determination. Simply, at least two observations must be made to assess if movement has occurred, the first to observe the position prior to change, the second to observe the new position subsequent to change. These observations must be recorded in time and determined by time. Some obvious examples of measurement explicitly based on movement are: voltage (flow of electrons), wave frequency, velocity, distance, direction, rate of diffusion, speed of light. Moreover, sophisticated instrumentation converts many measurements into movement, e.g., the simple thermometer records the movement of mercury between positions on the scale within the boundaries of the capillary tube, and the voltmeter records the movement of the pointer-needle between positions on the scale within the boundaries subtended by the arc of the pointer.

Certain measures appear not to be movement-related when in actuality they are movement-related, as in the case of measures of angular displacement expressed as number of degrees. This type of measurement presumably is taken statically by applying the appropriate measuring instrument. Actually a reading of number of degrees is possible only by scanning and comparing the extreme values on the instrument (180° or 360°) with the recorded values of the angle. This process involves the movement of the perceptions of the scientist. Of course, if the instrument is precise enough it may have such movement encoded in its design, i.e., the scientist can read the number of degrees of an angle at a glance. However, never is instrument design sufficient to supplant perceptual movement of the scientist in reading the instrument. He is always forced to make perceptual comparisons of this type. These comparisons imply his own movement.

So movement is a primitive of most measures in one of two ways. First, it may be an integral part of the measurement. Change in position, however specified, may be a measurement dimension. Second, movement may be extraneous to the measurement but necessary for the scientist to read the measurement. Movement may be implied by the reading of the measure in the sense that its reading is impossible without perceptual comparison.

Movement is a ubiquitous measurement primitive. Movement has been defined as change in position. As discussed in the first chapter, any definition of change must include specification of the steady states before and after the change, the transition point of the change, and the controlling factor or variable of the change. This definition of movement is at the metalevel and will be called change^M. The steady states are the two positions; the transition point is the instance at which the controlling variable takes effect; the controlling variable can be either an attribute of the space or an attribute of the scientist using the space. If it is an attribute of the space, then another measurement dimension and identification must be introduced into the space to account for the controlling factor or variable. If the controlling variable is an attribute of the scientist, it is interpretable as some aspect of the scientist's action; perceptual movement has been the action subset so far mentioned.

However, other aspects of scientist action are similarly interpretable. This includes any of the aspects mentioned previously: location, isolation, selection, transport, or arrangement of events and scientist observational action. Location is interpretable as a perceptual or, more correctly, observational phenomenon, as is scientist observational action. These cases have already been dealt with. Selection, isolation, transport, and arrangement will necessarily involve movement in the space because they imply manipulation of the events defined as positions in the space. In order for the scientist to isolate events he must select them. Selection also implies isolation; the scientist must have isolated the events in order to have selected them. Isolation is a broader term, because the scientist may select only several events out of the range he has isolated. For example, to study the attractant of social amoebae the scientist must isolate social amoebae, but he will select aggregated amoebae in order to isolate the attractant. The point is that both selection and isolation produce the change of position of the appropriate events. The scientist must move the amoebae around. Similar arguments apply obviously to transport and to arrangement because arrangement implies transport.

The application of measurements by the scientist is a final class of scientist action that is specifiable as the controlling variable of movement as change in position. In applying a measure a scientist must adjust its position. He must move the measure to the events. To measure length, the yardstick must be brought to the events, which of course involves movement of the yardstick. To measure volume, the scientist must move the events and the container in proximity. To measure certain quantities, the scientist must move the events into the container. And so on.

Movement as change^M therefore underlies all measurement. Further, all of scientist action is interpretable as movement related and therefore as measurement. The primitives of measurement thus underlie identifications, measurements, and scientist action. It is in this sense that measurement is primary for all phases of science.

Circularity

There is an apparent circularity here: action requires measurement, measurement requires action. This circularity was also implied with identification: identification requires measurement (the ST-rule), measurement requires identification. Confusion arises from failing to distinguish between metatheory of science and science. The primitives of measurement are being asserted at the metatheory level. They are not synonymous with measurement dimensions, scales, or units. They are the common deductive base of all particular measurements. The apparent circularity of the ST-rule is not real. To say identifications empirically must be based on these primitives does not deny that there is more to identifications than measurements. It does say that both identifications and measures have the same deductive base predicated on science as communication.

With respect to the apparent circularity with scientist action, the situation is more complex, but the resolution is basically the same. Movement was defined as change^M or change at the metatheory level. This is distinguishable from movement or change in position at the scientist level or change^S hereafter. The controlling factor in change^M was scientist action. The controlling factor in change^s is usually not conceived to be scientist action, that is, scientist action is implicit. The controlling factor is usually construed as some other measured identity. The steady states in change^s are usually positions on scales of dimensions. To assert that all scientist action is deducible from movement as change^M is a different assertion than that change^s is also deducible from change^M. Again what is an apparent circularity is only a commonality of deductive bases. Simply, scientist action is deducible from measurement primitives just as measurement is. And it is in this sense that measurement is at the core of science as communication.

Is it not therefore misleading to assert the primacy of measurement? No. If measurement is deducible from these primitives and if identification and scientist action are also deducible from them, then it follows that measurements must exist or must be constructible as the communicative medium of identification and scientist action. Hence measurement is ubiquitous, and the apparent circularity implied is not real. Again, the implicit nature for the scientist of this principle's manifestations says nothing about the utility or actuality of the principle for the metatheorist.

Dimensions, Scales, and Primitives

The primitives of measurement permit the deduction of interval and ratio scales. That is, scales of this degree of sophistication can be developed in science because of these primitives. Obviously, if position and boundary are interpreted as space and time and if space and time are measurable by scales at this level, then interval and ratio scales are deducible from these primitives. This suggests that lower-level scales, although mathematically feasible, are actually of limited use in science. This, in fact, is the case.

Savage's criticism[39] of Stevens' concept of nominal scale is quite appropriate. In brief, Savage maintains that the concept interprets all labeling processes as exercises in measurement and that it is therefore too broad. If nominal scale is defined so broadly, it must include identities. This means that in those identifications in which nominal scales are the measurement expression, that nominal scales as identities will be related to nominal scales as measures. Unless the two are distinguished, every independent expression is interpretable as a unit on a nominal scale.

Therefore, nominal scales will be those in which numbers are used specifically to distinguish between expressions that are understood to be object expressions. The traditionally defined mathematical relation between numbers is substitution: any nominal scale admits a one-to-one substitution of the assigned numbers. Identities that are not nominal scales will be any metaexpression that is related to a measurement expression, including scale and unit. Measurement dimensions have been shown to satisfy this definitional criterion. Any metaexpression will suffice.

The question of the use of nominal scales in science is separable from the question of the use of identities. Unfortunately, measurement theory has tended to confuse the two. Many familiar examples of nominal scales are actually identities. Classificatory systems in which labels are used to sort events are identities, not nominal scales. The same is true for most categorizing systems in science. For example, to say [[mammalia] are animals with X, U, and Z common characteristics]] is to identify [mammalia]. The confusion arises because nominal scales are simply special identifications. But they can be distinguished not only definitionally, but also by their use. Those nominal scales that are not identities will be used as predicative expressions in identifications and will not be identified by other measures. The first part of the rule is a consequence of the necessary predicative role of measurement in identifications. As measurements, nominal scales must identify. If the latter part were not true, then nominal scales could be identities identified by other measures.

Nominal scales can be and are related to other measurement scales, but this relationship characterizes a law or test of a hypothesis, not an identification. The nature of laws and hypotheses will be fully discussed in the next chapter. Briefly, identifications including component measurement expressions are related in hypotheses. In identifications, expression components are related, one set of which must be measurement expressions. The notable exception to this distinction are dimensions that are identities. In this case, the dimensions are empirically confirmed by predictable differences in their identifying measurement scale and unit and object expressions. Such identities are an exception because, as previously discussed, many of the expressions that scientists call "laws" are actually identifications of this type. However, it will also be recalled that so-called "higher-order" identifications (or derived measurements) actually fit this new definition of laws, for in them identifications are related to identifications—albeit that these identifications are of measurement dimensions.

Unfortunately, one is hard put to give any examples from science of identifications in which the measurement expression is a nominal scale. Only trivial examples come to mind in which category labels are assigned numbers. The phylogenetic class "mammalia" may be assigned a number, and this number may be a nominal scale unit. This case is trivial in the sense that it is a simple translation of an identification into a nominal scale. It may have developmental significance for science; it certainly does not have analytic significance. The important question is what the utility of such expressions is. If it is to develop and permit the use of expression types, then it is not as important as the use of these expression types, because analytically the use of the evolved expressions is most significant.

Such a translation is also trivial because the measurement dimension that is the base of the translation is the crucial component. To assert [[[mammalia] is unit N]] implies that the nominal scale dimension exists full-blown. The numeral N would be meaningless otherwise, for it would not be a unit. The translation is possible only because the dimension [[phylogenetic scale of animals]] preexists and provides the necessary comparative base. This type of translation expression therefore is little more than a communicative exercise.

Most nominal scales do not function as measurement expressions in the sense that they are identified by other measures. This identification process is true formally according to previous arguments and functionally according to the practices of scientists. All nominal scales must be further identified by other measurements. Even numerical classification must satisfy the ST-rule and the primitives of measurement. Before mammalia at unit N can be distinguished from reptilia at unit $N + n$, the common characteristics of the individuals of each class must be determined by isolating and selecting those individuals with those common characteristics; the identities demand the corresponding observation of these individuals, and so on. Further, the individuals and common characteristics must be located within space and time, be assigned positions within boundaries as it were. As the measurement primitives and ST-rule are at the interval or ratio level or imply the interval or ratio level, the argument is suggested that what are called nominal scales cannot be formulated without interval and ratio scales. This denies the traditional view of nominal scales as the beginning of a progression toward ratio scales as the highest level of scales.

Again the need arises to rebut an apparent circularity in this argument. Must not it be true given this reasoning that all measurements will imply other measurements, as any given instance of the use of a dimension and scale will demand reference to the measurement primitives, and these, in turn, imply other measures? If a yardstick is applied to the appropriate events, does not the component ratio scale still imply other measures because of the process of its application and the necessary location, isolation, selection, movement, and the like? No, the yardstick in its form and use is the deductive manifestation of the primitives. Its form and use can be analyzed in terms of these primitives, but it is the consequential terminus of them.

Formally, any nominal scale, on the other hand, is at best

an incomplete deduction. The dimension of any particular nominal scale will be the boundary, and the unit will be the position. Yet, these are imperfect approximations of the geometric-mathematical constructs of true space and time. The most obvious manifestation of this imperfection is the well-documented limitations on the mathematical operations that can be used with nominal scales: even addition and subtraction cannot be performed. The boundary and positions are not precisely fixed because the dimension is often an ill-defined attribute: ill-defined in the sense that the extensivity of the attribute is incomplete. For example, assuming appropriate numerical representation, even a familiar classification like life and death, whose dimension is "state of an organism," fails to discriminate among many subjects in the domain. The positions and boundary are not fixed in such a way that the scale can be unambiguously applied and read. Finally, movement as change in position cannot be fully certified at either scientist or metatheory level with nominal scales because of the insufficient specification of boundary and position. If the change is said to be controlled by another nominal scale dimension, all that can be said is that one unit value is associated with another unit value, a low-level statement. Where the change is controlled by scientist action and this action is known according to a nominal scale there is the same result.

It is not circular, therefore, to argue that nominal scales require interval and ratio scales for sufficient precision as well as for their very construction and use.

This formal argument about the necessary restrictions on the use of nominal scales in science is buttressed by the actual use of such scales. Never do nominal scales occur without further measurement specification to interval or ratio scales or without further measurement specification to interval or ratio scales or without being supplemented by interval or ratio scale measures. The most common example in science is frequency counts, the units counted per given dimension, where the units are nominal scale values or translatable as such and the dimension is measured on an interval or ratio scale. Some common examples are the number of animals of a given sex per unit area; the number of parts per million of a chemical; the number of organisms with a characteristic per the total number of organisms (e.g., the number of mice with a type of antigen per the total number of mice in the experiment,[40] or the number of plants with developed wounds per the total number of treated plants[41]); and the number of types of subjects, chemicals, or objects per given time interval (e.g., number of aggressive acts per hour of observation[42]). Frequency counts per area or time interval are examples of the supplementation of nominal scales with ratio-scale dimensions. And if the counts are of isomorphic events, the nominal scale is being specified to an interval or ratio level: an interval or ratio scale is formed by counting numbers of events with nominal-scale unit values.

The paucity and insignificance in science of the examples of nominal scales that are true measurements and not identifications and the formal and empirical fact that nominal scales do not occur in science without identification with ratio or interval scales lead to the conclusion that nominal scales *qua* nominal scales really do have limited utility in science. What are called "nominal scales" by measurement theorists have their true significance for the scientist as identities. Real nominal scales that are sufficient as such are almost nonexistent in science; their legitimatization as a separate type of measurement scale has resulted from their confusion with identifications.

The implicit primacy of interval and ratio scales can also be rebutted by referring to presumably legitimate ordinal scales. Yet, many of the same arguments negate their utility in actual scientific practice. Basically, there are few examples of ordinal scales in science. Further, those that are cited are usually interval or ratio scales from which ordinal scales have been retrieved for the sake of illustration. Kerlinger,[43] for example, must appeal to the most abstract level: ". . . if we have three objects, 'a', 'b', and 'c', and 'a' is greater than 'b', and 'b' is greater than 'c'; and if we can justifiably say, also, that 'a' is greater than 'c'; then the main condition for ordinal measurement is satisfied." Although the dimension is implicit, "greater" implies a physical quantity, and physical quantities are generally measured only at the level of interval and ratio scales. The use of such an abstract dimension conceals the fact that the illustration of the ordinal scale is derived from scaled-down interval and ratio scales. Simon[44] provides another example: "If I live at 1105 South Busey, you live at 1111, and Bill lives at 1115, we know that you live between Bill and me." The implicit dimension here is distance, a dimension that can be measured by interval or ratio scales. Generally, the quantities used to specify ordinal scales in the research literature refer to concealed interval and ratio scales —more or less, sooner or later, faster or slower, heavier or lighter, bigger or smaller, longer or shorter—as if the examples were derived to justify a scale type that exists mathematically or logically but not practically for the scientist. These examples are constructed to match the scale type. It is important that such fabrication proceed on the basis of preexisting interval or ratio scales.

An exception to this assertion is the Mohs scale of hardness of minerals. This true ordinal scale is often cited by theorists of methodology: e.g., "F. Mohs worked out a system by which a given mineral would be rated for hardness by comparison with other minerals. Harder stones scratch softer stones, and any given stone is given a rating between a stone it can scratch and one that can scratch it."[45] This scale is a very special one in science, the exception that proves the rule. The invariance of the ordinal dimension is a consequence of the imperviousness of the scratching operations to variations in other dimensions that can be measured by interval and ratio scales. It is an empirical fact that even if pressure and length of the scratch or angularity of the surface of the scratching and scratched stones are extensively varied the dimension of the scale is unaltered. In effect, the ordinal scale is produced by the stability of ratio and interval parameters.

Yet this is not to say that the scale will not be shown eventually to be deducible from interval and ratio scales. At the moment, it is not deducible from higher-level scales, i.e., relative pressure or length of scratch or angularity of stone surface cannot be used to transform this ordinal scale into a higher-level one. If, for example, scratchability correlated with pressure, the ordinal level of scratchability could be assigned ratio units corresponding to degrees of pressure. However, just because these dimensions do not provide deductive convertibility, it cannot be concluded that some other dimensions yet to be discovered will not do so, i.e., level of scratchability may correlate with molecular weight, atomic structure, chemical structure, or the like.

More importantly, this scale must still satisfy the ST-rule. It may not be reducible to the movement primitive: scientist interval or ratio level action like pressure or length of scratch or selection of stones according to degrees of angularity of surface has no effect on the change of position, "scratch-nonscratch," but the ST-rule must be satisfied. The minerals must be identified and the identification will be predicated by interval- and ratio-scale measures. This is true not only of the implicit space and time boundaries and positions necessary to locate and observe the minerals, but also of the identification of the minerals themselves. They are identified by the following ratio measures: molecular weight and structure, chemical composition as determined by sophisticated tests like chromatography and chemical reactivity, and crystal structure that implies other ratio measures like average surface area and number and degrees of angles of facets.

So even given that this ordinal scale is a very special one in science and as such is only partially reducible to interval and ratio scales, it still requires interval and ratio scales for its operation. It is still deducible—albeit not completely—from the interval and ratio scales and dimensions implied by the primitives of measurement.

The conclusion is suggested that the important principle of the primacy of measurement in science translates into the primacy of ratio and interval scale measures. Stated formally, this important principle becomes: fundamental to all of science are measurement dimensions and units that are at interval or ratio scale level; it can be argued that they are necessary for the communicative function of science. Another reason for this primacy derives from a consideration of the precision of measurement.

Precision of Measurement

The object expressions referencing the action of scientists are, by definition, tautological and therefore maximally precise. Measurement expressions also tend to be tautological. Dimensions and units approximate maximum precision. The equivocation in asserting this relationship stems from possible exceptions that arise from developmental considerations. Historically it is possible to find examples of dimensions and units that were vague or ambiguous even though they have subsequently approximated tautology. Scriven[46] has given the example of temperature; more generally, Cardwell[47] provides examples from the engineering sciences of heat transfer and thermodynamics. However, even in fully developed or "completed" sciences, this principle varies in applicability. In Bastin,[48] for example, can be found arguments about the interpretability or level of precision of the measurement process in quantum theory. The validity of the principle is therefore more assured if slightly rephrased as a consequence of these possible exceptions: measurement dimensions and units in science *qua* measurement dimensions and units tend to be interpreted unequivocally given extensive development.

Such equivocation does not appear to be so necessary when considering the level of precision of scales of measurement. Numbers and their mathematical relations are unequivocally interpretable. Scales, having encoded precisely interpretable numbers and their mathematical relations, tend to be tautological and therefore maximally precise. Their utility in science arises from their unequivocal interpretability. This maximal precision arises from the general precision of formal mathematical theory. In effect, this precision is transferred to science via measurement scales. It is in a slightly different but similar sense that Kemeny has elaborated on the crucial role of mathematics for science.[49] Again, however, it would be a crucial mistake to overlook the fact that this principle is far from ubiquitous and without exception. One of the most profound changes in formal mathematics came first with the development of Boolean algebra and then with the mapping of this pervasive mathematical theory onto a symbolic logic by Whitehead and Russell.[50] These important transformations resulted in part from the reinterpretation of traditional mathematical notions.

All this is to emphasize that tautology and unequivocal interpretation are best conceived of as the maximum level of precision that can be approximated but never absolutely achieved. The postulation of such an absolute standard would negate the developmental facts of science. It is not inconsistent with this cautionary note to assert that action object expressions and measurement dimensions, units, and scales approximate maximal precision in science and tend to be tautologically interpreted.

On the other hand, the compounds of all these expression types can by no means be said to be maximally precise of themselves. This is especially true of identifications. Maximal precision of these compound expressions is achieved after extensive research via the identification cycle. However, assuming the adequacy of the application of this cycle, it can be asserted that identifications in science tend to be unequivocally interpretable if not tautologically interpretable in the extreme. For example, the identification expression [[electrons] are negatively charged subatomic particles that move at the [speed of light] in specific orbits around the [nucleus of atoms]] has itself as its own interpretation. Scientists use it tautologically. Of course, it can be further specified by other identifications or measurement and object expressions that interpret the [speed of light] or [nucleus of atoms], but these expressions are supplementary to the original interpretation.

They are not independent alternative interpretations; they are additions to the initial identification by way of qualification or specification. This specification proceeds to exhaustion in science; it has a well-defined terminus according to the hypotheses or laws of which the components are a part. But each component is characterized by close approximation to unequivocal interpretability. After all, such approximation is the explicit purpose of the identification cycle.

Precision and Compound Measurement Expressions

There are two types of compound expressions that can be formulated with action expressions and measurement expressions. Although they have been previously noted, they will be exhaustively analyzed here. In the first type of compound, the measurement expression is the consequence and the action expression the antecedent. These compounds refer to the necessary scientists' actions to apply the measures: [[if I isolate and select the appropriate events, and if I bring the measuring instrument into proximity with those events, etc., etc., then I have [measured] those events by [scale X with unit U and dimension Y]]].

In the second type of compound the measurement expression is the antecedent and the action expressions are the consequence. This compound refers to the scientists' actions having to do with the reading of measures and the actions possible given these readings. For example, the scientist may read a measure and certify that he has successfully performed some contingent action, e.g., he has landed a vehicle on the moon, he has bombarded the nucleus of an atom with a stream of electrons, he has isolated DNA. In this sense, the measurement reading functions as feedback to the scientist, assuring him that he has done what he set about doing. To the extent that all identification is predicated by measurement and all measurement by scientist actions, all identification requires this feedback. The scientist may also perform certain actions contingent on the measurement readings. For example, he may arrange or rearrange objects contingent on the measurement: he may reset the orbit of the satellite or reaccelerate the electron stream, or reaggregate the social amoebae, or provide more feed for the animals, or reinject them. In other words, the scientist may manipulate in some way the events in his domain contingent on the measurement readings. He may also make certain assertions on the basis of the readings: e.g., "the measurement process worked or did not work," "the hypothesis is true or false," "the phenomena were too labile to be measured," and so on. In this sense, the measurement reading provides not feedback but a new class of information[51] that can be acted upon.

With neither type of compound expression can maximum precision be achieved without the existence of certain supplementary conditions extraneous to the compound expression. Level of precision will be contingent in this case on reality. There is no guarantee, for example, that multiple applications and readings of a measure at different times will yield the same readings. The variance in the phenomena may be sufficient to produce different measurement expressions. True, the dimension and unit will not change, but the scale value will change.

There is an often-cited relationship in research methodology that contradicts this relationship: reliability in reading a scale is said to be correlated with the degree of precision of the scale.[52] "Reliability" is defined as the degree to which multiple readings of a measure yield the same results or simply as the degree of consistency of readings of a measure. "Precision" here is defined as the number of demarcations or gradations in the scale or, in present terminology, as the number of scale values and relative unit size: a scale with a greater number of demarcations is said to be more precise than one with fewer demarcations. "Precision" as defined here is not to be confused with "precision" as used in this text. The given relationship can be restated with these definitions as follows: the greater the number of demarcations in a measure, the greater the number of different readings given multiple applications and readings of the measure with the same phenomena.

In the present context this relationship can be translated as a certification that it is possible to assure invariance of the readings of repeated measures of the same phenomena with appropriate modifications of the measurement. In other words, if the measurement expression is varied in its components as specified, then there will be a limited range of possible readings: i.e., the maximum level of precision of this form of compound is understood to be achievable with controlled variations in the component expressions of the compound. This of course contradicts the specified relationship having to do with precision of compounds. Yet it seems to be an obvious fact in science that phenomena vary and that this variation will produce variations in the range of action expressions—in this case specifically measurement readings—that can result from any given measurement expressions. The scientist may try to control the phenomena or may refine the measures by varying the unit value, but the lability of the phemomena can produce great variations of the readings. The traditional relationship must take this fact into account, i.e., given repeated application of a measure to the same phenomena *and* a known range of variation in the phenomena, it is possible to decrease the size of the unit within this range of variation so that consistent readings cannot be attained. This restatement expresses the essence of both relationships: "level of precision" as relative size of units can produce maximally imprecise compounds with antecedent measurement expressions and consequential reading action expressions *if the unit value component of the measurement expression is decreased below the range of variation of the phenomena.* However, this does not imply that readjusting the measurement expression components alone will effect the semantic level of precision of the compound expression. Basically it is true that multiple applications and readings of a measure at different times cannot be expected to result necessarily in the same readings because of the variation of events.

If this is true about the readings, it must also be true about the action expressions contingent on the readings either as corrective feedback for the scientist's action or as a new class of information that can be acted upon. For example, the scientist cannot assert that he has moved two events into proximity if his measurement readings do not certify that he has done so. Nor can the scientist readjust the positions of two events according to his measurement readings if these readings are inconsistent; he cannot move a droplet of saline solution containing a chemical attractant to a position of 3 mm. from a glass slide containing social amoebae if his measures read that they are 5 mm., 1 mm., 4 mm., and 8 mm. apart on respective readings. Again, without introducing other expressions about the lability of the phenomena and the relative control of the phenomena by the scientist, the corresponding compound expressions of themselves can never be maximally precise.

This principle can be applied to the different measurement scales with a resulting demonstration of the overwhelming importance of interval and ratio scales for science. Generally, even with appropriate specification of the parameters of the phenomena, nominal and ordinal scales in this form of compound will never be maximally precise, which follows to an extent from the previous discussion of nominal scales. As identifications they must be supplemented with interval and ratio scales; as measurement scales they provide no empirically confirmable information about the identifications they supplement. They, in effect, cannot even categorize events without being further specified by higher-level scales. It follows that no limited range of contingent action expressions can be predicated on these scales alone. Consider for example the compound expression: [[If [organisms] are [butterflies] then scientist A can do X]]. Even assuming that the antecedent identification contains a legitimate nominal scale unit, i.e., [butterflies], which is a tenuous assumption, what can the "X" be? The scientist does not have sufficient information to locate, isolate, or select [butterflies]. He cannot know whether they can be manipulated, for they may be as large as the earth or as small as a grain of sand. No contingent action is possible because all contingent action is possible. Perhaps the point is clearer if the desired contingent action were specified as changing [butterflies] into [caterpillars], which is equipollent with suggesting that the contingent action is changing the events a unit value on the nominal scale. Clearly this cannot be done because the scientist has insufficient information to accomplish the change. However, performing the change would be possible with further identifications including ratio scale measures: i.e., the scientist could locate and manipulate the amount of hormone necessary to accomplish the change, which presumes further identifications of the hormone and of caterpillars and butterflies and ratio measures of quantity of hormone and the passage of time necessary for the production of the change. Therefore, it is easily shown that nominal scales do not permit specification of limited action expressions in the sense that the scales function as either feedback or new information as the basis for further action.

Basically, the same argument can be made about ordinal scales. Again, the most obvious illustration involves the use of readings of ordinal scales to change the events in question. Suppose the scientist desires to change the ordinal scale value of two events, for example, to produce the state $A > B$ from the state $B > A$. This can be accomplished given the appropriate ordinal scale, but there are infinite alternative scales that can produce the same result. An infinite range of ordinal units can be inserted between A and B, and the determination that $B > A$ has been changed to $A > B$ will be the same. This suggests that there can be no unequivocal determination of the requisite actions to produce the change in scale value. In fact, at any one point in time it can be asserted that $A > B$, but there are theoretically infinite numbers of actions available to produce this reading. To give a concrete example that is more appropriate to engineering than science but still pertinent: if an instruction is given to plane the surface of a board straight and the only available feedback is that the prior planing was less straight than the subsequent planing, it is impossible for the person so instructed to stop planing and certify that he is done. Likewise, whenever the scientist is supposed to change events according to values on ordinal scales, there is no limit to the range of actions available. Generally it is true that ordinal scales as antecedent expressions cannot possibly produce of themselves any limited range of scientist action expressions. Consequently, the corresponding compounds can never be maximally precise even if supplemented by all necessary action expressions.

Interval and ratio scales, on the other hand, can result in unequivocal action and therefore in maximally precise compound expressions. Consider the simple example of counting, which may express an interval or ratio scale if the events are isomorphic and depending on whether a zero set of counted objects is recognized. The instruction to count X number of events can be satisfied by unequivocal action. Therefore any compound expression in which this instruction is antecedent will have a limited set of action expressions as consequence. In fact, such a compound would be tautological. This is generally true of all compounds involving action predicated on interval or ratio scales, providing provision is made for the addition of all the necessary supplementary action expressions.

This argument has been anticipated in previous considerations of identification and of the primacy of interval and ratio measures. It is another manifestation of this primacy. What began as an exposition of the role in science of perception, identification, and measurement ends with a principle of great importance. Elsewhere I have labeled this principle the rule of substitutivity, meaning that in science interval and ratio measures are in practice and sometimes in theory substituted for the events they are intended to measure.[53] This rule, although too strictly stated, can be illustrated with some profound examples. It has been pointed out that the child counting five objects does not see five objects, which may be one reason that counting develops relatively late vis-à-vis the child's ability to verbalize or even to recite the alphabet. This fact escapes the adult trying to teach the child to count five objects, and this omission is significant: the adult does not see five objects any more than does the child, but he thinks he sees five objects. Actually a complicated cognitive process— i.e., counting—must intervene between the visual recording of the objects and the determination that there are five objects. The number 5 has been substituted for the perception. In essence, the same can be said of certain measures in science.

Other examples are easily derived from everyday experience. Imagine sitting in a chair facing a long hallway with someone seated at the opposite end. Perceptually that person appears relatively small. Suppose you are told he is 30 feet away. The ratio scale measurement of distance functions to assure you that the distortion in your perception is due to distance and not to the actual dimensions of the person. The measurement standardizes the perception in the sense that it is substituted for any possible distortions in the perceptual process that might account for the variation in size. Again, the inference of distance based on the reduction in perceived size is so commonplace as to be an accepted fact. And this is so because the ratio measure of distance that codifies this inference is in practice substituted for the variation in perceived size. A very common function of measurement in science is to standardize perception in exactly this way: hence the provision of scales on micrographs to allow relative sizes to be judged, the use of contour maps of land topography as well as "people" topography,[54] the citing of measurements to supplement and substitute for the vagaries of depth perception, and so on. Basically, when interval and ratio measures are used in this way they are substitutes.

The rule of substitutivity is too strict in the sense that there are instances in which interval and ratio measures do not function in this way in science. Most notable and important are those cases in which the measurement dimension is the identity. Obviously, the dimension(s), scale(s), and unit(s) cannot be substituted for the dimension as identity for the dimension is a necessary prerequisite for their expression as identifiers. The substitutivity rule is best conceived as a consequence of the general primacy of interval and ratio scales in science: a consequence applying to a limited domain. The fundamental principle does not change: the life's blood of science consists of interval and ratio scales. However, identifications should actually be conceived of as units with minimally two components. The measurement component should be an interval or ratio scale, and this component is more of a complement than substitute. More correctly, this description is generally true.

Interval and Ratio Scales Compared

A minor addendum to this rule is necessary. Ratio scales actually permit the formation of more precise compound expressions than interval scales. This attribute is due to the key difference between the two scale types, the zero point on ratio scales that is missing on interval scales. Obviously, with interval scales the scientist cannot act to adjust events in one way or another to ensure that they correspond to the zero value because that value does not exist. An important consequence of this truism is that there will be no terminus of any sequence of actions predicated on an interval scale. Suppose that the scientist is attempting to reduce the temperature of an object to zero. This presupposes the feedback function of measurement in which the scientist will perform a succession of acts, depending on the successive measurement readings. There can be no last act if there is no zero reading on the temperature scale or, more correctly, if there is no absolute zero point for temperature. Historically, this example is quite appropriate, for the zero point has yet to be reached, although it is approximated with ever-decreasing error. Without this determination no succession of acts can change temperature value to zero. Of course, if there is no terminus to the actions, then there must be an unlimited number of action expressions that can be consequential to the scale, and the precision of the compound will not be maximal no matter what the number of supplementary action expressions. Conversely, given a zero point and a ratio scale there will be a terminus, and maximal precision could be achieved with the requisite supplemental action expressions. The same distinction will hold if the measures are a new class of information, as opposed to feedback as in this example. Generally, then, interval scales are inferior to ratio scales.

It should be emphasized that the specification of a terminus to the action is being considered within the context of the particular scale. On the other hand, it is possible that the action can be terminated because the interval scale is found to be inapplicable. The variation in the events may correspond to no point indicated on the scale. A ratio scale would permit the inference that the events do not have any of the dimension because in this case the "no point" would equal the zero point. An interval scale would permit the inference that the events are not measurable according to this dimension. In this case the terminus to the action would be specifiable if and only if the particular scale and dimension were declared irrelevant. Therefore, in this sense also, ratio scales are more precise than interval scales. Despite this superiority of ratio scales over interval scales, no claim will be made for the exclusion of the latter from "good" science for such scales abound (e.g., temperature).

Conclusion

An ordinal scale of scales according to precision has emerged: in ascending order the scale reads nominal, ordinal, interval, and ratio. The basis of the ordering is the interpretability of the compounds derivable on the basis of the scales by juxtaposing relevant action expressions having to do with the application or reading of the measures and action contingent on the reading. The scale is therefore not of measurement scales per se, for these by definition are maximally precise. Hence, this principle is not to be confused with advocacy of lower-order scales. Generally, ordinal and nominal scales are of limited utility in science; and no paradox is implied because the ordinal scale of scale precision is at the level of metatheory, not science.

3

Prediction
and Control

It has been established that much of science involves activity best described as the identification cycle. Within the context of this cycle it proved impossible not to mention hypothesis formation, although such hypotheses were of a special class. The remainder of the rules of science can be presented by discussing the same general cycle (i.e., from unshared nonsymbolic to shared nonsymbolic) as it applies to hypothesis formation and testing per se. It will be reemphasized that the identification cycle also can be interpreted as a component of what will be called the hypothesis cycle. It will be necessary to systematically reinterpret some of what was said about measurement in terms of hypothesis formation.

129

First, however, the suggested form of hypotheses must be discussed.

HYPOTHESES AS IMPLICATION STATEMENTS

Cause and effect statements are a possible form of expression of theoretical relationships. Presumably they are ubiquitous enough to incorporate all other forms, and scientists certainly use them extensively. It has been maintained in fact that they are crucial to all thought, that people in general and especially scientists seem to think naturally in terms of cause and effect.[1] These statements are problematic, however. The precise definition of "cause" has yet to be formulated. More importantly, "cause" has no limited set of corresponding action or interpretive sequences for the scientist, which is in part the result of and in part results in the lack of a precise definition. That is, causal statements are not empirically interpretable for the scientist because of the imprecision of the term "cause," and this empirical indeterminacy results in the imprecision of the term. This dilemma has been resolved in one way by Bunge's suggestion[2] that causal statements, although indispensible for inquiry, must be translated into associationistic statements to be testable or confirmable. Logical connectives are the medium of expression of associationistic statements. As the two most relevant logical connectives for this discussion are implication and equivalence, causal statements are not so much rejected as they are shunted to the rear.

Why not accept equivalence ("if and only if") statements as opposed to implication statements as the preferred hypothesis form? Just as Tarski asserts the primacy of equivalence statements in definitions, there is ample precedence for their use in metatheoretical hypothesis statements.[3] In stating hypotheses, provision must be made for error; no hypothesis will be applicable or true all the time. It is quite the opposite with Tarski's specification of the requisite linguistic form for definitions. He is concerned with a logic of truth, and by definition any logic as distinct from any theory is unbounded by rigorous empirical test. This means that he is free to stipulate the form of definitions without considering error due to empirical testing. The necessary provision for error in hypotheses is an artifact of their necessary empirical test. The equivalence relation makes no provision for error. Hence, it is inappropriate for hypothesis formation even though it is appropriate for definition formation.

The equivalence relation makes no provision for error in the sense that it does not directly imply the expressions necessary to codify the error if and when it occurs. The "ceteris paribus" (all other things being equal) clause must be appended to account for possible error, and this escape hatch still does not provide the form for the expression of this error. [[A if and only if B, ceteris paribus]] asserts only that there will be possible error and that all other things must be held constant to minimize error. This does nothing to assure that those A's that occur when B does not (error) will be codified in other suggested expressions. In fact, all other things are never equal and [[A if and only if B]] will not apply all the time. When it does not the instances of its negation will be extraneous logically and linguistically to the expression. In other words, equivalence relations are in too stringent a form to allow for the vagaries of empirics, and the ceteris paribus clause is effectively a myth that can conceal the ubiquity of error.

A final suggested form of hypothesis expression utilizes probabilities. Galtung[4] for instance has stated that all hypotheses will include probabilities and that those that do not are not hypotheses. [A] and [B] would be associated with a certain level of probability. Specifically, according to Galtung, assuming [B] to have a number of values, [$B_{1 \ldots n}$], the hypothesis relating [A] and [B] would read, P_A (B_1, B_2, ..., B_n), where P_A would be the probability of A's association with various levels of B. The difficulty with all such probability notions is the ambiguity of the interpretation of probability values. Is the probability to be interpreted as a priori or a posteriori? If a priori, the probability value is a numerical projection derived from hypothetical distributions of test outcomes postulated by probability theory. If a posteriori, the value is based on repeated tests. Therefore, any hypothesis stated in this way has two possible interpretations: A and B may have been found to be associated a certain percentage of the time, or A and B will likely be found to be associated a certain number of times assuming large (or unlimited) numbers of strings of tests. This ambiguity entails a problem if the two types of probabilities are confused. The problem involved is analogous to the transposition of reality problem. A priori probabilities pertain to a metatheory of proof while a posteriori probabilities refer to the empirics of testing. When Galtung asserts that certain hypotheses will have a probability value of 1.0 as a component, he is confusing the two types of probabilities, for his assertion is tantamount to saying that fully determined or errorless hypotheses are possible. They may be possible at the level of metatheory, or a priori, but they are not possible at the level of empirics, or a posteriori. Errorless hypotheses have never been produced in science. This point will be elaborated at the end of this chapter; for the moment, it is sufficient to note that the truth of this assertion results from the previously discussed necessary variation of events. More generally, for this and other reasons as Popper[5] suggests, the notion of probability because of this ambiguity is quite problematic for a theory of science.

The weaknesses of these relationship expressions are the strengths of the implication statement with supplementary conditions. This preferred hypothesis frame reads, [[Given $[C_{1 \ldots n}]$, *if* $[A]$ then $[B]$]], where the $[C_{1 \ldots n}]$ are the necessary conditions to validate the hypothesis with minimal error. First, it has been established that casual statements must be translated into this relation or into the equivalence relation to be testable. Second, the $[C_{1 \ldots n}]$ are the necessary linguistic and logical mechanisms to codify the error when it occurs. In a very important sense, science progresses through the successive formation of additional C_n's until the hypothesis has minimal error. As the range of applicability of the hypothesis is bounded by the supplementary conditions, the error is reduced to manageability. This important point will be elaborated in the section on "proof" in this chapter. Third, the implication relation is considerably more flexible than the equivalence relation in the sense that A and B are not always posited as being associated: alternative antecedents can account for B, and A can account for alternative consequences. Another important growth mechanism of science is implicit here: science's progression is very much the search for alternative antecedents and consequences. Fourth, if probabilities are necessary, the flexibility of the implication relation is such that they simply can be inserted: [[Given [$C_{1 \ldots n}$], if [A] then [B] at [$P(N)$]]].

Finally, and perhaps most importantly, implication relations are the basic medium of logical thought. They are the essence of deductive reasoning: they are necessary for the formation of deductive or axiomatic theories. As Galtung suggests,[6] such theories are chains of implication hypotheses (or can be so translated) in which each hypothesis is implied by each preceding one to the upper bound of one or several general hypotheses that imply the rest. These are the axioms. Interestingly, there is some doubt whether causal statements can be employed in such deductive chains, and probability statements certainly cannot.[7] Thus, it should be remembered that, even though this analysis focuses on hypothesis formation and test and consequently has a distinct horizontal bias, the mechanism for the formation of deductive theories is inherent in the form of hypothesis expression selected.

Types of Implication Hypotheses

Several forms of hypotheses have already been dealt with. These have included hypotheses relating the action of the scientist and identification, hypotheses that relate measurement with scientist action in the sense of either the application or the reading of the measure, and hypotheses in which measurement dimensions are related. However, these were not systematically analyzed as hypotheses of this form. Generally, all hypotheses can be divided into those that the scientist specifically and systematically tests and those necessary for the testing. The relationship between measurement dimensions and between scientist action and identification are examples of the former; the relationship between scientist action and measurement reading or application is an example of the latter. The first class of hypotheses will be called "main hypotheses." The second class will be called "auxiliary hypotheses." The situation is complicated by the fact that with the progressive development of science auxiliary hypotheses may become implicit according to the rule previously cited. Further, some of these auxiliary hypotheses are always implicit. Before going on to consider main hypotheses, it will be necessary to state and restate certain facts about auxiliary hypotheses.

Generally, those auxiliary hypotheses will be implicit which relate well-accepted aspects of scientist action with identification or measurement or with the production of the necessary conditions for either. For example, the scientist need not be presented with a set of hypotheses telling him how to perceive events. These events will be located, and the scientist as man will be capable of readjusting his perceptual apparatus so as to detect them. However, it would be a mistake to imply that this is always the case. As the detailed discussion of observation in the last chapter demonstrated, the location and confirmation of the events may demand explicit hypotheses about perception. Yet, there is a range of actions that the scientist as man can perform without explicit instruction, and this range usually has to do with perception.

Those auxiliary hypotheses will become implicit that describe scientist action which the scientist has been thoroughly trained to perform. For example, scientists are trained to use certain instruments like microscopes, voltmeters, and thermometers—the hardware of their specialties. The purpose of the training is to make implicit the necessary hypotheses regulating the scientist's action with respect to these instruments. That is, the scientists' actions are standardized with the consequence that mundane hypotheses regulating action need no longer be stated. The overall effect is a simplifying of the process of inquiry. If a scientist is instructed that an electron microscope was used to photograph a particular chromosome, he immediately will be capable of reproducing the photograph if he has been instructed in the use of electron microscopes, which reduces the complexity that would be involved in instructing him to enable him to reproduce the action. The situation is analogous to the ease with which one drives a car after being instructed how to do so: the original instructions need not be repeated each time, as they are implicit for the driver.

The standardization of measurement has the same results and is a subset of this type of implicit auxiliary hypothesis. Measurement procedures are standardized in such a way that, even with differing communication components, scientists can reproduce or replicate the measures. Scientists may change, laboratories may change, the events in question may change, but the standardization of the measure guarantees reproducibility and replicability (with error of course).

As auxiliary hypotheses become implicit when they are maximally precise, standardization of measurement procedures and instruments is interpretable as a technique for producing maximal precision. The two ways of assessing level of precision actually correspond to the content of the procedures for assuring standardization. If scientists agree to high percent levels how a measurement procedure or instrument is to be used, that procedure or instrument is said to be standardized. The high agreement can be imposed extraneously to the communication process by the establishment of absolute standard measurements, as is done by the Bureau of Weights and Measures in this country. The ultimate test of the standardizing is the degree to which unequivocal action contingent on it is attained. The action referred to here has to do with the application of the measure. To refer to the reading of the measure as was previously mentioned it is necessary to append the assumption of the stability of the events. Given the satisfaction of this assumption, the standardization will result in unequivocal measurement readings. Standardization thus can be understood as an explicit precization procedure applied to a particular class of expressions.

The ultimate effect of the advanced technologies in highly developed sciences is the transfer or incorporation of some of the once-explicit auxiliary hypotheses into technical apparati, thereby transforming them into implicit hypotheses. Standardization proceeds along this track, as does formal scientific training. To take a simple example, the scientist who must reliably observe the behavior of his animal subjects must be instructed in how to categorize the behaviors in question, how to record instances of their occurrence, where to locate the animals, how to identify the situation in which the behaviors occur, and so on. Put a motion picture camera in the same scientist's hands, and the instructions can be minimized. Some of the necessary auxiliary hypotheses have been replaced by the technology of the camera in all the advanced sciences. Other examples of automated recording systems are easily found in any science. To an extent, this substitution or incorporation process is one meaning of the truism that science advances geometrically, contingent on the geometric advance of scientific technology.

One class of auxiliary hypotheses usually must be stated explicitly, and they do not follow the developmental progression from being explicit to becoming implicit. This class consists of the hypotheses that are necessary to control those factors that could confound the measurement procedure and thereby produce compound expressions of low precision. The compound expressions are those involving the reading of the measures. The control hypotheses specify what the scientist has to do to minimize possible disruptions in his measurements and thereby minimize the concomitant alternative compound expressions generated by discrepancies in the measurement readings. Notice that the measurement expressions per se are not in question; the unit, dimension, and scale may be relatively unequivocal. Yet there may be other factors that produce variation in the measurement and therefore variation in the expressions derived from the measurement. Control hypotheses must be explicitly stated to allow the scientist to reduce this variation.

Generally, the exact content of the control hypotheses will vary from measurement context to measurement context. The scientist attempting to measure gravity waves must bury his instrumentation deep within the ground in at least two locations if he is to be sure that his measurement readings are of gravity waves and not of "noise" produced by seismic shocks due to earth surface events. Similarly, the scientist measuring change in human muscle tension must quiet his subject if the electromyograph readings are to record the muscle tension produced by the relevant action, e.g., "tensing up" as opposed to "shifting in seat." However, there is a well-known class of extraneous events that requires a special subset of relatively uniform control hypotheses: uniform in the sense that researchers give a name to the class of events in question. This class is called "reactive measurement": the disruptions in the measurements and the resulting alternative compound expressions are inherent in the application of the measurements themselves.

Reactive measurement can be defined as a special case: i.e., certain measures in their application may alter the events and hence the subsequent measurement readings. The measures are therefore disruptive factors that must be controlled. The corresponding control hypotheses will tell the scientist how to use the measure to minimize its disruptive effects. For example, the animal ethologist may observe his subjects from behind a blind according to the auxiliary control hypothesis: if you conceal yourself from the animals, then you can observe them without altering their natural behavior simply by your presence.

Reactive measurement can also be defined as a constant: i.e., all measures are reactive; they differ only in the degree to which they require explicit control hypotheses. Presumably, there is a range of tolerable variation of the readings. As long as the reactivity of the measurement does not exceed this range, no control hypotheses will be needed. In other words, if all measurement is reactive, then there will always be a range of alternative compound expressions derivable from the application and reading of the measurement. The level of precision of these compounds will never approximate unequivocal interpretability. However, the level of precision can be tolerable or intolerable. Contradictory and vague compounds would clearly be intolerable. Imagine a measure that yielded contradictory readings or one in which the range of possible readings could not be predicted. Remember that the contradictory and vague consequences are the result of the application of the measure and not the measure itself; presumably the component measurement expressions could be tautological with the same overall results. Clearly the reactivity of such a measure would make it practically useless. Further, a measure that produced ambiguous readings because of its reactivity would be tolerable or intolerable depending on the level of ambiguity: one whose readings were two ways ambiguous would be more tolerable than one whose readings were ten ways ambiguous. Auxiliary control hypotheses would be explicitly introduced when the level of precision of the reading expressions were conceived to be intolerable. The purpose of the hypotheses would be to eliminate contradiction, to transform vagueness into ambiguity, or to limit the range of ambiguity of the reading expressions. These goals would be accomplished by controlling the reactivity of the measures.

Heisenberg's principle of indeterminancy[8] can be translated into these terms. In translation, for Heisenberg the constancy of reactivity and therefore the upper bound on precision short of the maximum value suggest that there are limits to man's knowledge. These limits are defined as the range of tolerable variation in the compound expressions. For him, the range of variation can never be reduced beyond a certain value, so it is not possible to formulate the requisite control hypotheses. No set of necessary control hypotheses can be formulated that will permit the control of the reactivity to the level that maximally precise compound expressions can be produced. His famous example is that the position and velocity of an electron cannot be measured simultaneously. If the position is measured, the velocity reading must be altered; if the velocity is measured, the position reading is altered. In this example, the reactivity is interdimensional and interscale. Because one measure is applied another measurement is altered. The possible compound expression obtained by reading one measurement is two ways ambiguous: one reading will yield a pre-change steady state; a second reading will yield a post-change steady state with the controlling factor being the measurement of the same identity with a different dimension, scale, and unit. According to Heisenberg, no control hypotheses can eliminate this reactivity. The scientist cannot reduce the ambiguity further. It is in this sense that reactivity can be conceived as a constant of all measurement. Control hypotheses can be employed when the reactivity disrupts the measurement process, and science can progress. But reactivity cannot be totally controlled. Heisenberg's principle then is interpretable as the limiting case of reactive measurement as a constant of all measurement.

The conclusion suggested here is the same one mentioned previously. A reason for this conclusion is added. Compound expressions in which measurement expressions are juxtaposed with the scientists' application or reading of the measurements or actions contingent on the readings can never of themselves be maximally precise because of the variation in the events. The added reason is that all measurement must be reactive, minimally as in Heisenberg's principle and maximally to the extent that the measurement process is disrupted. Both of these reasons emphasize the overwhelming importance of auxiliary control hypotheses. These hypotheses must be explicit because they are necessary to precisely apply and read the measurements. They are in fact tested and retested with each use of the measurements in question.

All of the types of hypotheses mentioned so far have had to

do with measurement. They are auxiliary to the main hypothesis, but certainly not ancillary to it. Much of science involves the testing of these auxiliary hypotheses. They exist to facilitate the formation and confirmation of the main hypotheses; they do not exist as an end in themselves. It is possible, however, to conceptualize all hypotheses in the same way, and this conceptualization serves to underscore the exact interrelationships between auxiliary and main hypotheses.

MEASUREMENT CHANGE AS HYPOTHESIS FORM

Change is the essence of science. That is, the specification of change is the main task of any science. At the metatheoretical level this specification will include codification of implicit and explicit auxiliary hypotheses, main hypotheses, the interrelationships between these two hypotheses sets, and certain metahypotheses and principles having to do with these interrelationships. At the scientific level this specification of change will include codification of explicit auxiliary hypotheses like control hypotheses and certain hypotheses necessary for identification, the main hypotheses, and the interrelationships between the explicit auxiliary hypotheses and the main hypotheses. Also included at the scientific level will be explicit expressions about test results. At the metatheoretic level there will be a corresponding set of expressions, including hypotheses about evidence and proof. The distinction between levels is blurred here because the scientist frequently refers to this same class of expressions, which will be considered in detail further along.

All measurement implies comparison. In order for the scientist to know whether or not he has applied a measure correctly, he must compare his application with previous applications. This, in turn, implies his comparison of his results with other results. More generally, the singular instance of measurement application and reading is an absurdity; all measurements are repeated according to the communication rule of replication and reproduction. Also, in the reading of a measure comparison is implicit. The unit has significance only in comparison with other units and the dimension, and the scale value has significance only in relation to the scale and unit. For example, the expression [[This pen is two centimeters long]] is interpretable and can be an antecedent to action expressions only because the dimension of length, the unit of centimeter, and the ratio scale that are implicit have been interpreted previously. They have been used successfully as the basis of other comparisons. The reading of a singular unit and scale value actually implies multiple comparisons. A previous example is also pertinent here, the reading of number of degrees of angular displacement.

Comparison is inherent in all measurement, and change is implied by comparisons. That is, comparison has as a minimal necessary component a change of observation. Again, the example of angular displacement measurement is appropriate. It was shown that taking a reading of degrees requires an explicit change in the observation of the scientist, but that is the limiting case. Any observation implies change. The scientist must reorient his perception and instruct others how to accomplish the same reorientation and hence the same observations. Minimally, this can involve an explicit change in attention. Interestingly, there is a great deal of current psychological research on attention as an important class of human and animal behavior.[9] Significantly, it is conceptualized as a necessary component of learning. Maximally, the necessary changes in scientist behaviors to accomplish observation can involve complex actions like isolation, selection, transport, and arrangement of events. Finally, comparison and change may be explicit components of the measurement instruments rather than attributes of the scientists. That is, the measurement instrumentation may record change in events and its reading require the comparison of the change values. This will be true generally of any measuring instruments that use some form of electrical conversion process: e.g., electromyographs convert change in muscle tension into a series of electrical impulses; neural discharge is converted via electrical impulses into graphic displays or pointer readings.

All this is to say that change and comparison are primitives of measurement that are implied by measurement. This situation is so characteristic of science that in the last chapter movement as change in position was defined at the metalevel as a primitive of all measurement. The relationship was also previously implied with reference to the importance of difference expressions. It can now be seen that this class of expressions is the codification of change and comparison as the fundamentals of science. Difference expressions are the communicative correlates of this fundamental relationship.

Auxiliary Hypotheses as Change

The process of identification implies measurement and therefore implies change. The hypothesis expressing the change has the form: $[[If [I_1 M]$ at $[T_1]$ and $[I_1 M_1]$ at $[T_2]$ then $[M_1$ is the identifier of $I_1]]]$, where I_1 is the identity, M_1 is the necessary and sufficient measurement that completes the identification, and the antecedent expression is the assertion of the identification. The measurement components here are to be understood as the ST-specification of the identity if that identity is perceptual or as any other measures if that identity is not perceptual. A most important case of the latter is where the identity is a measurement dimension.

This hypothesis codifies change in measures as a function of time. Repeated measures are taken of identities, and the relative stability of the identification expression is noted. If there is minimal change, then the identification expression will be asserted as if it were invariant. "Minimal" change is defined as tolerable change: the resulting alternative identification expressions have a range sufficiently limited that they are maximally precise. As there will always be some variation in measurement readings as a function of variation in events or reactivity of the measures, there will always be a range of identifications. This is one meaning of the often-cited truism in the philosophy of science that events are never completely stable; stability is an assumption of the scientist. Much of his behavior is therefore interpretable as an attempt to impose stability on the world or at least to seek it out within the limits of its occurrence.

To acknowledge the variation in the identifications and at the same time assure invariance in the identification expression, the scientist appends an error term to his identification expressions. This error term is usually a numerical expression. It is based on the measurement unit and scale values and tells the scientist what values are the upper and lower bound within which all identification expressions may be expected to lie, what the range of alternative identifications will be according to the range of component unit and scale values that is the error. The incorporation of such an error term is most pronounced in some branches of physics when scientists labor to decrease the error in identifications whose identities are measurement dimensions. For example, physicists have used three different experimental procedures to lower temperature to absolute zero, yet the range of error in this approximation is within the millidegree (.001 degree Kelvin) or submillidegree region on the scale.[10] In fact, the third law of thermodynamics asserts that there will always be a range of error in this measurement.

Typically, scientists will express satisfaction with identifications in which the error term can be unequivocally asserted. If it can be unequivocally asserted to a certain value (e.g., plus or minus some quantity), the range of variation in the alternative identifications is known. If it were not known, the identifications would be vague. As it is known, they are ambiguous. Of course, even with a known error value those identifications that are most precise (least ambiguous) will be preferred to those that are least precise (most ambiguous). Some error values are better than others because they are smaller than others.

This statement must be qualified somewhat to be descriptive of actual scientific practice.

Even if the error value is precisely specified and is the smallest available, the scientist may still not be satisfied with it. This will occur if the change in measurement readings signified by the error value can for whatever reason be attributed to other than time. In other words, if the error value is a function of something other than time, it will not be considered satisfactorally specified by the scientist. If the error value is a function of time alone it is accepted as a necessary result of repeating the measurements of phenomena that vary themselves over time. If the error is not a function of time, it means that the initial identification hypothesis must be amended to include expressions referencing the other sources of error; hence it is no longer an identification hypothesis in the strict sense.

One such source of error can be the reactivity of the measures. To reiterate, if this reactivity is intolerable it must be explicitly stated. If it is conceived of as a constant of the measurements *qua* measurements, then it will be signified by the error term. Other sources of the error besides reactivity are specifiable. Generally, if they lower the precision of the identification sufficiently, they will be explicitly stated. The form of their statement will be explicit control hypotheses. These auxiliary hypotheses are also codifications of change.

The prototype of these hypotheses is: $[[$If $[C_1 \ldots n]$, then $[I_1 M_1]$ at $[T_1]$ and $[I_1 M_1]$ at $[T_2]]]$. The error term is not stated but is understood, and the $[C_1 \ldots n]$ are the conditions the scientist must produce to assure highly precise identifications. The consequence, $[[I_1 M_1]$ at $[T_1]$ and $[I_1 M_1]$ at $[T_2]]$ implies the identification hypothesis just mentioned. It is clear that the consequence must imply change because it includes measurement expressions. The antecedent expression, $[C_1 \ldots n]$ also implies change, but this change is not related to the measurement in the identification expression. This change is measurable, but scientists may not measure it. If they do, the change will be measured differently than the identity. Even if scientists do not measure the change, that of course implies nothing about its measurement by the metatheorist. Presumably, all conditions can be measured just as any event set is measured: i.e., the specification of dimensions, units, and scales should be achievable to high levels of precision.

Without exploring these metatheoretical measurements further, it is still possible to specify the change implicit in the $[C_1 \ldots {}_n]$. Simply, in order to set these conditions, the scientist must change his behavior and change the state of the events that are the conditions. For example, in order to measure gravity waves the scientist must relocate his measuring instruments below the earth's surface. He must also relocate himself to this new position. Interestingly in this example the event-related condition is precisely measurable and would be explicitly measured by some measurement of distance. However, the action-related condition is not explicitly measured. This rule appears to be general: those conditions that are events will require measurement specification, albeit measurement extraneous to the $I_1 M_1$ set; those conditions that are scientist action will not be specifically measured by the scientist. It is as if the measures of the event conditions is sufficient feedback for the scientist about the efficacy of his actions: e.g., if the necessary depth and dimensions of the underground station is specified, presumably all scientists will be able to perform the actions necessary to construct such a station and relocate the measuring instruments.

Therefore, with the specification of the $[C_1 \ldots {}_n]$ there will always be a specifiable set of sometimes explicit, sometimes implicit hypotheses. The antecedent will be the action of the scientist and the consequence the measurement of the event-control conditions. When this second set of measures provides sufficient feedback for the scientist action, that action will not be measured and, in fact, will be implicit for the scientist. When this second set is not sufficient feedback, then the scientist action must be explicitly stated. It may also be independently measured. Simply, the second measures will not be sufficient feedback if, for whatever reason, the scientist cannot perform the requisite action on their basis alone. Although one can speculate about the causes of this insufficiency—e.g., what actions must be trained or need not be trained—the fundamental fact is that some scientist actions can be standardized on the basis of measurement procedures while others require explicit instructions, independent measurement, or training in order to be standardized. This, of course, is a corollary to the explicit-implicit rule mentioned previously: certain compound action expressions must be explicitly stated for the scientist while others need not be; also, explicit expressions can become implicit given sufficient precision, while implicit expressions can become explicit if the scientist's expectations based on the confirmation of the compounds are violated, i.e., if the compounds that are hypotheses are falsified.

Control hypotheses are a special subset of auxiliary hypotheses. It is important to distinguish control hypotheses from those auxiliary hypotheses whose antecedents are scientist action and whose consequences are the measurements. The basic distinction is that control hypotheses function primarily to assure relatively precise readings of the measures, while these action hypotheses function primarily to assure the application of the measures. Gravity-wave measures can be applied on the earth's surface: the scientist has the requisite actions in his repertoire to apply the measures. Because these measures will have imprecise readings because of the disruptive conditions, control hypotheses are necessary. But despite these disruptive conditions, the measures can still be applied. Precise application, as opposed to reading, of measures is therefore the consequence of another subset of auxiliary hypotheses. These previously have been called action hypotheses. The explicit-implicit rule was originally applied to action hypotheses.

The prototype of these action hypotheses is [[If scientists do X, Y, Z, then they can [measure] events $[U_n]$]]. The classes of action expressions mentioned include: isolation and selection of events, rearrangement of events, transport of events, change in scientist action to observe events. Obviously, the measurement consequence involves change. The action-hypothesis antecedents also involve change. The scientist action may change, or the events may change, or both may change. In order to isolate and select events in the domain the scientist minimally must reorient his behavior; maximally, he must move the events. In order to measure the mercury concentration in fish a weighed sample of the fish first must be extracted and sealed in a quartz ampule.[11] In order to rearrange events the scientist must reorient his observations or move the events, both of which imply change. The scientist may choose to take radioautograms of certain sections of brain tissue in a certain order or may store the sections in a certain order. Obviously, the transport of events and change in scientist action to observe events also are special subsets of change.

These action-hypothesis antecedents may be explicit or implicit, and they obey the explicit-implicit rule. Furthermore, if they are explicit, they may be independently measured or not. It should be obvious that one class of action hypotheses has just been discussed: those whose consequences are control conditions. These action hypotheses are necessary for the statement of control hypotheses but are not control hypotheses: i.e. [[if scientist does X_n, then [$C_{1 \ldots n}$]]] as the former vs. [[if [$C_{1 \ldots n}$], then [$I_1 M_1$] at T_1 and [$I_1 M_1$] at T_2]]] as the latter. Generally, however, action hypotheses are necessary for the application of any measure, including measures of control conditions as well as measures in main hypotheses.

Main Hypotheses and Change

An analysis of main hypotheses is a straightforward extension. Simply, in these hypotheses a change in one measurement is related to a change in another dimension. The prototype hypothesis is [[If [$I_1 M_1$], then [$I_2 M_2$]] where [$I_n M_n$] is an identity and its associated measurement. These are what are most commonly meant by hypotheses. Presumably it is the job of science to test these hypotheses. As measures are being predicted on the basis of other measures, this hypothesis is predicting from and to change. One of the favorite ways of presenting these types of hypotheses is graphically. On the ordinate are arranged the dimension, scale and unit of one identification, and on the abscissa are arranged the dimension, scale, and unit of another identification. The types of scales need not match: ratio scales can be related to interval and interval to ratio. For reasons previously discussed, nominal and ordinal scales are omitted because they are not "true" scales.

Essentially, there is no difference between this type of hypothesis and one mentioned previously in which a dimension as identity is related to other dimensions as identities. It was stated that some of the basic laws of science have this form: e.g., $E = MC^2$. The only discrepancy between the two types of hypotheses is that in main hypotheses the identities are conceived of as separate from the dimensions. For example, mean annual evaporation of water can be related to mean annual precipitation, and both are measured by the same dimension, the number of centimeters. If these identities were the same as the measurement dimension, obviously the hypothesis would be a tautology—centimeters would be related to centimeters—which would be a logical absurdity. Thus, it is the explicit purpose of main hypotheses to relate different identifications that have identities separable or independent from measurements.

Main hypotheses, if defined in this way, must include control hypotheses and action hypotheses in which the antecedent conditions or antecedent scientist action are measured. In the former, the measures of the control conditions are related to the basic measures. In the latter, the measures of the scientist action are related to the measures of the control conditions or to the main measures. Control and action hypotheses, then, are types of main hypotheses. However, this should not blur the importance of the basic distinction. Main hypotheses are a crucial component of science. They have a very special relationship to auxiliary hypotheses even though the latter can be interpreted partially as special types of main hypotheses.

Main hypotheses can be tested if and only if the requisite

auxiliary hypotheses have been confirmed. Obviously, since main hypotheses relate identifications, auxiliary identification hypotheses must be provided. In order for the component measurements to be applied, action hypotheses must be fully confirmed and accordingly will be implicit. Finally, in order to be precisely read these measurements must be supplemented with any necessary control hypotheses.

This relationship has been fully described as the process of scientific inquiry as it moves from quadrant 1 to quadrant 3: from unshared nonsymbolic experience to shared symbolic experience. The implicit and explicit auxiliary hypotheses provide the linkage between quadrants as diagrammed at the end of Chapter 1. They have the same role in the identification cycle as in the hypothesis formation and testing cycle. Furthermore, the identification cycle and all the implied auxiliary hypotheses are necessary for the hypothesis cycle. The identification cycle, then, has two roles in science. It is an independent and legitimate form of scientific inquiry in and of itself. As such, it is analogous to the hypothesis cycle in the sense that auxiliary hypotheses function in a similar manner in both and the stages in the process are the same. It is also descriptive of the development of a form of auxiliary hypothesis that is necessary for the hypothesis cycle.

Specifically, these interrelationships can be stated as a series of deductively related metahypotheses:

1. [[[If [[action hypotheses]], then [[control hypotheses]]]]].
2. [[[If [[control hypotheses]] then [[identification hypotheses]]]]].
3. Therefore, [[[If [[action hypotheses]] then [[identification hypotheses]]]]].
4. [[[If [[identification hypotheses]], then [[main hypotheses]]]]].
5. Therefore, [[[If 1, 2, and 3 then [[main hypotheses]]]]].

With the specification of these deductive relationships, much of the description of science is complete. Before considering questions of proof which will require the introduction of an additional expression type, several more general issues must be considered.

Main Hypotheses and Multiple Measures

Main hypotheses can be complicated by the inclusion of more than two identifications or by identifications that include more than one measure. This complication can be analyzed as a straightforward extension of simple main hypotheses. There is an important exception, however, that requires further comment.

It is a common misconception in current research theory that identities are measurable in science in alternative ways. To convert this misconception to set-theoretic terms, an identity is construed as a set and the associated measures as either set members or as other sets. If the measures are interpreted as set members, then the identity is usually seen as incomplete and the process of inquiry as cumulative in the sense that the identity will be completed via application of the scientific method. If the measures are interpreted as other sets, then the process of identification is seen as the union of sets. In the strictest interpretation, the measures are construed as substitutable and equivalent to the measures. Phrased in these terms, this problem is analogous to the specification of the relationship between definiendum and definiens or interpreted expression and meaning. Here there are two interpretations of the relation between identity and multiple measures.

Operationism has used both interpretations. Theoretical constructs that are identities have been analyzed as equivalent to the operations necessary for their measurement. In less strict form, operational definitions of terms have been construed as additive or multiplicative: the identity term is defined by multiple alternative measurement operations that, in toto, are the definition of the term. An extensive critique of operationism has developed in the literature. Rather than beat a dead horse, it should be emphasized that what is being criticized here is not operationism per se, but operationism as an example of a more general misconception about measurements and main hypotheses.

This conception of measurement and identification produces the logical possibility of main hypotheses in which the related identifications have alternative measurements. This implies, in turn, that these hypotheses would have as many alternative interpretations as there are relationships between the alternative measures. For example, consider the following abstract hypotheses: $[[\text{If } [I_1 \ M_1; \ M_{1A}] \text{ then } [I_2 \ M_2; \ M_{2A}]]]$. Logically, this hypothesis would have four interpretations: $[[\text{If } [I_1 \ M_1] \text{ then } [I_2 \ M_2]]]$; $[[\text{If } [I_1 \ M_1] \text{ then } [I_2 \ M_{2A}]]]$; $[[\text{If } [I_1 \ M_{1A}] \text{ then } [I_2 \ M_2]]]$; and $[[\text{If } [I_1 \ M_{1A}] \text{ then } [I_2 \ M_{2A}]]]$. Of course, with the addition of certain restrictive assumptions this need not be true. Yet the conception of multiple measures usually does not employ any restrictive assumptions. Thus the legitimization of multiple measures as a research concept is tantamount to the legitimization of imprecision of main hypotheses. As the number of multiple measures increases so does the ambiguity and imprecision of the main hypotheses of which they are components.

This misconception is not only a logical absurdity. It can also be faulted on more substantive grounds. The identification relationship in science is a wholistic one. Measures neither replace identities nor cumulatively specify them. Measures identify identities and are inseparable components of the corresponding identifications. More concretely, there is no case in science in which an identity is identified by different measurements and the resulting identifications are independently interpreted. The abstract example just given has no substantive counterpart in science. By way of contrast, it is most certainly true that any identification can have multiple measurement components. But these components are not interpretable as independent identifications. They are conjunctive and not independent. For example, measures of wave length may appear with measures of wave frequency, mass with velocity, distance with direction, weight with size, length with depth, or volume with mass. These measures are not independently interpretable identifiers of the particular identity, they are different measures of the same identity and as such form one complex identification.

Part of the confusion over multiple measures is due to the apparent similarity of identifications in which measures are conjunctive and identifications in which measures are independent. This similarity is the deceptive product of a set-theoretic logical interpretation of identification. Accordingly identifications can be *constructed* in which the multiple measures appear to be independent. Furthermore this logical construction does correspond to two special cases in science. In the first case, the identities are measurement dimensions and the identifiers are other measurement dimensions, e.g., density equals mass per unit volume. Apparently, multiple measures do exist as independent components of identifications. But as has been mentioned twice before, these identifications are actually main hypotheses, or, more correctly, they have the status of scientific laws, i.e., they are main hypotheses that scientists call "laws." This first substantive correlate of the logical construction is better interpreted as a special form of main hypothesis relating two or more independent identifications rather than an identification with independent measurement components.

The second special case in science that can be misconceived as a case of multiple independent measures is implied by the first. Suppose that density is hypothetically related to pressure (force per unit area). The resulting hypothesis will have an antecedent and a consequence with multiple measures. Again the set-theoretic logical construction appears to have a substantive counterpart. However, if the antecedent actually is a main hypothesis and the consequence also is a main hypothesis, the misconception becomes apparent. The main hypothesis is a compound hypothesis relating two component hypotheses; it is not interpretable as a simple main hypothesis relating two identifications.

The confusion apparent here is a general one. Multiple independent measures of the same identity can be logically stated, but some relationship between the multiple measures is implicit. Some relationship between multiple measures must always underlie any formal expression in which multiple measures are components. Webb, et al.,[12] provide the perfect example of this schizophrenic dilemma. They argue for "multiple operationism, that is, for multiple measures which are hypothesized to share in the theoretically relevant components but have different patterns of irrelevant components."[13] And further, "Once a proposition has been confirmed by two or more independent measurement processes, the uncertainty of its interpretation is greatly reduced."[14] They are unable to substantiate this argument with concrete examples. The example they do use violates the argument by explicitly demonstrating that multiple measures can never be independent. "A consideration of the laws of physics, as they are seen in that science's measuring instruments, demonstrates that no theoretical parameter is ever measured independently of other physical parameters and other physical laws. Thus, a typical galvanometer responds in its operational measurement of voltage not only according to the laws of electricity but also to the laws' of gravitation, inertia, and friction. By reducing the mass of the galvanometer needle, by orienting the needle's motion at right angles to gravity, by setting the needle's axis in jeweled bearings (etc.) . . . , the instrument designer attempts to minimize the most important of the irrelevant physical forces for his measurement purposes. As a result, the galvanometer reading may reflect, *almost* purely, the single parameter of voltage (or amperage, etc.)."[15] This example illustrates the rules of science: first, where multiple measures are postulated they must be rigorosly related; second, one form of relationship is via scientific laws; third, control hypotheses can be scientific laws that function as control hypotheses, in which case the multiple interrelated measures will be components of the control hypothesis and the identification hypothesis. This example is more important in what it does not demonstrate: it is not illustrative of multiple independent measures as it purports to be. Clearly, even an explicit advocate of multiple independent measures cannot produce an example. Simply, the rule in science is that multiple measures exist only as components of main hypotheses, albeit well-confirmed and perhaps quite complex main hypotheses.

The situation is also confused because of the historical fact of the development of scientific measurements. It is possible to point to multiple measures of the same identity that have existed at different stages in the development of the science. Again, however, these multiple measures are not independently interpretable. Minimally, their interrelationship is mediated by time. Maximally, the fact of their dependence can result from developmental necessity, e.g., time measured by the spring watch was predecessor to time measured by the vibrating quartz crystal, and the latter employs the same principles but with several additions. This means there are two concealed main hypotheses that define the lower and upper limits of the variation of the interrelationships of the multiple measures in these historical examples. The first has the form, $[[\text{If } [I_1 \ M_1] \text{ at } [T_1], \text{ then } [I_1 \ M_{1A}] \text{ at } [T_2]]]$. The second has the form, $[[[\text{If } [I_1 \ M_1] \text{ at } [T_1] \text{ and } [[H_1]], \text{ then } [I_1 \ M_{1A}] \text{ at } [T_2] \text{ and } [[H_1 + H_2]]]]]$.

The multiple-measure rule can be stated as follows. The same identity can have measures with different dimensions. These must be complementary or conjunctive, in which case they form one complex identification. If they are not complementary, then the measures must be interrelated via main hypotheses that are called laws by scientists. Therefore, the dimensions are other identities, or the other identities are concealed. In any case, the different measures cannot be conceived of as independent identifications.

Definitions, Multiple Measures, and Main Hypotheses

This presentation of science appears to slight hypotheses whose antecedents and consequences are not expressed as identifications. Such hypotheses are usually conceived of as containing abstractions that are linked to measurement via definition. The extensivity of the definitions is generally recognized as varying: a particular abstraction may require multiple definitions to reach the level of measurement. Also, many forms of definition are recognized; operational definitions, nominal definitions, real definitions, dispositional definitions, recursive definitions; this is but a partial list.[16] Generally, definitions are defined as specifying meaning. When those meanings are measures or measurement procedures, the definitions are called "operational definitions." But this label for a special class of definitions should not cloud the relation between definitions and measurement. The philosophy of science usually specifies the terminus of definition at the level of measurement. One can avoid a strict interpretation of all definitions as operational by asserting that definitions of every variety at some point or other in their specification either suggest measurements for substantive abstractions or facilitate the assertion of such measurements. This implies main hypotheses in which definitions can be provided for antecedents and consequences. The hypotheses via this mechanism initially need not be stated as the relation between changes in measurements. A freedom of linguistic usage is implied: hypotheses can be stated at whatever level of generality, and their testability, which implies identification and measurement, can be assured independently of their assertion. Or to put it simply, the antecedents and consequences in main hypotheses need not be identifications according to this conceptualization.

Definition has previously been considered as a subset of the process of interpretation and precization. This is perfectly congruent with traditional usage. As such, definition is terminated with maximum precision. Any expression type is subject to precization via successive interpretation. This means that any expression type is subject to the process of definition. And any expression will be considered sufficiently defined when it is maximally precise. Measurement expressions are by definition maximally precise. Most identifications in science are processed according to the identification cycle until they achieve maximum precision. Much of this process can be conceptualized as the establishment of invariant relations between identities and measures. Definition can be conceived of as part of this process. The traditional concept of definition is thus modified but not substantially altered. It is viewed as a necessary technique for attaining maximum precision by linking identities to precise measurements. Furthermore, the identification process can be interpreted as progressing from incompleteness to completeness. Identities are successively defined and redefined until measurements are derived. Or identifications are defined and redefined until measurements are derived. In either case, there is no reason not to posit these identities as abstractions. Conversely, the process can be conceptualized as fully applicable to abstractions. Hence, freedom of linguistic usage is also assured with this type of analysis.

The application of these principles to main hypotheses provides the mechanism necessary to treat hypotheses that are abstractly phrased. Basically, the antecedent and consequence expressions can be phrased to any level of generality. Again, these expressions can be precizated via definition or, more generally, interpretation until they are linked to measurement. Notice that the assumption is implicit that the initial abstract expressions will be identifications or will be transformed into identifications. The transformation is possible because of the fundamental similarity between interpretations and identifications. Identifications are a special subset of interpretations that are themselves subject to the process of interpretation. However, not all interpretations are interpretable as identifications. Hence the necessity of the assumption of the continuity of the abstract expressions and identifications.

Definitions can be handled by this conceptual scheme while preserving much of their traditional analysis. However, these machinations are really not necessary. The bulk of the scientific research enterprise involves testing and formulating main hypotheses whose components are relatively precise identifications. It is really quite misleading to think of measurement as the result of defining abstract expressions that are components of hypotheses. This "top-down" bias distorts what science is about. Identities and measures develop simultaneously as identifications, and identifications are rigorously synthesized via the identification cycle and the necessary hypothesis components thereof. Even though philosophers of science have had much to say about definition formation, definition is relatively rare in science.[17] When it occurs, it is a precisely circumscribed technique for codifying transformations in identifications that have been discovered and developed. It does not exist as a procedure that can be applied to all expression components of hypotheses. It is an encoding procedure for symbolically storing interpretive transformations that involve identifications and more general interpretations. In this sense, it is a fallacy to consider definitions exclusive of the hypotheses in which they are used. For it is only in this context that their function can be fully understood. In fairness, it must be stated that most philosophers of science emphasize this interdependence. On the other hand, part of the significance of Wittgenstein's later work[18] lay in his completely relying on this principle rather than paying it lip service as an afterthought, i.e., his concept of meaning of terms being their use, and their lack of meaning as independent words.

The distinction between an "organic" concept of definition and a "top-down" one bears emphasis. It is really difficult to provide examples of definition from the physical sciences. Kaplan in his discussion of definition[19] provides no such examples. There is a simple reason for this: as science does not use definition in the "top-down" sense, any examples to be had do not conform to this model. Be that as it may, consider the definition of pressure as force per unit area. It is not unreasonable to assume that this can be called a definition with little if any contrary argument. This definition is the codification of a well-confirmed identification. That is, the formal symbolic representation of this identification is labeled a "definition." The identification-definition is useful because [pressure] is a component in several main hypotheses that are scientific laws: e.g., [[the [pressure] of a gas varies directly with its [temperature]]]. A stronger word than "useful" is called for here: this definition has been formed and is used by the scientist because the identification formally codified therein bears a well-confirmed relationship to other identifications. Also this definition is itself a well-confirmed law relating identification dimensions.

Definition in this "organic" sense is quite distinct from definition specified as a "top-down" procedure. "Definition" is not a procedure, technique, or mechanism; it is a form of record of the outcome of a procedure, technique, or mechanism. [Pressure] is defined as [force per unit area] because [[pressure] is [force per unit area]]. This contrasts to the notion of [pressure] existing as an abstract expression that through the process of definition is made equivalent to [force per unit area]. To borrow phraseology from Gertrude Stein: [[pressure] is [force per unit area]] is [[pressure] is [force per unit area]] is [[pressure] is [force per unit area]]. It is quite clearly an error to reify definition-as-name-for-a-symbolic-mode-of-representation to definition-as-procedure-to-specify-meaning. Scientists use definitions in the former sense, not in the latter.

Again, the metatheorist has tended to transpose his view of scientific reality onto the scientific reality. Main hypotheses that relate changes in identifications encoded (perhaps) as definitions are the stuff of science. Hypotheses which relate abstractions and which use definitions to link the abstractions to measurements are the logical constructs of some metatheorists. That a conceptual scheme has been developed which permits a congruent analysis of both versions of "hypotheses and definitions" is really beside the point.

The Significance of Hypotheses as Change

Hypotheses have been defined according to the types of changes they predict. Yet, "change" has been treated merely as an appended label. To say, "Hypotheses are predictions of change," really has little analytic value of itself. It is true, but so what? The consequences of the assertion are quite profound. Perhaps this is most obvious in considerations of proof and testing hypotheses, but the force of the concept emerges in two ways.

First, if hypotheses are expressions about change, then further weight is added to the previous argument that perceptual identifications or observables do not exist. Change cannot be observed in the strict sense. Certainly, the eye can see the movement of an object, but that movement has no enduring visual representation. It is an event that is fleeting. More strictly, the argument can be made that movement could not be perceived at all without boundaries or frames of reference. Therefore, it is not too strong a statement that movement per se is an inference and not a perceptual event. This point is most obviously made with movement as change and has been frequently applied to such movement-related constructs as velocity. Velocity, it is said, can be perceived only as a series of points in space with the distance and time necessary for its determination being nonperceivable measurements.

And even though the truism of change being nonperceptual is most obvious with movement, it is in many ways less problematic with other changes. Generally, any change that occurs through extended time periods is nonperceptual. The terminal steady state can be perceptually fixed, but the original steady state must be a product of memory or, more appropriately for science, a product of measurement recordings. And the transition point can be fixed only as a point in time and space. Such longterm change must occur in part beyond perceptual purview.

However, it would be a mistake to assume that perceiving change is problematic only because time intervenes. Even those changes that can occur within perceptually bound time periods are not perceptually relizable for basically the same reasons. The origin of the change must disappear with the inception of change, and its necessary disappearance makes all change necessarily nonperceptual.[20] A witness can be present as a man passes from life to death and can certify that he "saw" the man die. But that the man was once alive is a memory or perception passed into memory and not an active perception. Moreover, the exact transition point cannot be perceptually known. Hence, there exists the great problem with specifying the perceptual criteria for death that presently confronts medical science.[21]

The argument can be made much more simply if the role of time in the recording of change is not taken for granted. Time is necessary to certify change. True, this may not be time as sophisticated measurement, but time must be a component even if in its most primitive form. That is, the perceiver must have some sense of beginning and end, origin and terminus. Change is by definition a, passage from one state to another. The perceiver must recognize these two points. This recognition, in turn, is not perceptual. Even in this most primitive of forms, time is a measurement and not a perception. It is a record of transition and not the perception of transition. Of course, if the time is sophisticated measurement, this is obviously true.

All this is to say that change is an inference, not a perception. If change is a crucial component of hypotheses, then perceptual identities really have a rather insignificant role in science. Perception is not the primary mode of knowing. The basis of knowledge is inference even at the level at which perception has been assumed to be operative. If change is primary and change is nonperceptual, how is change recorded? Measurement is the principal mode in science, although as in the example of time more primitive modes are possible. Not only is change inherent in measurement, measurement is the principal record of change in science. Therefore, the atomistic components of knowledge are not perceptions but measured changes and changes in measurement. As previously argued, then, measurement is again seen to be primary.

Note that the function of measurement is slightly altered as a consequence of this notion of hypotheses as changes in measurements. Importantly, the argument about the primacy of measurement is buttressed. Almost as important is the emergence of the concept of measurement as records of change that do not so much substitute for perception, but rather place it in a subordinate confirmatory role. Measurement according to this interpretation is a storing device of memory. It codifies and stores the fleeting perception. Perception confirms the measurement: perception is necessary to determine whether or not the records of change are accurate. This relationship between perception and measurement is analogous to the relationship established previously between events and measurements in identifications, where the events confirm the measurement and therefore confirm the identification. Here the perception is seen as confirming measurements as records of change. Basically, the measurements are not representations of change in events so much as they are the translation of that change into a codified enduring form. With the adequate completion of this translation, the records become the events, so that main hypotheses predict from and to change in measurements.

An important question is suggested about measurement interpreted in this way: What is the best form of measurement as record? This question is equivalent to asking what records codify change most effectively. As the criterion for effectiveness, again, is precision, the question becomes: What measurement form is the most precise for recording change? Because dimensions and units vary widely in content in science, to answer this question by referring to appropriate categories of dimensions and units would seem to be unfruitful. Part of the answer lies in appealing to the primitives of all dimensions and units. All changes must be recorded as position alterations. Hence changes must be precisely fixed in space. All changes must entail by definition a temporal component. Hence, changes must be recorded by reference to time. Space and time, then, must be the base for all measurement of change.

This truism implies a full answer to the question. As space and time are interval and ratio measures, interval and ratio scales are the most precise measurement forms for recording change. Certainly changes can be recorded on nominal and ordinal scales, but these records will be minimally precise. This argument parallels previous arguments about the level of precision of nominal and ordinal scales, and need not be reiterated in detail. Even impressionistically, the truth of this assertion becomes apparent. Change must involve the specification of transition points. These points must be plotted as a function of space and time. They can also be plotted on other dimensions as well (e.g., change in weight), but space and time are essential functions. If other dimensions are used to plot the transition, these dimensions must be expressed by interval or ratio scales. Transition points can be plotted only on interval and ratio scales. Conversely, transition points cannot be determined by reading nominal or ordinal scales. Simply, interval and ratio scales can be used to plot the transition, while nominal and ordinal scales cannot. Substantively, this means that nominal or ordinal scales do not permit the graphic recording of the change: they do not permit this transformation because of the limited mathematical operations they imply.

One preliminary gain to be had from this conceptualization of hypotheses as change is the buttressing of the aforementioned principles of science, including the primacy of interval and ratio scales. A second more fundamental benefit contingent on this concept is the reshaping of the objectives of science.

PREDICTION AND CONTROL

There is considerable argument over what the objectives of science really are, but we shall avoid the morass. Two supposedly independent objectives can be shown to be interdependent when hypotheses are conceptualized as different types of changes. Prediction and control are demonstrably interdependent. They imply each other. If precise predictions are formed, then control must be possible. If control is possible, then precise predictions have been formed. The argument can be brought forward on two tracks: one general, without defining control; the other more concrete, with a definition of control.

Generally, no science does not aspire to control the events in its domain. Actual manipulation may not be technically feasible at a given time, but this is the fantasy of all scientists. Astronomers would like to change the orbits of the planets; meteorologists would like to control the weather; geologists would like to control earthquakes. The objection can be made that control in certain sciences may not be feasible because the events are not manipulable. Planetary orbits, the weather, and earthquakes may not be manipulable by God's fiat, so this objection is well taken. But what is overlooked in this counterargument is that knowledge can provide man with the option of altering his behavior contingent on the attributes of nonmanipulative events. The scientist's theories, then, can permit man to control his own behavior so that he is, in effect, controlling the nonmanipulable events. Astronomers can give sufficient information to man to orbit planets. Meteorologists can tell man how to avoid or plan for certain weather patterns. Geologists can locate earthquake-prone areas and tell residents how to earthquake-proof their residences.

The fact that certain events cannot be manipulated does not alter the fact of scientists' striving for control and providing it in the sense that men can control their behavior contingently. However, it should not be overlooked that this statement is relatively weak. Metaphysically, it can be asserted that there is no logical reason why all events should not be manipulable. If the laws of nature are discoverable by man, these laws should provide requisite knowledge for control. It can also be argued that no list of attributes that result in nonmanipulability can be specified. Barring these metaphysical arguments (which does not negate their utility), the weaker argument can be disputed on definitional grounds. Is control through contingent action the same as control of events? This question demands the definition of control, which leads to the concrete assertion about the interdependence of prediction and control.

Control can be defined as planned change. The question of definition reduces to: When can it be asserted that man has controlled events? The assertion is possible under two conditions: a person asserts he can change events, and he proceeds to change them. Both of these entail the use of plans: the person must be aware of the contingencies about to be implemented; he must be capable of stating the contingencies; and he must be capable of behaving in accordance with the contingencies. Simply, he must plan change and implement the plans.

The specification of the form of the plans completes the argument. The plans can be conceptualized as hypotheses. Generally, to conform with traditional usage of "control", the hypotheses are auxiliary ones in which the antecedent is some aspect of the scientist's action and the consequence is the change of certain events. In this case, "control" is synonymous with change of events between steady states in which the controlling factor is the scientist's behavior. These types of hypotheses have been called action hypotheses. "Control" in this case involves the person's explicitly stating a specific action hypothesis, and, in effect, testing that hypothesis by performing the requisite actions and recording the predicted changes.

The metatheoretical and the scientific levels of analysis are all-important here. The action hypothesis and implementation of change must be formulated by the scientist as his interpretation of the expression: "I controlled events X, Y, Z." Conversely, he must be capable of labeling the hypothesis and implementation as his "control" of events. Control as action hypotheses and implementation of change is at the level of a scientist communication; control as the label of these is at the metatheoretic level. Consequently, the assertions of control in the former sense should be bracketed and assertions of control in the latter sense should be double-bracketed. Control would be defined as planned change at the metatheoretical level. The metatheorist could legitimately say that the scientist had [[controlled]] events if he as metatheorist could reproduce the scientist's action hypotheses and certify their predictive adequacy. A chain of infinite regress in the definition of control is possible with each metalevel. Infinite regress is avoided by drawing the boundaries of the metatheoretical inquiry.

Control as planned change in which action hypotheses are the scientist's plans conforms most closely in definition to traditional usage when the scientist action specified is the transport of events. For example, the assertion "scientist A has accelerated the electron speed or controlled the speed of the electron" would be translated, "if scientist A has transported a source of ions at the center of the chamber of the cyclotron and has accelerated the ions by means of a high-frequency alternating electric field of the same frequency, etc., then the electrons will be accelerated to speed X from speed Y."

"Control" can also be defined according to other possible scientist action antecedents: isolation or selection, arrangement, or change of observations. With these definitions, traditional usage is being bent somewhat. The scientist may passively isolate or select events for study in the sense that their space-time regions remain invariant but his space-time region changes. Or he may arrange events passively in a similar sense by using instruments in which the events have been previously arranged: e.g., in the cyclotron the chamber is mounted in a certain fashion while the ion source is placed in a fixed position in the chamber. Or the change in his observations may in no way affect the absolute position of the events even though it affects their position relative to previously observed events or positions.

"Control" in any of these senses would probably violate traditional usage. Yet, these definitional variants do not violate the essence of the scientist's actions. Any act of "control" defined in the narrow sense would definitely have to be supplemented by other actions in order to be descriptive of what scientists do. In other terms, "control" as action hypotheses and tests or implementation of change in which the scientist transports events is so strictly defined that other contingent and equally important classes of action are omitted. The difficulty is analogous to the fallacy identified by Wittgenstein of searching for meaning in isolated words. Transport, selection, isolation, reorientation of observation, and arrangement of events are all necessary components of the gestalt of scientist action. "Control" as transport alone overlooks the crucial context of scientist action that gives the act of transport its significance and purpose.

Carnap[22] introduced the concept of "perceptual realizability" to make a parallel argument about too narrowly defining "control." In brief, he argued that scientists could be said to "control" events in the sense that they make them perceptually accessible. Perceptual realizability as a subset of this expanded definition of control is demonstrably sufficient to create adequate hypotheses and theories, so that control as transport can in fact be dispensed with as a necessary criterion of "good science."

A final expansion of the definition of control is possible and fruitful. The auxiliary hypotheses as plans may be supplemented by main hypotheses. Subsequent human action may be the consequence of this compound antecedent. This returns to the concept of control in which man's action can be regulated contingent on knowledge of events albeit that these events may be nonmanipulable. The knowledge is expressed formally as the verified main hypotheses while the auxiliary hypotheses are components of the scientist's methodological lore and are not usually considered as part of the knowledge developed by science. However, the technology of science that is the manifestation and codification of these auxiliary hypotheses has had important consequences in extending man's control over his environment.

The concept of control can be seen to be inextricably bound to that of prediction. The expanded definition of control based on hypotheses as change demonstrates that, in fact, control cannot be defined independently of prediction. The assertion that one set of objectives of science is prediction or is prediction and control overlooks this important interdependency. Another important rule of science can be gleaned from this discussion. It is at least equally true that scientists can develop precise predictions because they can control the events in their domain as that they can control the events in their domain because they have developed precise predictions. The purpose here is not to reproduce a novel version of the chicken and egg dilemma: "which came first, prediction or control?" The purpose rather is to emphasize that the question really has no definitive answer. A precise definition of "control" must refer to prediction, and as previously discussed, a precise definition of prediction (as hypothesis formation) must refer to control.

An interesting relationship is implied by this gestalt-like interdependence. Most hypotheses are predictions that predict change in measurements. Those that do not, like certain auxiliary hypotheses, can be transformed into hypotheses that predict change in measurements. If the analysis is carried far enough, in fact, it can be argued that all hypotheses that are explicitly stated must have antecedents and consequences that include measurement expressions. To be explicitly stated a hypothesis must have antecedents and consequences that are identified. By definition, all identifications imply identifying measurement expressions. It follows that all explicitly stated hypotheses must have measured antecedents and consequences. The initial premise about the ubiquity of identification is open to question. Certainly, some scientific expressions may not definitionally or deductively imply measurement. Developmentally, however, the case for such ubiquity can be effectively argued. Be that as it may, the strict form of the argument is irrelevant for the purposes at hand. Those hypotheses that predict change in measurement are also used as the basis of the definition of control. The relationship suggested by this definitional interdependence is that levels of control should be associated with levels of measurement:

types of scientist action should be related with level of measurement scales.

This relationship has been specified in great detail elsewhere.[23] Unfortunately the terminologies used do not match. A summary presentation congruent with the present analysis is in order. Initially it should be emphasized that this hypothetical relation is speculative. Its value lies in its suggestiveness. One possible set of hypotheses in a developed metatheory of science would probably have to do with the relation of classes of scientist action contingent on classes of measurement. The theme has been preliminarily developed with previous discussions of the role of measurement in auxiliary hypotheses having to do with the application and reading of measures.

The caution duly noted, the first step necessary in establishing the relationship is to scale the measurement scales and scientist action. This operation is relatively straightforward with the measurement scales. Ratio scales entail all others; interval scales entail ordinal and nominal scales; ordinal scales entail nominal scales; nominal scales entail no others. In other words, interval, ordinal, and nominal scales can be retrieved from ratio scales; ordinal and nominal scales can be retrieved from interval scales; nominal scales can be retrieved from ordinal scales. A chain of transitive implication relations expresses this relationship: ratio $\supset$ interval $\supset$ ordinal $\supset$ nominal, where the "$\supset$" symbolizes the implication ("if . . . then . . .") relation. A similar scale can be constructed using action components: transport $\supset$ arrangement $\supset$ selection $\supset$ isolation $\supset$ change in the perceptual orientation of the researcher. Unfortunately this constructed scale is arbitrary because the entities being scaled are primitives. They were not chosen as the undefined components of scientist action on the basis of a rigorous analytic or empirical rationale. They are not completely arbitrary, for they make good intuitive sense, but the arbitrary component in their selection must carry over to any scaling of them. Simply, transport seems to imply arrangement, arrangement seems to imply selection, and so forth, but it is a long way from "seems to" to empirical confirmation of the scale. Presumably, such empirical confirmation would be one task of a metatheory of science. Again, this relationship is suggested, not confirmed. Both scales can be juxtaposed in a graphic presentation: the measurement—scale scale is placed on the ordinate, the action scale on the abscissa.

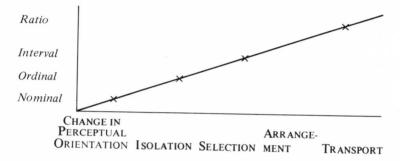

The derived relationships corresponding to the points on the graph are as follows: if the scientist has ratio scales, then he can transport events; if he has interval scales, then he can arrange events and transport them; if he has ordinal scales, then he can isolate and select events; if he has nominal scales, then he can change his perceptual orientation.

The only empirical evidence for any of these hypotheses exists for the last hypothesis. There is much evidence in perception research that perception is binary. Generally, in fact, there are two schools: one that says perception is binary, another that it is continuous.[24] Given that binary discriminations are expressible as nominal scales, if perception is binary, it follows that perceptual orientation would be contingent on nominal scales. To reiterate, however, it is a stretch from preliminary evidence for one hypothesis to confirmation of the suggested relationship. The whole thing could be speculative fantasy. This is not to negate the utility or possibility of such an endeavor. One important fact deserves emphasis: the possibility of such a relationship is suggested by the previous analysis of control, and the previous analysis of control is suggested by the concept of hypotheses as predictions of (primarily) measured or (secondarily) unmeasured changes.

PROOF AND TESTING

Comparison is necessary to test any hypothesis. This comparison is not between known values of measurement change. It is between known and expected values of change. The essential question is, Did the measurements change in value as expected? The expression type that is minimally necessary to answer this question is the negative of the particular measurement expressions. The comparison then is between the affirmative and the negative of measurement expressions. For example, if the hypothesis to be proved is $\triangle A \supset \triangle B$, which reads [[if there is a change in measure [A] then there will be (is) a change in measure [B]]]. The minimal necessary comparison is $\triangle A \supset \sim \triangle B$, which reads [[if there is a change in measure [A], then there will be (is) *no* change in measure [B]]]. Every hypothesis to be tested minimally implies this comparison hypothesis for its proof. By "minimally implies" is to be understood that any hypothesis may require much more for its test and proof, but that in principle this it the general rule of proof of any hypothesis phrased as an implication expression.

Again the importance of difference expressions is evident. These expressions codify this comparison as change just as they did change-measurement values. The only difference here is that the essential difference is between affirmative and negative.

Obviously, there are four logically possible outcomes in the test of any hypothesis phrased in this way: $\triangle A \supset \triangle B$; $\triangle A \supset \sim \triangle B$; $\sim \triangle A \supset \triangle B$; $\sim \triangle A \supset \sim \triangle B$. These outcomes can be expressed in a two-by-two table. The table summarizes the minimal possible comparisons given one hypothesis of the aforementioned form, assuming the partitions to equal the implication relation.

	△ B	∼ △ B
△ A	1	2
∼ △ A	3	4

Cells 1 and 2 are the minimal comparison needed for the proof of the hypothesis summarized in cell 1. Combinations of the other outcomes can be used to express other types of proof relationships often mentioned in the research literature. One possible interpretation of the proof of the assertion, $[[\triangle A]$ causes $[\triangle B]]$ is the following: $[[1$ and 4 and time order$]]$. That is, one can be reasonably certain it is true that $[[\triangle A]$ causes $[\triangle B]]$ if the distribution of outcomes with repeated testing is such that $\triangle A \supset \triangle B$ and $\sim \triangle A \supset \sim \triangle B$ are repeatedly confirmed and if $\triangle A$ always precedes $\triangle B$. Note that two additional assumptions are necessary: repetitive testing and the time ordering of $\triangle A$ and $\triangle B$. Furthermore, the assertion $[[\triangle A]$ is correlated or associated with $[\triangle B]]$ can be interpreted as follows: $[[1 > 2$ and $3]]$. One can be reasonably certain that the correlational assertion is true if the distribution of outcomes with repeated testing is such that $\triangle A \supset \triangle B$ is confirmed with higher frequency than both $\triangle A \supset \sim \triangle B$ and $\sim \triangle A \supset \triangle B$, and that 2 and 3 occur as outcomes at least once. Note that the same assumption of repetitive testing is necessary, but the specification of time order is irrelevant. Finally, the probability of the truth of $\triangle A \supset \triangle B$ can be expressed as a proportion or ratio of combinations of these outcomes assuming again repetitive testing:

Proportion:

$$\frac{F (\triangle A \supset \triangle B)}{F (\triangle A \supset \triangle B + \triangle A \supset \sim \triangle B + \sim \triangle A \supset \triangle B + \sim \triangle A \supset \sim \triangle B)}$$

Ratio:

$$\frac{F (\triangle A \supset \triangle B)}{F (\triangle A \supset \triangle B + \triangle A \supset \sim \triangle B)}$$

"F" symbolizes the frequency of the truth of an outcome, given repetitive testing.

The reader is referred elsewhere for the proof of these translations.[25] The arguments are extensive and complex and really not relevant to the object of this analysis. What is important, however, is the necessity of the assumption of repetitive testing and frequency distributions of outcomes of tests. This underscores the importance of direct replication and reproduction for science. These two aspects of the identification and hypothesis-testing cycles have been mentioned. Now their overwhelming importance is apparent. As the two procedures of repetitive testing they are one necessary condition for the proof of a hypothesis. The other condition is the minimal comparison of cell 1 with cell 2. Even though this section is dealing with the progression from quadrant 3 to quadrant 4 in the hypothesis-testing cycle, the gestalt-like interdependence of all the quadrants is underscored by the importance of reproduction and replication. The relationship should be formally stated. The progression from hypothesis (quadrant 3) to hypothesis test or confirmation (quadrant 4) involves a feedback loop to quadrant 2 (identification and measurement) and to quadrant 1 (perception). The path closed by the first loop is replication, the path of the second is reproduction. These are "direct" when the components of the cycle are not substantially altered. Direct replication and reproduction are not to be understood as simple additions to the cycle that provide closure. They are necessary components of the proof of any hypothesis. They are not only triggered by falsification as stated summarily at the end of Chapter 1. They are necessary for the proof of any hypothesis.[26]

PROOF AND FALSIFICATION

The negation condition necessary for proof can be called the "falsification" expression, after Popper.[27] This expression is to be understood as different from any of the others mentioned previously. As will become evident, it can be conjoined with many of the others by way of formulating the proof comparison. But it is a distinct and independent member of any such pair. This fact is underscored by examining the necessary condition for falsification. The relationship that will be discussed is the same that emerged with a consideration of falsification and identity. This relationship will now be expanded to cover the case of hypotheses in general.

In order to assert a falsification expression, the affirmative expression with which it is paired must be maximally precise. This is implied by the principle: in order to know what something *is not* you must know what it is. If "know" is interpreted as "can unequivocally assert," then it follows that before the negative expression can be unequivocally asserted, the affirmative expression must be unequivocally asserted. Tautology is maximum precision. Therefore, tautological expressions are the most easily falsified. An inconsistency is apparent here: tautologies by definition should be nonfalsifiable. Herein enters the importance of the independence of falsification expressions. The negation of a tautology is a different expression than the tautology. The falsification of a tautology therefore becomes the matching of the tautology with its negation expression. The tautology is not transformed; it is paired with another expression that is its negation. Understood in this way the apparent inconsistency is fully resolved, for tautologies of themselves may be inviolate and at the same time falsifiable.

The logical difficulty is really not important because tautologies as the upper bound of precision have been defined as nonachievable. The issue is moot. Attention can be turned more fruitfully to the exact relationship between precision, falsification, and expression type.

Within the context of the identification cycle, identifications and measurement expressions can be freely falsified. The purpose of the identification cycle is to confirm the identifications and measurements. Confirmation is equivalent to the degree of nonfalsifiability. The expressions are considered satisfactorily confirmed when they have been exposed to the possibility of falsification. This exposure is a function of the implicit and explicit auxiliary hypotheses that are used to develop the identifications and measurements. In other words, the identifications and measurements can be falsified by the falsification of the auxiliary hypotheses necessary for their development. What is being described here, of course, is the identification cycle progression. The final product of that cycle if it is successful is maximally precise identifications and measurements.

Within the context of the hypothesis formation and testing cycle, measurement expressions as components of identifications are nonfalsifiable. Another inconsistency is apparent. If these expressions previously have gone through the identification cycle before being injected into the hypothesis cycle, then they by definition must be maximally precise. If they are maximally precise, they must be maximally falsifiable. Yet they are being asserted to be (relatively) nonfalsifiable. The inconsistency is easily resolved if the separability of the contexts is remembered. These expressions are (relatively) nonfalsifiable in the hypothesis cycle because they have not been falsified in the prior identification cycle. Therefore their maximal precision and nonfalsifiability are not contradictory assertions.

The parenthetical "(relatively)" before the "nonfalsifiable" is the result of the possibility that within the hypothesis cycle the identifications and component measurements could conceivably be falsified. This possibility is accounted for by the error term in the identification. It means that within a certain range of applications the identification can be falsified.

It must be strongly emphasized that all of this is true about measurements as components of identifications. Measurement expressions of themselves are never falsifiable. This fact is the result of logical and developmental necessity. The purpose of standardization is to assure the nonfalsifiability of measures. Standardization may be a developmental fact and therefore is one result of the identification cycle. But as a fact it imposes the logical necessity that measurement expressions be nonfalsifiable. The component error term therefore does not symbolize the degree of falsifiability of the measurement. It symbolizes the degree of falsifiability of that which is being measured: the identity. When the identity is a measurement dimension, the falsifiability of the application and reading of the measurement is represented by the error term. This means that the error term does not represent the falsifiability of the measurement; rather it represents the relative variation in the events being measured.

This distinction deserves an example. In the abstract identification expression, [[The object weighs [10 g. ± 3 mg.]]], the [± 3 mg.] is the error. The figure does not represent the degree to which weight is inaccurate: it does not suggest that the measurement of weight can be falsified within a certain range of error. An object may not be measurable on this dimension and scale, or such measurement may be irrelevant to the purposes (i.e., hypotheses) of the scientist. But it is logically absurd to say that "weight is false" or formally that "not weight" is a meaningful expression. The ± 3 mg. is a representation of the degree of inaccuracy to be expected in weighing that object. It implies that the identification can be negated within the range ± 3 mg. with repeated measurements. One identification can be expected to read [[[The object weighs [10.001 g.]]]], another, [[[The object] weighs [10.002 g.]]], a third [[[The object] weighs [10.003 g.]]]. The first identification is negated by or falsified by the second and third identifications, the second by the first and third, the third by the first and second. These alternative interpretations of the identification form its "falsification set." This concept will be elaborated below. Important at this point is the fact that the error term is not the expression of the range of potential falsification of the measurement, but of the range of the potential falsification of the identification.

Another example is necessary to deal with the case in which the identity is a dimension: [[[a calorie] is the [heat] necessary to raise the [temperature] of water [1° C]]]. Assume the appended error term of ± .03° C. The error does not represent the falsifiability of the measurement dimension [calories]. Rather it represents the range of values within which the identification will vary. Given that the identity is a measurement dimension, this range of variation is of the phenomena or events being measured. It may also reflect the inaccuracy of the instruments, but that is really another way of saying the same thing, i.e., that the instruments are inaccurate to the extent that they do not reflect the variation in the phenomena (remembering that the upper bound of this inaccuracy is the reactivity of the measurement, and all measures will have some error term). Clearly, it is a fallacy to assert that [calories] can be falsified. The identification has no alternative interpretations that can form the falsification set: the error term does not imply alternative interpretations of the identification. It does imply alternative interpretations of the application and reading of the measure. In this case, the error term is misplaced in the sense that it really belongs as an appendage of the auxiliary hypotheses necessary for the scientist to apply and read the measure. Its appearance as a component of this special identification is the result of the arrangement of symbols: because the auxiliary hypotheses are implicit and the error term must be specified, it is included by conviction in the identification. Of course, the error in the auxiliary hypotheses can be the result of many factors: for example, reactivity, limits of accuracy of available instruments, variation in phenomena, and scientist perceptual or action error.

The Hypothesis Cycle, Falsification, and Precision

The identifications and measurement expressions form the relatively invariant comparative base necessary for the proof of hypotheses. Their (relative) nonfalsifiability accounts for the necessary difference between the identification and hypothesis formation and testing cycle. In the latter, the identifications and measures are not subject to falsification; the purpose of the sequence is the falsification or, conversely, the confirmation of the logical relation between the identifications. Therefore, it is the relation that is being tested and not the components of the logical frame that expresses the relation. This subtle distinction between the cycles is indispensable for understanding the proof of hypotheses.

A fully confirmed or nonfalsified hypothesis would have a deterministic form. It would be expressed in terms of cause and effect with zero error. Or, if implication is the hypothesis form, the test results would never falsify $\triangle A \supset \triangle B$ or $\sim \triangle A \supset \sim \triangle B$, and $\triangle A$ would be observed to always precede $\triangle B$. Conceivably, error in the identifications and therefore their potential falsifiability can occur in such fully determined hypotheses.

That is to say, the error terms in the identifications are interpretable independently of the error term in the hypothesis. In this extreme case, the error term in the hypothesis is zero, while those in the identifications can be greater than zero, because hypotheses relate classes of events and the identifications must be applied to classes of events. The component measures will be made across events and time and not time alone. The difference is the same as repeatedly measuring one event and measuring many events of one class. Admittedly, there will always be some measurement error in the identification, but this measurement error may not be sufficient to disrupt the relationship. The relationship can be said always to occur irrespective of the inherent error in the identifications. In a sense, the fact of the relationship between classes supercedes the fact of the variation in the identification of the members of the classes, which explains the frequent omission of the error terms from the component identifications of a hypothesis. They are implicit because they do not have any effects on the relation between the identifications. For example, the errors in the measurements of the distance any object travels and its speed do not alter the relationship between distance and speed, and depending on the objectives of the scientist, the errors in the measurements may be insignificant and unspecified because the relationship is primary.

The independent interpretability of the error terms of the identifications and of the hypotheses illustrates the distinction between the identification cycle and the hypothesis cycle. However, the case of fully determined hypotheses and identifications with error terms should be understood as the limiting one of this distinction. It is never achieved, only approximated. It has been previously stated that no hypothesis can be fully determined. In terms of proof, even in the most advanced sciences the outcomes of hypotheses tests will be a distribution among all four proof cells: $\triangle A \supset \triangle B$; $\triangle A \supset \sim \triangle B$; $\sim \triangle A \supset \triangle B$; $\sim \triangle A \supset \sim \triangle B$. The more advanced the science, the higher the frequencies in the cells $\triangle A \supset \triangle B$ and $\sim \triangle A \supset \sim \triangle B$ and the lower the frequencies in the cells $\triangle A \supset \sim \triangle B$ and $\sim \triangle A \supset \triangle B$. Presumably the cell frequency of greatest concern would be $\triangle A \supset \sim \triangle B$; in the more advanced sciences, this would be a negligible frequency. The events to be controlled can vary freely and the objectives of science be met as long as the scientist can control the events according to prediction; the $\sim \triangle A \supset \triangle B$ frequency therefore would be less bothersome for the scientist.

The fact that all hypotheses must have some error throws new light on the relation of this error to the identification error. The error terms may be independently interpretable, and in the extreme unrelated, but the extreme is seen not to exist. In fact, error in the identification (or "measurement error") can have an effect on hypothesis error (or error in the relationship). It should be emphasized, however, that this effect does not negate the fact of their basic independence. The extreme case is where the range of error in the identifications is not known; the effect of the failure of specification of the range is an error term of unpredictable magnitude in the hypothesis. Simply, the total frequency distribution of test outcomes cannot be determined in this case. Some tests will be inconclusive and not yield one or another of the outcomes because the measures simply will not apply. They will not register. Or more correctly, this non-outcome is a logical possibility because the range of measurement outcomes is open-ended. A more likely outcome is one in which the cell frequencies approach equality so that the joint outcome is indeterminant. This too is possible because the results of the measures will not fall within specific limits; every outcome therefore is equally likely.

The case of an unknown range of identification error is the

other limiting one in the effects of hypothesis error. Between this possibility and the one of no effects between error types is arrayed most of science. Within this array lie those cases of greater to lesser effects of identification error on hypothesis error. The degree of effect is contingent on the magnitude of identification error. Generally, the larger the error, the larger the error in the hypothesis. This relationship is well known. In terms of proof, it can be specifically quantified. The larger the identification error, the greater the frequencies of the $\triangle A \supset \sim \triangle B$ and $\sim \triangle A \supset \triangle B$ although, to reiterate, the latter frequency tends to be trivial, given the objectives of science. The size of these frequencies should approach some as-yet-unknown upper limit that is lower than equality in all four cells. The determination of this upper limit would be yet another task of an empirical metatheory of science.

A rather elegantly quantifiable relationship emerges. If hypotheses are unfalsified and fully determined, the joint frequency distribution of test outcomes would be divided between $\triangle A \supset \triangle B$ and $\sim \triangle A \supset \sim \triangle B$. Given the independence of hypothesis and identification error, this result would be fully compatible with known but negligible error in the identifications. But as hypotheses are never totally unfalsified, the question becomes, what is the relation between identification and hypothesis error? This relation is arrayed between the extreme of no relation and the extreme in which identification error is indeterminant and hypothesis error is indeterminant as a result. In the latter case, the frequency of test outcomes is equal in each cell with an unspecified (but specifiable) frequency of non-outcomes produced by failures in the results of applying and reading the measures. In between the extremes, generally, the greater the identification error, the greater the hypothesis error. Correspondingly, the frequencies of test outcomes should be greater in the crucial cells ($\triangle A \supset \triangle B$; $\sim \triangle A \supset \sim \triangle B$) and lesser in the remaining cells, particularly $\triangle A \supset \sim \triangle B$. These frequencies should approach an unknown but determinable upper limit depending on the error magnitude that is less than equality in the four cells. If the error magnitudes are minimal, then the frequency in (especially) the $\triangle A \supset \sim \triangle B$ cell should be minimal, and the frequencies in the $\triangle A \supset \triangle B$ and $\sim \triangle A \supset \sim \triangle B$ cells should be maximal. In other words, the difference in frequencies of the two pairs of cells should depend on the magnitudes of the identification error and resulting magnitude of the hypothesis error.

The magnitude of the error in identifications or hypotheses leads to a range of permissible interpretations of them contingent on their repeated testing. This range corresponds to the range of test results obtained. For example, the identification $[[X]$ *is* $[3° \text{ C.} \pm .003° \text{ C.}]]$ has as many interpretations as there are values within $\pm .003°$ C. This range of interpretations is to be distinguished from the range of alternative interpretations that make up the "falsification set." The "falsification set" of any testable expression is the full range of alternative interpretations that arise subsequent to the initial falsification of the expression. Testable expressions include identifications, main hypotheses, and auxiliary hypotheses. The initial member of this set must always be the falsifying expression (falsifier). Formally, this will be the negation of the expression, if this negation is understood to be an independent expression and not an interpretation of the initial expression. The falsifier is not the set, but a member of the set. Therefore, the interpretations are not of the initial falsifier. They are triggered by it. The falsification set, then, is the associated expression set of any testable expression associated as a consequence of testing and falsification of the expression. In other words, if an expression is falsified, the falsification set consists of the initial falsifier and any possible interpretations of the fact of falsification, e.g., $[[H_1$ was falsified $(\sim H_1)$ because the measures were faulty]] or $[[I_1$ was recorded as $\sim M_n$ because events varied]].

The range of interpretations corresponding to the magnitude of the error in identifications or hypotheses is a function of the ability of measures to unequivocally measure. That is, this range is due to variation in the measures or the measured events. The numerical quantity corresponds to scale values and the range in values is assessed with repeated measurements. This empirical necessity is to be distinguished from the logical necessity of the falsification set. The falsification set is related to this range of interpretations due to error magnitude only at the lower extreme. If the testable expression (hypotheses or identifications) is errorless, then the falsification set will be a null set. Since no testable expression is errorless, the null set does not, in fact, occur. Beyond this initial marginal relationship, the falsification set is unrelated to this range of interpretations. An expression may have maximum or minimum error, and it may still have a falsification set with only the falsifier as member. Or an expression may have an open-ended falsification set and have minimum error.

On the other hand, the falsification set is directly related to the level of precision of the initial expression. If that expression is tautological, then the falsification set member will be tautological. This is the formal restatement of a previously cited relationship: maximum precision in the initial expression provides for unequivocal falsification of that initial expression. Accordingly, if the expression is vague, the falsification set will be vague, i.e., open-ended. Also, the degrees of ambiguity in the expression correspond to the degrees of ambiguity in the falsification set. It follows that with the control of the level of precision of testable expressions, the level of precision of their falsification sets can be controlled. However, it must be reiterated that this implies nothing about the magnitude of the error of the measurement expression components of these expressions. Nor does it say anything about the probability of their initial falsification. Both are empirical, not logical, questions.

It is necessary now to parenthetically correct previous arguments by this author with respect to the same point.[28] I have stated elsewhere that vague hypotheses must produce unestimable error and ambiguous hypotheses estimable error that corresponds to the level of ambiguity of the hypotheses. The present argument directly contradicts this point. Magnitude of error is empirically determined. It is quite possible that a vague hypothesis could have minimal error because that hypothesis fortuitously fits the events in question. Furthermore, with repeated testing this hypothesis could register the same minimal error. However, three things mediate against this likelihood. First, the hypothesis itself could be interpreted differently with each subsequent test, making repeated testing extremely difficult. Second, as the falsification set is open-ended, whenever that hypothesis was falsified, the results would be interpretable in many different ways, the range of which would be unknown. The error could be minimal, but it would not be unequivocally accepted as such, because alternative interpretations of what that error "meant" would always be suggested. Third, in those tests in which the hypothesis was not falsified (was confirmed), the scientist could never be certain which interpretation was not falsified. Therefore, even though the correspondence between vague hypotheses and unestimable error could be falsified because of empirics, the correspondence between vague hypotheses and vague falsification sets, vague hypotheses and difficulty in replication, and vague falsification sets and indeterminate interpretations of error would seem to mediate against this. The same arguments apply to the assertion of relation between levels of ambiguity and magnitude of error.

Besides, to construct a metatheory of science with emphasis on fortuitous circumstances is to build on sand. Everything is possible, but predictable relationships are the essence of knowledge about the range of possibility. Taking the possibility of fortuitous circumstances into account, it would seem reasonable to cautiously resurrect and reinterpret these previously cited arguments in the fashion just given. Another part of these prior arguments was that, with proper control over the level of precision of the hypotheses, control could be exercised over the potential estimability and size of the component error term. The control procedure most heavily advocated was definition.[29] Again, this relationship must now be qualified in accordance with present arguments.

The concept of definition as language control is too narrow.

With the proper emphasis on the identification cycle, the (relatively) maximally precise communicative base of the hypothesis cycle is guaranteed. It is hard to see where definition as procedure plays a part in establishing this precision within the context of the identification cycle. Definition, on the other hand, as codification of identifications is extensively used in the hypothesis cycle. Precization, on the other hand, *is* descriptive of the identification and hypothesis cycles. It can be viewed statically as providing level of precision as a metric of communicative adequacy. It can also be viewed developmentally as the core requirement of either cycle. In neither case is it so much a tool or control procedure as it is a communicative process. Therefore, it is not imposed from above, but must be approximated for the sake of communicative clarity.

On the other hand, levels of precision of testable expressions do correspond to levels of precision of the falsification sets of these expressions. Unequivocal falsification and, conversely, unequivocal confirmation can occur only with maximally precise testable expressions. One interdependency that tends to satisfy this relationship has already been emphasized: maximally precise identifications tend to produce maximally precise hypotheses, and measurement expressions are used to establish maximally precise identifications. These hypotheses may be totally false, but their falsification is contingent on their precision. Similarly, identification auxiliary hypotheses must be maximally precise to be falsifiable. If they are not falsified, they lead to the formation of identifications that are maximally precise. If the identifications are not falsified, they can be used to establish maximally precise hypotheses that will in turn be falsifiable. And the argument comes full circle. The auxiliary hypotheses in the identification cycle must also be maximally precise and falsifiable in order to establish maximally precise main hypotheses. This contributory condition along with maximally precise identifications completes the argument. However, the subset of auxiliary hypotheses that usually receives the most attention along these lines in metatheories of research are control hypotheses. They, therefore, deserve special (but brief) attention.

Falsification, Proof, and the Logic of Control

"Control procedures" is a phrase that is generally used in research to refer to the use of control hypotheses. A logic of control in this sense as opposed to control as the objective of science can be described according to the relationship between control hypotheses and main hypotheses. This relationship implies certain things the scientist has to do in order to test it.

First, the scientist may elect to control certain potentially disruptive conditions by keeping them constant. In the extreme, he may keep them constant at the zero level. This can be called control by exclusion. The scientist excludes the potentially disruptive condition, thereby eliminating its possible effects. Suppose, for example, that the scientist is testing a hypothesis in which noise level (C_1) or light intensity (C_2) could disrupt the requisite measurements. If controlling by exclusion, he would try to reduce the noise level and light intensity to zero and to keep them constant at that value throughout the test. Exclusion is one subset of control by constancy.

Another subset involves reducing the potentially disruptive effects of the control conditions to a negligible value so that they have no influence upon the antecedent or consequent condition. The control conditions are operative in the domain, but their effects have been negated. This can be called control by negation. It is distinct from control by exclusion in that the control conditions are not deleted from the research; they are present, but their effects are neutralized. For example, the scientist may elect to control light intensity and noise level by negation with the use of unpatterned noise and light. This is a common practice in research with human subjects. Note that noise and light are not excluded. As the human being can produce his own noise and light or his own perceptions (and misperceptions) of noise and light, it is doubtful whether they can ever be reduced to the zero level.

If one were to nit-pick, it could be argued that this example of control by negation is actually one of control by exclusion: the patterning of the noise and light is being eliminated. Although this argument makes sense, control by negation and exclusion are two different control strategies that are related as subsets of control by constancy.

Perhaps a clearer example from social science research involves the use of statistical techniques to implement control by negation. Suppose the control condition to be sex of human subjects. Obviously, sex cannot be eliminated in the research. Instead, sex is controlled statistically by making it irrelevant in terms of potential influence on the antecedent or consequent condition. Whatever the particular statistical device used, the general technique is to collapse the male-female dichotomy in any relevant comparisons: put differently, relevant comparisons are made within male-female categories rather than between them. The use of such statistical manipulations are familiar examples of control by negation: the effects of the disruptive conditions are negated by reducing them to statistical irrelevance.

Random selection of subjects or events can also be interpreted as a subset of control by constancy.[30] As the logic of randomization has been extensively treated in the research methods literature, another restatement is unnecessary here. It should be recognized, however, that the basic rationale of randomization is to reduce the disruptive potential of an unspecified range of control conditions to a constant and negligible value. As a technique its overwhelming importance is due to its negation of the necessity of specifying the conditions being controlled. The assumption is made that every subject or event consists of a constellation of attributes that could singly or in interaction adversely affect the test of the main hypothesis. Randomization dictates that the influence of these attributes will be diluted if each subject or event is selected according to a random probability model. The attributes will tend to exert an equal and constant and negligible effect if subjects or events are randomly selected or assigned to different treatments.[31]

Control by constancy also can be described according to the form of hypothesis that implies it as procedure. It has previously been stated that control conditions can be symbolically represented in the following fashion: $[[\text{Given } C_{1 \ldots n}], \text{ if } [A], \text{ then } [B]]]$. Suppose there are two conditions, $[C_1]$ and $[C_2]$. The symbolic representation will be:

$$[[\text{Given } [C_1 \cdot C_2]]].$$

where the "$\cdot$" signifies the conjunction "and" in conformity with the usage of symbolic logic. If the scientist is controlling two conditions by constancy, then the following possibilities pertain:

1. $\sim C_1 \cdot C_2$
2. $C_1 \cdot \sim C_2$
3. $\sim C_1 \cdot C_2$

where the brackets are understood but implicit and the "$\sim$" stands for negation as in symbolic logic. The scientists can control by constancy by holding C_1 constant (case #1), by holding C_2 constant (case 2), or by holding both C_1 and C_2 constant (cases 2 and 3). That is, he can control either or both of the conditions by constancy. Cases 1, 2, and 3 are to be understood as separate hypotheses rather than alternative interpretations of the main hypothesis. The scientist may elect, in effect, to test each one separately. The importance of this fact is that the requirement of maximal precision must be applied to each hypothesis in turn. Of course, if this requirement has been satisfied for the identifications in one, it will have been satisfied for the identifications in the others. Thus, the real question for the scientist to answer is how precise are the C_1 and C_2? Or more strictly, how precise are the auxiliary control hypotheses that they imply? Because each control hypothesis will require different antecedent scientist action contingent on whether he elects to do 1, 2, or 3, the precision of each alternative must be considered separately. Again, maximum precision of these alternatives will contribute to the maximum falsifiability of the main hypothesis.

Randomization as control by constancy would assume C_{1+n}, but not specify them. The resulting compound expression would be:

$$[[\sim C_{1+n}], \text{if } [A] \text{ then } [B]]$$

This would be procedurally translated:

$$[[\text{Given [random selection], if } [A] \text{ then } [B]]].$$

This translation most closely approximates the satisfaction of the ceteris paribus clause, because an attempt is being made to control all other things by constancy and equality.

The scientist may elect to control certain potentially disruptive conditions by including specific, measured values of them in the test of his main hypothesis. This can be called control by inclusion. For example, if light intensity and noise level are the control conditions to be included, the scientist will test his main hypothesis while systematically varying measured values of light intensity or noise level. What values he chooses will, of course, depend on his measurement dimensions, units, and scales. More importantly, it will also depend on any prior knowledge he has of their hypothesized effects. Some values may be more disruptive than others; and if he knows what these values are, he will approximate them. This is not to exclude the possibility that he can freely vary the values in order to assess the relative disruptive effects of all levels of noise and intensities of light. This possibility is one important growth mechanism of science.

The form of hypothesis that implies control by inclusion is in the two-condition case:

$$[[\text{Given } [C_1 \cdot C_2], \text{ if } [A] \text{ then } [B]]]$$

That is, the scientist is explicitly dealing with values of these conditions in his test. If he were looking at more than two conditions, each subsequent one would be appended to the main hypothesis. This increasingly complex hypothesis is to be understood as a single expression. The requirement of precision thereby applies to the total expression.

It should be apparent that control by inclusion is the approximation of the hypothesis with minimal error. And here is the important conceptual bridge between logical and empirical necessity. True, a hypothesis without specified and included control conditions can have minimal error, but this is not the case in science. The approximation of minimal error has proceeded by the successive specification and active control of possibly disruptive control conditions. This procedure traditionally has been the empirical correlate of maximal precision. That is, the increasingly exhaustive inclusion of relevant control conditions usually has resulted in the increasing precision of the main hypothesis to which these conditions are successively appended. This in turn implies that, with increased specification of included control conditions, the main hypothesis should have fewer members of its falsification set and therefore should more closely approximate unequivocal falsifiability. Again, whether or not that hypothesis is falsified is an empirical question, but the degree of certainty in its validity if it is not falsified increases proportionately as its falsification set is decreased.

What appears therefore to be a means of control auxiliary to the main thrust of science is actually a crucial tool in the acquisition of knowledge. The relationship bears emphasis. The successive control of conditions by inclusion is a cumulative process whose utimate goal is the maximal precision of the main hypothesis to which they are appended. This process is very much empirical in the sense that it is done in order to unequivocally test the main hypothesis. Hence, it is a bridge between procedure and logical expression, even though the fact of the error in the main hypothesis is ultimately an empirical one. This strategy of inquiry is all the scientist can do to reduce that error to manageable limits. Although error may not be actively controlled, the scientist is actively controlling his process of inquiry to increase the likelihood of minimal error. The prior statement at the beginning of this chapter that the $[C_{1 \ldots n}]$ have the cumulative effect of reducing the error in the main hypothesis to manageability should be duly amended by this important qualification.

Control by inclusion is more powerful than control by constancy because of the relationship just stressed. The effect of constancy is the testing of alternative hypotheses, each of which must separately satisfy the requirement of maximal precision. The effect of inclusion is the successive approximation of maximal precision through the inclusion of control conditions. The distinction is the analog of the prior distinction between increasing the precision of an expression through the conjunctive addition of component qualifiers and increasing the precision of an expression through the elimination of alternative, independent interpretations. In brief, control by constancy allows the scientist to say what conditions did not make a difference in the test of the main hypothesis, while control by inclusion allows him to say which conditions made how much of a difference. Diagrammatically, the distinction is quite obvious. Control by constancy with $C_{1,\,2}$ minimally would require the following table for the presentation of results:

	B	$\sim$ B
1/ $\quad C_1 \cdot \sim C_2, A$		
2/ $\sim \; C_1 \cdot C_2, A$		
3/ $\sim C_1 \cdot \sim C_2, A$		

The B and $\sim B$ are the necessary comparison for the proof of any hypothesis. The partitions represent the implication relation between A and B. Importantly, each column cell represents a separate test, and in each column cell one or the other or both conditions are held constant. The possible comparative statements are restricted to the assessment of relative proof contingent on one or both conditions being shown to have no effect.

On the other hand, control by inclusion with two conditions

minimally would require the following table for the presentation of results—assuming that each condition provides the minimal necessary two-valued comparison:

		B	$\sim$B
A	C_{1A}		
	C_{1B}		
	C_{2A}		
	C_{2B}		

Each cell represents the outcome of a single test, and the possibe comparative statements are that one or another value of C_1 or C_2 made more of a difference in the proof or disproof of the hypothesis. The inferential power of this comparison therefore is increased eight-fold over any single inference derivable from control by constancy.

MATHEMATICS, THOUGHT EXPERIMENTS, CONCLUSION

The basic description and metatheory of science is now complete. Attention will be turned in Part II to the adequacy of social science in terms of the satisfaction of these rules. First, however, one final aspect of science must be presented.

Significantly, no mention has been made of the role of mathematics in science. Its importance of course is indisputable. Without embroiling this account in a long and complicated treatise on mathematics, the role of mathematics is two-fold. First, it is a symbol system that permits the codification of the quantifiable relationships of science. The important point is that these relationships are primary and that mathematics codifies them. Before mathematics can be used in science, the necessary empirical and logical operations must have been performed. In the terms of this analysis, before mathematics can be introduced into a domain of inquiry, the demands of the identification and hypothesis cycle must be fulfilled.

But the power of mathematics is the ability it gives to the scientist to perform operations on these symbols, to formulate hypotheses, and to facilitate their testing. Again, avoiding unnecessary complexities, mathematics in this sense functions to project the identification and hypothesis cycle for the scientist. Put differently, in this second role, mathematics allows the scientist to escape the immediate confines of any one identification and hypothesis cycle. He can project beyond and anticipate future tests and outcomes via mathematics. In no branch of mathematics is this more apparent than in probability theory, in which the scientist can calculate the probability of future outcomes of future tests on the basis of well-established probability distributions of outcomes. Despite this overwhelming importance of probability mathematics, it must be remembered that the ability of the scientist to utilize mathematics in its second role is contingent on the initial adequacy of the identification and hypothesis cycle. Even this cursory discussion is sufficient to place mathematics in proper perspective.

"Thought experiments" are often much heralded in the philosophy of science for their fulfillment of a role analogous to the second one of mathematics. They permit the scientist to project into the future and correct past mistakes. Unfortunately, no extensive analysis exists of the thought experiment, even though its importance is known. Without proving my statement, I would like to conclude Section I by asserting that much of the process of thought experiments can be analyzed congruently with this presentation. Specifically, precization seems to be a crucial component of the process. Notably, the extremes of tautology and contradiction seem to provide the guideposts of this process just as they do for communication. Implication relations also seem to be a natural component, and auxiliary and main hypotheses complement each other as they were seen to in the earlier discussion. In short, thought experiments seem to be communicative enterprises in which the scientist is playing both roles of source and receiver while applying the requirements of precization. All the component expressions can appear in the thought process. The significant omission is the fact of the test, as empirically determined changes in measurement values. However, as knowledge of these changes can provide grist for the mill, all that is missing is the test of the derived relationships. Or, more formally, all that is missing is the specific proofs. This, of course, is speculation, but it is speculation based on introspection. Also, it would seem to be descriptive of great discoveries in science, most notably Einstein's formulation of the theory of relativity on the basis of his reinterpretation of the Michelson-Morley experiment.

PART TWO

4

Precision, Identification, and Measurement Problems in Social Science

Making general critical comments about social science is becoming increasingly risky. The field is burgeoning in the quantity and quality of research efforts. For those acquainted with the spectrum of specialties and subspecialties, the very task of generalization is arduous at best. The substantive gamut runs from macroeconomics and cross-cultural research to human communication and physiological psychology. The range of differences covers not only theoretical content, but also research practices. Surveys are conducted with sample sizes in the thousands while at the other extreme simple frequency counts are taken of eye-glance exchanges. And the methodological rigor of most research across the whole range is becoming geometrically more stringent.

However, neither quantity nor quality should deter critical evaluation. It is true that some specialties in social science are notoriously unscientific, to the point of making contrary claims quite preposterous. It is also true that in many instances increased methodological rigor has sacrificed theoretical significance, while in others theoretical significance has been pursued at the expense of empirical confirmation. All social scientists, I think, would nod agreement to these statements and proceed to tag the work of their colleagues accordingly. Yet, the purpose here is not to name-call. Suffice it to say that most social scientists would assent to the statement that their discipline is not so scientific or advanced as are the physical sciences.

This chapter and the next are designed to specify the points of nonarticulation of social science with the physical science model that were detailed in the first three chapters. The generalizations that will be made will be differentially applicable to the various specialties of social science because some specialties are more advanced than others and their concerns do differ widely. Yet, these generalizations will be broadly applicable across the discipline. If biases appear, they can be accounted for by the author's formal and informal education, which has been concentrated in the following areas listed according to relative emphasis of study: social psychology, sociology, psychology, anthropology, linguistics. The most glaring omission is economics, although much of sociology borrows heavily in theory and method from this specialty. Despite these restrictions, the discussion to follow will, I hope, be broad enough to overcome any inherent biases.

At the outset, it must be acknowledged that many social scientists would disclaim the physical science model. For example, sociologists at present are undergoing an intensive and enduring rethinking of their objectives by way of reaction to the empiricist influence that has shaped their discipline for the last thirty years. The most common disclaimer to be heard is that "understanding" is a sufficient objective for certain social scientists, while the more stringent objectives of science (i.e., prediction and control) are considered permissible for other social scientists interested in them. I have yet to see a sufficient specification of what this less-stringent objective entails and have serious reservations about the use of the label "science" or "scientists" by those who aspire to the objective. How, for example, does this breed of social scientists differ from professional journalists or historians, except perhaps in the jargon used? Or more appropriately, do these social scientists differ sufficiently from journalists or historians to warrant special names for themselves or their specialties? But these reservations about understanding as objective are not sufficient to negate the freedom of certain social scientists to embrace the objective as long as that freedom does not curtail the freedom of other social scientists to embrace the physical science model for their work. It is duly noted then that the arguments to follow assume the legitimacy and desirability of the physical science model for social science. A brief review of the highlights of prior discussions will precede and focus the critique of present social science.

A METATHEORY OF SCIENCE

Science has been analyzed as communicative action in the sense that within this context the minimum number of rules of play of the game have been presented. Two cycles or sequences of action have been discussed. Each entail the same core sequence: unshared nonsymbolically represented experience (quadrant 1) is translated into unshared symbolically represented experience (quadrant 2), which is translated into shared symbolically represented experience (quadrant 3), which is finally translated into shared nonsymbolically represented experience (quadrant 4). Different expression types function differently according to the particular quadrant and cycles involved. The two cycles entail the formation and testing of identifications or hypotheses. The basic communicative demand is precision. That is, in order for the sequence to proceed to quadrant 3, the demands of precision must be met.

This is so because the transverse from 2 to 3 is the transverse from asocial to social behavior. Of course, the parties to the communicative and, by definition, social behavior are scientists, while the medium of their communication is the total expression types of each identification or hypothesis cycle.

Precision is an ordinal scale of communication adequacy. Maximally precise expressions are tautological, while minimally precise ones are vague: in the first case, the expression has itself as a single interpretation; in the second, the expression has an indefinitely large range of interpretations. Ambiguous expressions are in the middle of the scale and are more or less precise according to the number of interpretations in their range. Level of precision can be empirically determined by calculating the percent agreement of usage or degree of equivocation of action contingent on the particular expression. Either of these standards of assessment can be phrased as a hypothesis in which level of precision of an expression is a predictor of the percent agreement of the expression's use or the degree of equivocation of action contingent on its use. These two hypotheses summarize the sense in which communicative adequacy is contingent on level of precision. Precision applies as the standard of adequacy of all scientific expression types.

The identification cycle entails the following expression types: identifications; measurement expressions consisting of dimensions, units, and scales; and action and control hypotheses having to do with the application or reading of the measures. Identifications are analogous to interpretations and definitions in form and function. An identity is juxtaposed with one or more measurement expressions. The resulting identification is a complete unit. Directly perceptual identities do not exist. All identities must entail measurement. An important form of identification in science is one in which the identity is a measurement dimension. Measurement is traditionally defined. Interval and ratio scales are primary; ordinal and nominal scales are insignificant in science. Measurement functions either as feedback to the scientist on the efficacy of his contingent actions or as a new class of information permitting different classes of actions. The primitives of measurement are analogous to the primitives of science: space, time, and movement as change in position. The space-time (ST) rule that all events are to be ultimately identified in space and time, and the movement primitive again emphasize the importance of interval and ratio scales. Action hypotheses can be expressed as implication statements in which the antecedent is some aspect of the scientist's action (location, isolation, selection, transport of events, or perceptual orientation) and the consequence is the application of the measurement or the change in measured value. Control hypotheses are essentially the same except that unmeasured as well as measured events are the objects of the action and unequivocal measurement readings are the objective. When the measurement functions as feedback or a new information class, the measurement expressions and the readings are the antecedent and the scientist actions are the consequence.

The progression of the identification cycle is contingent on these hypotheses. In other words, the development of identifications is contingent on the successful use and the adequacy of these hypotheses. The standard of adequacy is precision. If these hypotheses are maximally precise, then the ultimate identification will be maximally precise. The importance of measurement generally, and interval and ratio scales specifically, is their tendency to be maximally precise or tautological. They form the communicative base upon which precise identifications and action and control hypotheses are built. Therefore, the hypotheses and measurement expressions are severally necessary and in total sufficient for the formation of identifications that satisfy the demands of the communication cycle.

This relationship is more accurately phrased in the converse form. If the hypotheses and measurement expressions are maximally precise, then the resulting identifications will be maximally precise. And maximal precision results in the necessary prerequisite to proof: unequivocal falsification. In other words, maximally precise expressions will be maximally falsifiable in the sense that any occurrence of falsification will be unequivocally interpretable as a falsification of that expression. If the contributory expressions of the identification cycle are maximally precise, then they and the resulting identification will be maximally falsifiable. Interestingly, measurement expressions of themselves tend to be nonfalsifiable, but as components of derivative compounds (e.g., action hypotheses) they are falsifiable. Once identifications have been developed to maximal precision, they also tend to be nonfalsifiable. That is, one way of interpreting the identification cycle is as a testing ground for identifications, in which they are exposed to falsification continually; if they are proven, then they become nonfalsifiable by definition. Replication and reproduction are necessary in the sense that the cycle must be continually repeated to prove identifications in this sense. Finally, "meaning" questions are important because they provide feedback in the cycle. The prototypic meaning question, "What does this identification mean?" or, better, "How is this identification to be interpreted?" results in an activation or reactivation of the cycle, ensuring that ultimately the identification is tested and retested.

Maximally precise identifications form the relatively invariant comparative base of the hypothesis cycle. Main hypotheses in science—those that are the "body of knowledge" that science develops—are implication expressions whose antecedents and consequences are identifications. In essence, given that the component identifications are nonfalsifiable, if a test of the main hypothesis results in falsification, then it can be concluded that the hypothesis as a relationship between identifications was falsified. Auxiliary hypotheses are necessary for the successful completion of the hypothesis cycle: i.e., for the formation and testing of main hypotheses. These hypotheses can also be phrased in the implication form. They are analogs of action and control hypotheses and have to do with the application and reading of measures and the scientist action necessary for the formation and test of main hypotheses. To the extent that auxiliary hypotheses are maximally precise, they will be unequivocally falsifiable. If with repeated testing, they are proven (minimally falsified), then the cycle can be completed and the main hypothesis tested. To the extent that it is maximally precise, it too will be unequivocally falsifiable.

However, whether or not the main hypothesis is falsified is an empirical question. Generally all hypotheses will have a range of error, which means that at certain times under certain conditions they will be falsified. Proof then is a relative concept that can be expressed as a frequency distribution of test outcomes according to whether the hypothesis has been falsified or not. The overwhelming importance of replication and reproduction again becomes evident, for this distribution necessarily implies repeated testing. It is a mistake, on the other hand, to consider error entirely empirical. Maximal precision will yield unequivocal falsification, which will make estimates of error more precisely determinable. Also, the logic of control must satisfy the communicative demands and attain maximum control over the lability of events. This logic of control consists of two basic strategies: to keep all disruptive conditions constant at the zero value (exclusion) or above the zero value (constancy proper) and to include and manipulate the disruptive conditions (inclusion). Control by inclusion is superior to control by constancy because it yields greater information. Both strategies are linguistically codified as expressions appended to the main hypothesis with the subsequent formation of multiple independent hypotheses (constancy) or one compound hypothesis (inclusion). The formation of the latter type of compound expression through this control strategy can be interpreted as an attempt to minimize the error in the main hypothesis through the use of the necessary control hypotheses implied by the included control conditions. It is this dual interpretability that weds science, as communication, and error, as an empirical question: the formation and testing of the main hypothesis are truly interdependent.

Science is not as neat as this analysis would imply. One significant departure from simplicity lies in the existence of other important expression types. The identification cycle is a legitimate form of scientific research in and of itself. And the identification cycle does not interface with the hypothesis cycle as clearly as stated. The hypothesis cycle can spring from the head of Zeus fullblown. In this case, hypotheses and component identifications are developed inseparably. Herein enters the overwhelming importance of questions as a different expression type: they can initiate the hypothesis cycle or the identification cycle. They are the expression of problems and are fully answerable by hypotheses. Hence their role as cycle-starter. As expressions, they can be measured on a scale of precision, with maximally precise questions of certain well-established forms being maximally answerable in science. These substantive questions should be distinguished from meaning questions: the latter are fully applicable to the former and function in the hypothesis cycle generally as primers and as feedback.

Comparison is the essence of scientific knowledge in the sense that all hypotheses as the expression of scientific knowledge can be interpreted as predictions of change, and the assessment of change entails comparison. More specifically, the ubiquity of measurement translates most hypotheses into predictions of change in measurement values. This will not be true of those auxiliary hypotheses that are sufficient to guarantee unequivocal scientist action. But these hypotheses are seen to be a special case. Two important consequences result from viewing hypotheses in this way. First, measures are interpretable as records of change. Second, and more importantly, control as planned change is defined inseparable from prediction. This means that the objectives of science are prediction *and* control, and not one or the other.

Finally, the principles and rules of play of the communicative game of science form a metatheory of science. The criterion of empirical adequacy and testability or falsifiability of this metatheory is precision as a scale of communication adequacy. For example, hypotheses of a low level of precision should produce greater scientist disagreement over use and meaning and fewer successful replications or reproductions of the hypothesis cycle. Or relatively imprecise identifications should result in a greater number of scientist questions about their interpretations, formation, and test. The attempt to formulate such a metatheory of science distinguishes it from most other treatments of the subject which tend to develop logical, not metatheoretical systems of thought. One important advantage is a clear delineation of and attempt to avoid the familiar transposition of reality problem whereby metatheorists superimpose their metareality on the reality of science and assume their version of reality to be the correct one. By orienting this analysis toward the pole of testability and falsifiability, the necessary empirical corrective of this problem is provided, albeit in skeletal form.

A CRITIQUE OF SOCIAL SCIENCE— PRELIMINARY REMARKS

Certain criticisms of social science are implied immediately by this analysis. Many of these are known and their truth accepted. Others are less obvious. Among the latter are those having to do with metatheoretical solutions to the problems of social science that are to be found in a broad range of methodological literature. It will be shown that these solutions are not real, both in their insufficient approximation of science and in their perpetuation of some strategic social-scientific weaknesses.

The straightforward critique of social science will come first; the critique and analysis of various metatheoretical pseudo-solutions will form the bulk of the next chapter. It is easy to overlook the significance of what is being called for in this section—not simply a patch-up of existing social science, but rather a fundamental rethinking of current social science, a Copernican Revolution. If this sounds immodest, it is not meant to be for I make no pretense of being able to specify the parameters of this revolution. Only its initial stimulus and broad outline will emerge in what follows.

Lack of Precision in Social Science

In a previous book[1] my criticism of sociology was a first attempt to pinpoint the now (to me) obvious fact that sociological language suffers from great imprecision. In the more general terms of this analysis, most of the expressions of social science are of the lowest levels of precision. Little space need be devoted to demonstrating this.

Every attempt at definition in social science is in effect an admission of this fault. In sociology an excellent example is provided by my article[2] whose sole purpose was to define and explicate (i.e., redefine) the expression "status inconsistency." The term "status" alone, a key term in much of social science, has to my knowledge four different definitions: a person's differential behaviors or actions according to his position in a group; the differential actions of others toward a person according to his position in a group; the outward physical insignia or stimuli adhering to a person (such as uniforms and badges); and a person's ranking on certain generalized scales (such as income, occupation, education, and prestige). Moreover, many variations of these general definitions are derivable according to the subdefinition of their component expressions, e.g., the classes of behavior or the particular rankings used. This is not to say that these definitions cannot be deduced from a more inclusive abstract definition and that therefore one overall definition is not available. That was the purpose of my article, and the use of disposition concepts (à la Lachenmeyer or Kadushin[3]) greatly facilitates the task. However, [status] is used in these different ways by various social scientists without the benefit of an integrating generalized definition.

Similarly, Kroeber and Kluckhohn[4] provide fifty-two different definitions of [culture]. Mandler and Kessen[5] refer to and analyze the case of multiple definitions of terms in psychology. Machlup[6] systematically and elegantly analyzes certain key expressions in economics toward much the same end. Finally, Berelson and Steiner[7] in chapter after chapter note the problems of definition formation in different subspecialties of social science in an attempt to exhaustively list the finds of social science. So the emphasis on and formation and use of multiple definitions is common to most of social science.

This tendency is an indicator of imprecision in the sense that definition is a special precization process. Its extensive use means that social scientists are much concerned with certifying or determining the exact level of precision of their expressions. Its termination at multiplicity is evidence that their expressions are precise to the maximum value of high ambiguity. And this of course pertains to those expressions that have been subjected to precization. The case could be made that this is the top of an iceberg of imprecision.

One very important consequence of this imprecision that is the progenitor of the emphasis on definition formation is the relatively large number of meaning questions in social science. Much of social science is metacommunicative in the sense that social scientists continually ask questions about their expressions and their use of their expressions. No other science has been as concerned with its semantic and logical adequacy in its phases of development. In effect, social science has borrowed not only the methodology of the other sciences but also theories developed about that methodology. It is as if social scientists were attempting to increase the precision of their expressions by introducing the metalevel action sequence whose domain is hypothesis and identification cycles. In actuality, no other science has ever progressed by the introduction of this metalevel inquiry.

This is not to say that such metainquiry is not potentially useful, for that would negate the purpose of this book. However, a basic fallacy must be avoided: metainquiry cannot be substituted for the inquiry necessary to increase the level of precision of social science theory. There is a growing body of counter-metatheoretical literature in social science that is a healthy corrective for this fallacy.[8] On the other hand, it would be a great mistake to overlook the lessons of science. The best of both worlds can be had by wielding these lessons critically, by emphasizing confirmable metatheory, and by recognizing the transposition of reality problem of which this fallacy is a subset. This, of course, has been the justification of this book.

The other predicted consequences of a low level of precision besides emphasis on meaning questions are also obvious in social science. Basically, most social scientists do not have sufficiently precise theoretical expressions to guarantee unequivocal action on the basis of those expressions. This lack can be most clearly seen when social scientists are called upon to solve social problems, when the opportunity arises for them to show their wares. Working extensively in business and government research, time and again one hears strident complaints about the failure of social scientists to "deliver." This type of impressionistic evidence, which is very important to the applied researcher, is buttressed by well-documented failures like Project Camelot and the Rand Institute's research on the Vietnam War. Less popularized failures appear occasionally in professional journals. The simple truth is that social science has not generated precise enough information to permit unequivocal action by social scientists within the confines of their domain or, more importantly, by social scientists operating as problem-solvers in the everyday world of man.

This general criticism, of course, must be tailored with recognition of the impressive achievements of certain social scientific specialties. Nelson Rockefeller can become an "unbeatable" political candidate because of effective public-opinion polling. Likewise, media experts (some qualified social scientists, others not) can deliver votes to politicians seeking office, while market research analysts and attitude and mass communication experts can substantially increase the sales of products under the most adverse conditions. More significant (in terms of my personal values) are the achievements of operant conditioners in redesigning certain social systems, especially educational ones, and the work of certain social psychologists in research on conflict, cooperation, and war.

However, at this point in the history of social science it is best to minimize the probability of the Type II error of not criticizing the weakness in the discipline while thereby maximizing the Type I error of criticizing areas of strength in the discipline. It can be unequivocally stated that social science has not attained the objective of the prediction and control of human behavior with minimal and estimable error. The defense that this objective is somehow inappropriate (e.g., too stringent, ethically unacceptable, technically impossible) has been shown to be moot. This failure of social science is synonymous with its failure to be a science. It is the result of the general lack of precision of the expressions of social science.

Social Science as Pack Rat

The general lack of expression precision in social science has differing implications for the different expression types. There is, however, a very pervasive practice in social science that tends to perpetuate this lack of precision. Rather than initiating the identification or hypothesis cycle "from scratch", social scientists are heavy borrowers of identifications and question-problems. The source of this borrowing ranges from the physical sciences, to literature, to conventional or folk wisdom.

Borrowed identifications are the rule rather than the exception. Thus social scientists speak of "power," "roles," "bureaucracy," "violence," "play," "self," "personality," "aggression," "hostility," "conflict," "cooperation," and "exchange." The mark of these identifications is a failure of empirical underpinning. More specifically, measures must be created or found to fill the position of identifier, rather than being immediately suggested by the identification. And this process usually entails extensive definition and redefinition. In other words, these borrowed identifications are nothing more than words that have been reified to the position of identifications. Because the words are used, it is assumed that they must be identifications that can be fully determined with appropriate definition and correspondence with derived measurements. For example, [power] was previously analyzed as designative of complex action sequences as opposed to a fully identified event, which it is often mistaken to be.

Such borrowed identifications are quite problematic. They are often illustrative of the confusion of word and thing, the inappropriate use of definition including the operationist fallacy, and the violation of the restrictions of measurement that are crucial to the whole process of scientific inquiry. These and other problems will be analyzed in detail shortly when considering the slighting of the identification cycle in social science. Suffice it to say here that borrowed identifications are often pseudo-identifications in the sense that the identity tends to be a word that has not been fully identified by measurement. The freedom of usage of words that permits the detachability of identities has resulted in the confusion of identity and identification: i.e., because people can use [power], "power" must exist. Finally, the extensive definition of these pseudo-identifications even to the level of measurement (in the best cases) is a weak substitute for the identification cycle. In effect, these pseudo-identifications are injected into or imposed upon the identification or hypothesis cycle with the ultimate effect of depressing the level of precision of the component expressions.

The case of borrowed hypotheses is not as pervasive in social science. Basically, social science has always been deductively biased in that social scientists have freely hypothesized about the behavior of men. Perhaps it is easier to hypothesize than identify, or maybe the residue of borrowed identifications has facilitated original hypothesis formation. Whatever the reason, social scientists have not been reticent about formulating original hypotheses (see Berelson and Steiner[12]), although they are deficient according to this model of science, as will be presently seen.

However, borrowed problems and questions are, like identifications, more the rule than the exception. This pervasive borrowing is partially the result of borrowing of pseudo-identifications and the flexibility of the question frame. As Premack[13] notes, the interrogative is perhaps the linguistic frame easiest to construct. In the extreme, it can be formed by deleting an expression component from a declarative and attaching an appropriate marker, i.e., a question mark or appropriate voice inflection. For example, "Cats?" from "Cats are carnivorous animals." or "Status?" from "A person with high status will have more power than a person with low status." Although this extreme is inappropriate considering the textual restrictions of science, it emphasizes the relative freedom of question formation. This freedom is compounded by the accessibility of scientifically appropriate frames: [Why], [What], [How], [Is X related to Y]. Combined with readily available pseudo-identifications the ultimate result is the prefabrication of questions by social scientists that, in effect, initiate a hypothesis or identification cycle that is predestined to imprecision. These questions are borrowed in the sense that they are not implied by prior empirical investigations or relevant identification or hypothesis cycles, but are legitimated by human inquiry extraneous to the social science communicative sequence.

The seriousness of the deleterious effects of borrowed questions can range from research questions that are hopelessly vague to research questions that express pseudo-problems. The first result is not as serious as the second because all that is necessary is the precization of the question, i.e., its transformation through the successive application of meaning questions. For example, Lachenmeyer[14] had to transform the vague question, "Is X recreational program effective with mental patients?" through several levels before he derived the researchable question "Does X recreational program increase the verbal responsiveness of chronic schizophrenics?" However, the precization of vague research questions can be a dubious research practice. It stands in the same relationship to scientific research as does the use of definition as a sanctioned research procedure. Simply, the power of science derives from the formation of a limited set of precise questions via the replication of research. Questions are precisely interpretable prior to their initiation of the cycles of inquiry because developmentally the components of their hypothesis-answers have become precise. Requisite for this development has been prior cycles of inquiry. For example, the question [[How does [X] operate?]] will be answerable by hypotheses with precise identifications, including [X]. The vague questions of social science are vague because the requisite identifications for precise hypothesis formation necessary to answer those questions are not available. In the example, if precise identifications were available for [effectiveness] and [mental patients], the research task would have been analogous to a research task confronted by science as opposed to social science.

Even though vague questions are problematic, by far the most deleterious consequence of borrowed questions for social science is the expenditure of much time and energy researching pseudo-problems. A sociologist friend recently described his shift in research focus from studying the "sociology of deviance" to the "sociology of leisure" as a historical necessity: "Deviance no longer exists, so I shifted to studying leisure. Sociologists no longer study juvenile delinquency; this research is no longer funded. I figured leisure was the hot topic of this decade." Honestly said!

This trivial example has its more profound counterparts. The title of Szasz's original article questioning the reality of mental illness as a problem is illustrative, "the myth of mental illness." His arguments have become more strident and accusatory with time, and in his most recent book[15] he maintains that the mental health movement is a continuation of the Inquisition. In other words, the mental health movement is a political fact of repression of nonnormative behavior and not a national health problem. If one accepts the full implications of his arguments, it must be concluded that mental health research is the problem because it legitimizes societal repression. Short of this, it is evident that there are serious grounds for questioning the viability of all mental health research, if in fact mental illness exists more by societal definition than empirical reality.

Whether one accepts the more strict or less strict version of the argument, it is true that administrative decisions prompted by budgetary considerations have caused "revolving-door" policies in all federal and most state mental hospitals. The wards are being emptied and emphasis is being shifted to foster care and community mental health programs. That this change in policy occurred largely in spite of social-scientific mental health research (with the exception of Szasz's work) rather than because of it is evidence enough that mental health as a social-scientific problem is suspect. The questions to be emphasized should not have been "How can mental illness be cured?" or "What causes mental illness?" They should have been "What classes of mental patients can be and should be societally managed in what ways to assure maximum joint payoff for society and for the mental patient?" or "How can mental illness be prevented?" Although the issue is quite complicated, it is certain that "mental health" is not the problem as initially conceived.

Much the same thing has happened in criminological research with the current emphasis on "decriminalization." [Crime] traditionally has been defined legally, and researcher's problems have been expressed by questions including crime as legally defined. However, suddenly because of the exigencies of an overburdened criminal justice system, some [crimes] are by fiat more criminal than others. The definition of crime has or is being changed to permit the criminal justice system to concentrate its resources and to relieve the overburdening. For example, crimes of moral terpitude like public drunkenness, homosexuality, certain other sex offenses, and gambling have been "decriminalized" in the sense of a modification of the laws or, as with gambling in New York, by a shift in administrative police policy in relative emphasis of enforcement in certain areas. With the change in the definition of crime, there is a change in the questions that can be asked about it. In a subtle sense problems have been eliminated because of societal necessity. It is no longer fashionable or appropriate to ask "What causes crime?" The questions of this decade are "How can the Criminal Justice System be redesigned to handle effectively the task before it?", "What [crimes] have societally significant consequences and can be eliminated?", and "How can crime be eliminated, prevented, minimized, or managed?"

With respect to the last question, the research problem of current social science concern is how to design alternatives to prison or "diversion projects."[16] One type of diversion proceeds prior to adjudication, whereby the offender is diverted from the system before being arraigned and legally labeled as a criminal. This is practiced mostly with the young offender, 10 to 16 years of age, although in certain cases it also applies to those arrested who have youthful offender status, 16 to 19 years. So my friend is right, in a sense, for juvenile delinquency is not the same problem now that has been researched traditionally by social scientists. With the change in the definition of [crime] and the ways of dealing with it has come a change in the definition of the problem.

Operant conditioners who deal with human behavior have clearly recognized this problem of problem specification. They define their problems according to what behaviors should be modified. These behaviors are broadly classified as "appropriate" or "inappropriate." Appropriate behaviors are to be shaped up, inappropriate behaviors weakened or eliminated. The definition of these behavioral classes is conceived of as being determined by societal consensus. That is, behaviors are appropriate or inappropriate according to the prevailing conventions or norms of society. Clearly, if these norms change, so will the definition of the research objectives. As a consequence, the problem and questions to be answered will likewise change. In effect, the social problems tackled by operant conditioners have a well-recognized labile base.

What is frequently unrecognized is that this lability opens the door to pseudo-problems. For example, it can be asked whether the operant researcher should redesign the Criminal

Justice System and reformulate the societal administration, definition, and management of justice, or should he be running token economics for prison inmates to teach them certain basic learning and manual skills? This is the type of problem-question choice that human operant conditioners have failed to reckon with. They have legitimated problem borrowing by fully accepting societal definitions of problems with the possible consequence that their problems are not "real"; their questions are misplaced if their objective is to solve basic social problems like crime. They would do better to initiate their inquiry from scratch by fully identifying the problematic events.

Such considerations are directly related to the problems of precision. Borrowed questions and problems perpetuate social-scientific imprecision because they themselves are imprecise. Because they are the initiators of the inquiry cycle, this imprecision produces imprecision throughout the cycle. Mental health researchers and criminologists have failed to solve these social problems partly because they have been misled into asking the wrong questions expressing imprecise borrowed problems. The case of operant conditioners is illustrative of the fact that even despite a rigorous empirical foundation the whole cycle of inquiry can be questioned because of the imprecision of its problem-question formation. In effect, questions cannot be precisely answered if they are not precisely formulated, and they will not be precisely formulated if borrowed from the conventional or common-sense knowledge of men.

The Identification Cycle Slighted

An important corrective for pervasive imprecision is an emphasis on the process of identification. The examples given imply this, for a precise specification of the complex human behavioral events underlying such expressions as [mental illness] and [crime] would do much to make precise the relevant problems and questions. Yet, the overwhelming sin of social science has been the slighting of the identification cycle.

A general indicator of this tendency is the general failure of social scientists to engage in exploratory research aimed at measuring the events in their domain. Commonly, this research is simply not considered to be publishable. A deductive-nomological bias reigns which dictates that "good" research is hypothetico-deductive. "Good" articles contain an introduction section which specifies the research question and concludes with a hypothesis or set of hypotheses to be tested. This beginning is followed by a precedure section in which is detailed the particular methods used to test the hypothesis. Format usually dictates that this section refer to the attributes of the chosen subjects, how they were selected or disposed of, the definitions and measurements, the research design including the type of controls, what was done to or with the subjects or the data gathered from the subjects, and any special actions by the researcher to facilitate the test and the control procedures. Then comes a result section in which the data are analyzed (usually) statistically and the degree of corroboration of the hypothesis is discussed. A conclusion-discussion section in which the implications of the test are specified ends the article. Whether or not this format is followed, and it is widely accepted, these components usually occur. Hypothesis formation and testing therefore prevails as the espoused activity and product of social scientists.

This emphasis, with the concomitant de-emphasis of identification, partially results from the heavy residue of borrowed and pseudo-identifications. Identities and derivative hypotheses about human behavior abound, and the task of the social scientist becomes the application of sophisticated methodological techniques to the test of derived hypotheses based on these borrowed expressions. Whatever the cause, and others will be discussed presently, this nomological bias is all-pervasive. Yet, trends to the contrary should be noted. Most conspicuous is psychophysical theory, whose expressed purpose is to develop measurement scales of perception.[17] Much of human communication and ecological research also runs counter to this trend.[18] For example, Birdwhistell[19] has dedicated over two decades to developing elaborate codes to identify all features of nonverbal communication; Sommer[20] has done much work in the identification of aspects of human spatial arrangements and movement; and Barker[21] has done the same with everyday human activity. Finally, there have been metatheoretical calls to reemphasize this area like those of Webb, *et al.*,[22] and Glaser and Straus,[23] although the latter's call to "grounded theory" is a mixed argument advocating hypothesis formation first and identification second.

This partial list of counter-examples to the contrary, the pervasiveness of the neglect of the identification cycle is also evidenced by the emphasis of definition in social scientific research. The article format just presented usually includes a subsection in which definitions are to be listed. Basically, these definitions are of two general types. One type is devoted to clarifying the subsequent use of expressions. The other type is devoted to providing the measurement expressions that are the identifiers of the expressions. The two types are not mutually exclusive, i.e., measurement procedures may be the terminal definition in long definitional chains. The crucial difference is that with the latter type, measures are provided, (these are "operational definitions"), while with the former they are not. For example, Berelson and Steiner[24] define [stratification] as "the ranking of people in a society, by other members of the society, into higher or lower social positions so as to produce a hierarchy of respect or prestige." As it stands this definition is without specified measures. If it were operationalized the "higher or lower social positions" would be defined in terms of a specific measurement dimension ("respect or prestige") with specific units and scale type.

All social scientists are trained to define their terms. Definition is ubiquitous. Usually the edict is to make full use of both definitional types, but operational definitions are conceived as procedurally sufficient for the conduct of research. In this sense, definition is conceptualized very much as a component of good scientific procedure. Berelson and Steiner[25] preface each chapter with operational and nonoperational definitions, for example. Using definition in this procedural sense has been shown to be counter to the use of definition in science. More relevant here is that definition used in this sense is a poor substitute for the identification cycle.

The form of operational definitions is analogous to the form of identifications: in both, metaexpressions are juxtaposed with other metaexpressions and linked via some form of relation, usually equivalence. This formal analogy tends to conceal a crucial difference, and the resulting confusion leads to the faulty conclusion that the demands of the identification cycle have been met with operational definition. It is in this sense that definition in social science is used as a poor substitute for the identification cycle.

Generally, operational definitions are not conceived to be testable: there is no proscription to test them. Identifications on the other hand are repetitively tested in science until fully confirmed and highly precise. This is not to say that operational definitions do not have criteria of empirical adequacy; they can be said to "work or not work." However, their specification of the conjoined identity is beyond direct testing. Consider an example from Webb, et al.: "degree of fear induced by a ghost-story-telling session can be measured by noting the shrinking diameter of a circle of seated children."[26] Whether or not "degree of fear" can be measured in this way cannot be tested. Not only may children move closer together in ghost-story-telling sessions because of other factors—i.e., they are "supposed to," given societal expectations —but, more importantly, the testing of the definition is a logical absurdity. On the other hand, if this "definition" were a component of the identification cycle, it would be fully testable. Formally, it would be an identification in which the identity is a measurement dimension: "degree of fear". The identifying measurement expression would be another dimension and scale: physical proximity. The identification to be extrapolated, then, would have the form: [[[Fear] is measured by [physical proximity] with [X unit on Y scale]]]. It would be fully testable in the sense that [fear] would be an independent measurement dimension that presumably is certifiable as such due to its role in other identifications. That is, if this operational definition were an identification, ʃfear] would be a fully determined measure, and the relation between the two measures would be testable.

This point can be made differently by converting the operational definition to hypothetical form: assuming that ghost-story-telling sessions are fear-arousing, [[if [high induced fear] then [closer physical proximity of the targets or receivers] of the fear-arousing message]]. Physical proximity in this example is the shrinkage in diameter of a circle of seated children. This hypothesis is not testable because the antecedent is not fully identified: the relative fear-arousing potential of different ghost stories must be assumed, and fear is not an independent measure. On the other hand, if this definition were an identification, the antecedent would be identified and measured and the hypothesis would be testable: i.e., [[[if [[ghost-story] with [fear-arousing potential of X value]] then [[physical proximity] of [Y value]]]]]. More accurately, this main hypothesis would predict a change in physical proximity, "closer" being measured as a change of scale value, on the basis of a change in fear-arousing potential. Generally, all operational definitions when converted into hypotheses have unmeasured antecedents and therefore are untestable; while identifications likewise converted have measured antecedents and therefore are testable.

That operational definitions in social science can be conceived of as hypotheses with unmeasured antecedents is not a new insight. From completely different orientations, Blalock[27] has asserted it; and Webb, *et al.*, implicitly recognize the dilemma involved. The latter's emphasis on multiple operationism boils down to an advocacy of predicting testable relations on the basis of operational definitions by relating multiple consequential identities and measures via their hypothesized relationship to an unmeasured antecedent. To use another example from Webb, *et al.*, the popularity of different radio stations has been measured by having mechanics record the position of the radio dial in all cars brought into particular service stations.[28] [Popularity] is an unmeasured antecedent to the measured consequence of the position of the radio dials. [Popularity] was also measured according to more traditional questionnaire and interview-rating techniques. Again, the antecedent is unmeasured and the consequence is measured. Furthermore, it can be deduced that the two measured consequences would correlate, which would be a testable hypothesis. Finally, with respect to multiple operationism, Webb, *et al.*, do not rely solely on such intellectual machinations to circumvent the problem of the untestability of operational definitions. In many examples, they fully advocate stating the hypothesis involved so that it is testable, thereby converting the operational definition into a testable hypothesis. Many of their examples are, in fact, in testable hypothesis form: e.g., Middleton's study involved the correlation of fertility values estimated from the size of fictional families in eight American magazines with fertility values traditionally measured on the basis of actuarial data.[29]

Social scientists have at least anticipated this problem with operational definitions. Interestingly, as in the case of Webb, *et al.*, and also in the case of multiple measures, which will be presented shortly, the proposed solution to this problem is to in some way construct testable hypotheses on the basis of operational definitions. A type of reversion back to the identification cycle is being implicitly advocated. Yet this embryonic reemphasis of a crucial aspect of science is not sufficient. Even when operational definitions are converted into testable form, they are not falsifiable. This state, of course, contrasts with that of identifications, which are unequivocally falsifiable. For example, one favorite operational definition of status is [[[status]$_{df.}$ = a person's ranking on scales of occupation, education, and income]]. As everybody will have a ranking on these scales, everybody will have a status. To put it differently, there will be no class of individuals for whom [status] will be found not to be applicable. [Status] can never be negated and therefore is not falsifiable. This statement is also true in the more general sense that social scientists do not conceive of [status] as a falsifiable expression. It is not that [status] is true and has never been falsified; it is that [status] can never be falsified even if it were testable. The well-recognized problem with this definition due to the intercorrelation of the measures[30] is a subset of this nonfalsifiability. Because occupation, education, and income are correlated, people high or low on one scale will be high or low on the others. It is therefore recognized, even accepting the viability of the definition, that this intercorrelation makes the within-definition comparisons nonfalsifiable. As people tend to be high or low on all dimensions, people who are discrepant actually form a different class of individuals and not the negation of the particular constellation of status rankings. People who are consistent in one direction or the other can never be found to be inconsistent; or more correctly, if a person is consistent, he will tend to appear to be very consistent, even if this is not true. In this example, then, the operational definition of status is testable because testable hypotheses relating the dimensions can be constructed, but the hypotheses tend to be nonfalsifiable just the same.

If [status] were fully identified, this would not be the case. In an identification, the identity [status] would be falsifiable in two senses. First, [status] would be measured via an interval or ratio scale, and if a person had no status, the scale empirically would be inapplicable, if an interval scale, or would record zero status for some individuals, if a ratio scale. Second, and this is more important, if [status] were fully identified, it would by definition be locatable in space and time. Implicit in this location would be the ability of social scientists to form and test compound hypotheses in which scientist action was antecedent or consequence to the identification of [status]. These hypotheses are the basic medium for the testability and falsifiability of scientific identification: simply, if scientists cannot do what they say they can, then their identifications are open to question. For example, social scientists would be able to select and isolate people with specific values of status, to arrange them according to status value, to transport them accordingly, and to reorient their own perceptions so as to observe and compare people with these particular status values. This means that social scientists could test their identifications according to the success (unequivocal nature) of these actions and falsify them according to their lack of success (degree of equivocation).

The Identification Cycle: Measurement Demands and Data Types

The slighting of the identification cycle in social science is not evidenced only by the use of borrowed identifications and operational definitions as substitutes. It is also apparent from the low level of measurement in the social sciences. True interval or ratio scales are necessary for identification and are the product of the identification cycle. Two interdependent criteria merge for assessing the adequacy of the social sciences with respect to the identification of the events in their domain. The first criterion can be expressed as a question: How well do social scientists obey the ST-rule? Do they locate their events in time and space, or, more generally, do they apply the primitives of measurement in their quest for identifications? The second criterion involves an assessment of the level of measurement achieved in the social sciences. As the second criterion is relatively straightforward, it will be dealt with first.

True interval or ratio scales are rarely used in social science. There are exceptions to the truth of this statement (e.g., see Duncan[31]). However, it is generally true of most social scientific research from survey to experiment. It is a widely accepted tenet in survey research that interval and ratio measurement are assumed rather than real (see Labovitz[32]). Interestingly enough, although it is not often recognized by social-scientific experimentalists, their measures are not usually interval or ratio, especially if the measurements consist of frequencies of specific behaviors (see Burgess and Bushell[33]).

Numbers can be assigned to behavioral categories to produce interval or ratio measures of frequency if and only if the behaviors in particular categories are isomorphic. Isomorphy is, of course, always relative: There will always be some dissimilarity or within-class variance. However, at minimum, this dissimilarity must be estimable and within tolerable limits that are defined by the extent to which the research meets its objectives and provides adequate predictions. There are two general conditions producing this isomorphy: the behaviors must have the same typography and must occur in similar contexts. The context condition involves similar spatio-temporal reference, similar situational components ("place" variables), and similar transitional probabilities.

Often the within-class variance is too great or the transitional probabilities of two different behaviors in the same class too disparate to satisfy the general condition of isomorphy. A frequency analysis of social behavior is often problematic in this respect. For example, Milby[34] defines social behavior as "talking to, working with, or playing with another patient or staff member (by a patient) at any time during the 2-min. sample period." These three classes of behavior are obviously not sufficiently equivalent in typography to be all counted as single instances of social behavior. Moreover, the behavioral components of each subclass are too diverse to have similar transitional probabilities: e.g., even two greetings (as instances of "talking to") can have different transitional probabilities. A greeting in the context of ongoing conflict may be equivalent to an aversive stimulus meant to heighten the conflict, while a greeting in the context of friendship may serve as a stimulus to a more intense positive relationship. It is clear then that in this example the ratio level of measurement obtained by the calculation of frequencies of social behavior is at best an ordinal scale assumed to be a ratio scale. The same is true of many other studies using frequency of behavior to obtain interval or ratio measures of behavior.

Generally, therefore, true interval and ratio scales are hard to come by in the social sciences. There is a fairly widespread justification for this deficiency that unfortunately is fallacious. Many social scientists maintain that one of the necessary restrictions of their science is the inaccessibility of interval or ratio scales. Simply, it is said that human behavior may never be measurable with these scales. The fallacy is the assumption that the measurement scales form a continuous developmental progression. Nominal scales are assumed to be the lowest level developmentally while ratio scales are the highest level developmentally. More technically, it is assumed that the four basic measurement scales can be measured according to an implicit dimension of [degree of development] that has four units on an ordinal scale. (There are other possible units besides the four basic measurement scales, like partially ordered scales, but these four are basic in the sense that they are part of the deductive base of any others.) The justification of the low level of social-scientific measurement assumes this metameasurement in the sense that it is implicitly argued that social science cannot progress beyond the middle of the range of values. Human behavior is taken to be so complex and labile that its measurement is asserted to be forever developmentally blocked, possibly somewhere short of interval scales, definitely somewhere short of ratio scales.

This metameasurement scale is fallacious because it is the product of the transposition of reality problem. Measurement scales as first devised by S. S. Stevens[35] are mathematically defined, not empirically defined. The different scales are differentiated on the basis of the mathematical transformations permissible with each:

1. A nominal scale admits any one-to-one substitution of the assigned numbers.
2. An ordinal scale is transformed by any increasing monotonic function.
3. An interval scale is transformed linearly.
4. A ratio scale is transformed by multiplication by a constant.

Furthermore, interval, ordinal, and nominal scales can be retrieved from ratio scales, ordinal and nominal from interval, and so on. Importantly, the existence of this mathematical progression implies nothing about a historically necessary developmental progression. Nominal scales may be mathematically the most primitive and ratio scales may be mathematically the most advanced, but this implies nothing about their sequential development. Nominal scales cannot be deduced to have developmentally preceded ratio scales of the same dimension. Nor can it be deduced that the development of nominal scales generally must precede the development of any other scale type in any science. The same applies of course to all the scales in the mathematical progression. In other words, every scale is or can be interpreted to be historically unique, and any scale could be developed separately from the others. Ratio scales may have developed for some sciences, interval scales for others, according to the logical and empirical demands of the particular identification cycles. Thus, the imputation of this mathematical progression to empirical-historical necessity is a manifestation of the problem of the metatheorist's transposing his reality onto the reality of science.

Not only is the justificatory argument based on a faulty premise, but all prior arguments about the primacy of interval and ratio scales in science can be brought forward to challenge it. If interval and ratio scales are necessary (in all prior senses) for the development of science, then to say that social science cannot develop them is to say that social science can never be a science (in all prior senses). However, all this counterargument is really unnecessary, because some subspecialties of social science actually make extensive use of true interval and ratio scales. Duncan's review of the literature on nonverbal communication provides excellent examples.[36] Measures used include: duration of specific behaviors, rate, direction, duration, and distance of human movement, frequency and duration of eye glance, and spatial arrangements. Sommer[37] has presented an extensive analysis of research using spatial measures. Furthermore, there is research in psycholinguistics that uses these scales: e.g., studies of speaker switching, duration of hesitations and pauses, and phonemic length of certain utterances. Given the use of these scales, it is unreasonable to assert that they cannot be developed. There are good reasons for the lack of their development in most of social science, which will be examined shortly. But it is erroneous to suggest that they cannot be developed, for they have been.

The fact of the existence and use of these scales really should be no surprise because, in all the examples, the ST-rule is being invoked. That is, the scales involve time and space in some way, either directly or through derivatives thereof. Preformed interval and ratio scales are being used as the developmental base of social-scientific interval and ratio scales—a rather obvious solution. There is a component of the argument that this "obvious" solution does not address. These interval and ratio scales may apply only to a limited range of social scientific events. Beyond this range human behavior may still be too complex and labile to be measured in this way. In other words, these measures may be appropriate for only certain classes of human behavioral events, while it is entirely likely that the remainder of the events in the domain of social science may not be so measurable because of their lability and complexity.

This argument is almost impossible to rebut. A rebuttal would require an answer to the questions: What classes of events cannot be so measured; can these events be appropriately symbolically represented in order to be so measured; how can they be represented in order to achieve this; and finally, what is the limit of the range of application of these measures? The latter question is more than the converse of the first question because the implied activities necessary to answer it are different. The first question and the two subsequent to it suggest some translation or transformation procedure of those classes of events and corresponding expressions that are presumably not measurable with these scales. An analogous venture has been undertaken by Skinnerians (behavior modifiers) in sociology, most notably in the work of Homans[38] and the text by Burgess and Bushell.[39] The basic contention is that all sociological expressions can be translated using Skinnerian or operant conditioning theory. With a respondent conditioning bias, Cottrell[40] was one of the first sociologists to recognize this basic compatibility. An answer to the first question, on the other hand, would involve many of the same translation activities consisting of elaboration of sophisticated deductive-reductionist arguments and definitions or explications (redefinitions) and interpretations of traditional sociological expressions into operant conditioning terminology. As the question has to do with identifications, a sufficient answer would involve empirical testing of the proposed alternatives with emphasis on their adequacy of precision, falsifiability, and confirmation. In other words, the translation process must eventuate in the application of the identification and hypothesis cycle. In fact, operant conditioners have been faulted in their translation endeavors because they have not paid close enough attention to the requirements of these cycles—although this criticism is phrased differently. Chomsky's article[41] has become a classic on this basis.

An answer to the final question—what is the limit of the range of application of the interval and ratio scales mentioned? —would require the application of the requisite identification and hypothesis cycles using these measures. Therefore, the activities suggested by it are more positive in the sense that it is not necessary to rehash prior research endeavors, negate them, and translate them compatibly. The ultimate criterion of utility of these scales will be their ability to generate adequate hypotheses as answers to social-scientific questions. The crucial question, then, is what significant social problems/questions can be solved/answered with the use of these scales. This of course is an empirical question.

Thus, the supposed lability and complexity of social scientific events and inoperativeness of ST-derivative scales can be effectively rebutted only by developing hypothesis sets, including identifications using these scales, that adequately answer a significant proportion of social-scientific problems-questions. In other words, adequate research (in all senses) must be implementable on the basis of these scales. The difficulty in rebutting the original argument is straightforward; sufficient grounds for so doing remain to be developed. Suggestively, however, the argument can be partially rebutted. First, a study will be presented that demonstrates that certain social phenomena can be so measured. Second, one knotty set of social events will be translated sufficiently into identifications using these measures.

THE STABILITY OF A SET OF COMPLEX SOCIAL PHENOMENA

Several years ago I was hired at a Veterans Administration hospital to assess the effectiveness of a rather special voluntary program conducted for the patients there. The report and data that follow have not been published previously. The basic results of the study have been published elsewhere.[42]

The Bedside Network of the Veterans Radio and Television Guild is a voluntary organization that has for twenty-one years sent members on Wednesday evenings to entertain patients at various Veterans Administration hospitals across the nation. The music portion of the program consists of the playing of music and participatory singing by the hospital patients. The site of my research on this program was a large (1800-bed) V. A. hospital whose population was largely mental patients. The music activity took place at the same time on the same weekday evening every week. The volunteers were usually the same from week to week, although there was variation. The room in which the activity took place changed once during the period of the study. The volunteers would enter the room (a large dayroom or a large social hall) and set up their equipment. During the period in which the activity was observed, from thirty-four to fifty-eight patients were ushered in by the hospital aides and seated in chairs arranged in rows facing the microphone, recording equipment, and band. In the dayroom, there was no formal stage: the area used as a stage was separated by about five feet from the first row of chairs. In the social hall there was an elevated stage. The male and female patients were primarily longterm, chronic, and closed-ward.

After the patients were seated, songbooks were distributed and the names of those patients who wished to sing were recorded. These patients were called upon to sing as the evening progressed, and they led the singing by performing in front of the microphone. Their efforts were tape-recorded and played back on the hospital radio station the following morning. The entire procedure took an hour and a half.

During the performance, two female volunteers circulated among the audience, talked to patients, sang with them and generally attempted to get them to participate. The other volunteers played musical instruments, manned the recording equipment, or prompted the patient who was singing at the microphone. The quantitative description that follows is of the activities of the two circulating volunteers.

Method

The observer sat in a position from which he could record the activities of the volunteers unencumbered by any visual obstacles. He used an event recorder to record the frequency and duration of Bedside member to patient interaction, patient to Bedside member interaction, Bedside member to Bedside member interaction, and movement in zone *A* and movement in zone *B* by either volunteer. Movement consisted of any "walk" by a Bedside member of more than two consecutive steps in one direction. Zone *A* was the area just in front of the first row of chairs. Zone *B* was the area from the first row of chairs to the back of the room. "Interaction" consisted of any instance in which one party conversed with another. Each of these volunteers was observed for fifteen minutes after the singing program had begun as she moved among the patients. Because of a change in volunteers it was possible to collect data on four different people in this role. After several informal observation sessions, each volunteer was observed for five sessions with the exception of one who did not participate more than three times. One session was videotaped and three independent observers were used to assess the reliability of the observations. As a further check against observer bias, the data were not converted into numerical scores from the event-recorder graph until the reliability checks were repeated.

Results

For this research, reliability is defined as the proportion of shared observations to total observations for frequency and the proportion of shared within- and between-category duration in seconds to total duration in seconds. These proportions are expressed in percentages and represent, in effect, the percentage of interobserver agreement for each category. The reliability between observer One (the observer for the whole study) and observer Two for frequency was 100%, between One and Three, 79%, and between Two and Three, 79%. The reliability between observers One and Two for duration was 81%, between One and Three, 73%, and between Two and Three 67%. There was prior instruction before observers Two and Three viewed the videotape, but no practice. Observer Two was a graduate student in psychology, and observer Three was a high school student. Each observer viewed the videotape separately and used the event recorder to record the relevant behaviors. The low reliability for duration can be explained by the failure of adequate training and the fact that the videotape often did not permit clear discrimination of the initiation and termination of interactions.

Table 4-1 gives the mean and standard deviation in seconds for each behavior category and the total frequency for each category. These results reveal the remarkable stability of these behaviors for each of the four Bedside members involved. In each case, the mean duration in seconds of each behavior varies little between sessions and within sessions, as demonstrated by the consistently low value of the standard deviation. Also, frequency of each behavior varies little between sessions for each volunteer.

Table 4-1. Mean (X) and standard deviation (S) in seconds of duration of given behavior for each volunteer and frequency (F) of this behavior: "B-P" is Bedside member to patient interaction, "P-B" is patient to Bedside member interaction, "B-B" is Bedside member to Bedside member intraction, "A" is movement in zone A, and "B" is movement in zone B.

	B-P			P-B			B-B			A			B		
Volunteer	$\overline{X}$	S	F	$\overline{X}$	S	F	$\overline{X}$	S	F	$\overline{X}$	S	F	$\overline{X}$	S	F
1	16.0	2.4	9	3.6	—	1	6.9	.6	6	7.4	1.8	14	7.0	2.0	28
	14.0	1.3	10	5.0	—	1	8.6	1.0	6	6.0	1.3	15	6.0	1.6	25
	13.3	1.8	12	4.5	1.2	2	7.0	1.0	8	5.2	1.2	16	4.9	2.4	28
	15.4	2.6	8	5.1	1.4	2	8.2	1.5	7	5.8	.8	17	5.6	.8	28
	14.4	1.2	10	4.2	—	1	7.3	1.6	8	7.6	.3	14	7.8	1.2	26
2	6.8	1.4	13	3.8	2.8	3	8.6	.6	16	3.5	1.6	28	5.5	.9	22
	5.3	.8	14	3.2	3.1	4	5.1	.3	19	4.2	.6	23	6.1	.8	25
	3.1	.6	11	3.7	1.6	3	10.0	.7	13	6.2	.4	21	7.2	.5	29
	5.8	1.2	14	2.2	.2	5	8.2	.6	15	7.1	.5	25	6.8	.2	23
	7.8	.8	12	3.4	1.8	3	8.3	.6	15	4.4	1.7	26	6.1	1.2	26
3	17.6	1.3	22	4.7	.6	4	9.4	.9	5	6.1	1.4	15	6.9	1.0	13
	21.2	1.6	22	7.8	.5	4	9.8	.8	4	4.3	.9	12	4.2	1.2	13
	24.5	.9	20	17.8	.4	3	7.8	.9	4	4.6	1.3	11	4.9	1.4	17
	23.0	1.7	28	6.5	.4	3	11.6	.5	3	3.8	.7	12	4.9	2.1	15
	17.5	.2	24	7.3	.7	7	9.3	1.2	5	4.7	.9	13	5.6	2.0	18
4	7.2	.6	32	5.4	.7	3	7.3	.3	15	4.6	1.7	36	6.8	.8	39
	6.3	.6	38	5.7	.2	4	7.4	1.0	16	3.3	2.0	38	15.9	2.1	40
	7.9	.4	27	5.6	.5	4	7.0	2.0	12	4.7	1.7	37	6.5	.2	36

Discussion

The stability of these behaviors can be explained by the fact that each volunteer had been repeating the same activities over and over for several years. This stability existed despite potentially disruptive changes like the change in the site of the last two sessions for volunteers 2 and 3, the change of Bedside personnel from one session to the next, and the variation in the number and members of the patient audience. Unfortunately, data were not collected systematically on these variations, but the relative stability of the phenomena is evident.

"So what?" First, the very stability of these complex social phenomena gives the lie to the supposition that all social phenomena have an inherent amount of variation that precludes their highly precise measurement. Second, simple observational techniques have yielded stable quantitative measures of social phenomena. This would immediately suggest the relevance of other such measures: e.g., distance covered in each movement, content analysis of speech during interaction, or relative total frequency and duration of movement from and toward patients or from and toward other volunteers. Third, if one is in search of identifications of "social facts" or other behavioral phenomena that are analogous to the facts and phenomena of the physical and natural sciences, the stability of these phenomena and their ease of measurement would suggest them, and others that they imply, as likely candidates.

Finally, adequate hypotheses can be formulated in answer to questions that can be asked about such identifications. For example, it might be asked: "How can a volunteer increase the duration of her interactions with patients?" Volunteer 3 has the highest duration of Bedside-Patient and Patient-Bedside interactions. She is also consistently lowest in the frequency of Bedside member to Bedside member interactions, but approximately equal in the mean duration of these movements to the others. From these identifications the following hypotheses can be formed: if a volunteer does not talk to other volunteers too frequently (measured according to the maximum and minimum frequency of these interactions for any two volunteers) and if a volunteer does not move about in either the patient or nonpatient zone too frequently (measured according to the maximum and minimum frequency of these movements by any two volunteers), then the volunteer will maximize the duration of his interactions with patients and their interactions with him. Obviously, the next step would be to test this hypothesis.

This hypothesis is problematic because of the nonindependence of frequency and dration of these behaviors and of the behaviors themselves. The former relationship should be self-evident. The latter is less obvious. Given a preset time limit, any volunteer who spends more time in B-P and P-B interactions will probably have a low frequency of movement and B-B interactions because there is less remaining time in the interval to behave in these ways. This is not necessarily true, of course: a volunteer can spend more time in B-P and P-B interactions and also have a high frequency of movement and B-B interactions (and vice versa) *relative* to other volunteers. The degree of frequency ("high" or "low") and the length of time ("long" or "short") are empirically determined by the maximum and minimum values for any two volunteers, another illustration of the theoretical power that such measurable, stable phenomena give the researcher. However, this possible nonindependence is problematic. It can lead to obvious circularity.

Despite this problem, hypotheses of this form are far from trivial. The initial research problem was to assess the effectiveness of this voluntary organization. [Effectiveness] could be defined as the duration of both sequences of volunteer-patient interaction. The hypothesis is therefore one possible answer to the question: "Why is this program effective?"—a very common question in social science research. However, I think there is legitimacy to the argument that this definition of [effective] is really arbitrary and therefore the question-answer tailored to success. The issue turns on what is the most appropriate interpretation of [effective] or, in formal terms, on the precization of the expression. As discussed, this is one possible way of tackling research problems. In the actual situation, through a series of four meetings with the client (i.e., Bedside group) precization proceeded until consesnsus was reached on an interpretation of [effective]. The interpretation used, which in this case is an identification, was the ratio of volunteer-initiated verbal exchanges to patient responses: i.e., question: answer; statement: comment. Note that this identification is different from the previous one. It is this type of equivocation in identification determination that makes this semantic approach to social science research relatively imprecise. It can be de-emphasized by clearly identifying the objectives of the research beforehand: i.e., what changes in patient behavior are generally sought; does this program effect these changes, and if so, how? Semantic analysis can never be entirely dispensed with, but it can be de-emphasized so that words like [effectiveness] do not occur in questions, hypotheses, or identifications. Such words would be permissible in problem formation and speculation prior to the expression of that problem as a question or questions. Accordingly, the initial research question in this project would be not "What makes this program effective?" but "What changes in patient behavior can be attributed to what aspects of the program, assuming a scale of normality or appropriateness of patients' behavior such that the direction of change could be specified?"

THE MACROLEVEL—MICROLEVEL FALLACY

Attention turns now to the question of the demonstrable translation of certain social science identifications into equipollent identifications that use ST-derivative measures. Simply, are there any significant social science identifications that cannot be expressed by identifications using these measures? In answering this question the issue of the failure of social science to observe the ST-rule and other prerequisites of identification formation must be dealt with. This was the first alleged manifestation of the inadequacy of the identification cycle in social science. The second manifestation—the failure of social science to develop or fully utilize preexistent interval and ratio scales—was dealt with in the last section. Herein lies the interdependency of the two: fulfilling the prerequisites of identification is necessary for the development and use of interval and ratio scales in the identification. The failure of the latter is fully attributable to the failure of the former. Therefore, insofar as translation is possible or necessary, the inadequacy of the initial fulfillment of the identification prerequisites is demonstrable.

The most obvious source of identifications that are not measured by these or similar interval or ratio scales is macrolevel theory, which is important in history, sociology, and economics and increasingly in some branches of psychology. Briefly, macrolevel theory expressions have to do with properties of and relations between collectivities of individuals. These expressions have been called [[group terms]], [[emergent group properties]], or [[global properties]].[43] The following are some examples: [social system], [institution], [organization], [stratification], [bureaucracy], [society]. Macrolevel theory is usually contrasted with microlevel theory, whose component expressions have to do with properties of and relations between individuals: e.g., [role], [status], [personality], [interaction], [expectations], [rewards], [costs]. The distinction is not hard and fast. Certain expressions are used in both senses. [Power], for example, can be interpreted as an attribute of individuals or collectivities. However, the distinction is well known among social scientists and philosophers of science.

An appropriate test of the viability of these measures (ST-derivatives like frequency, duration, and movement) would be their utility in translating macrolevel identifications. This translation is a two-step process because of the level of abstraction of macrolevel expressions and the supposed ontic hiatus between these and microlevel expressions. The first step involves the demonstration that macrolevel expressions can be translated into microlevel expressions. The second step involves the specification of the requisite identifications. The task is simplified by the existence of prior research addressing both steps.

The first step can be interpreted as a question: does there exist a set of macrolevel expressions exclusive of the possibility of translation into a corresponding and equipollent set of statements containing microlevel terms? An affirmative answer would mean that there are macrolevel expressions that are not interpretable by reference to microlevel expressions having to do with properties of or relations between individuals. If the expressions are identifications, then this answer would reread: social scientists are properly concerned with those macrolevel identities that are not measurable by reference to an individual's action, responses, attributes, and the like. Both forms of affirmative answer are demonstrably false. With respect to expressions generally, Brodbeck and Wisdom[44] convincingly demonstrate that no social scientist has yet isolated such a set of untranslatable expressions. With respect to expressions that are identifications, it can be unequivocally stated that there is no instance of any macrolevel identity that in the course of research is not eventually identified by measurement expressions having to do with individuals, their actions, or their responses: e.g., macrolevel sociologists and economists employ survey methodology exclusively in their research with the necessary reliance on questionnaire or interview responses. For the moment the fact of this identification and not its adequacy is important. So, generally, the translation of macrolevel expressions to microlevel expressions is complete or completable.

A substantive example from the author's work illustrates one possible completable translation;[45] Brodbeck or Wisdom provide others.[46] For expediency the brackets in the example will be assumed. "If organization A does U, V, W, then organization B will do X, Y, Z" translates into "if actor A_1, who is a member of organization A with position D does U, V, W, then actor A_2 who is a member of organization B with position *E* will do *X, Y, Z*," where the membership of $A_{1, 2}$ and positions *D* and *E* are labels affixed to $A_{1, 2}$ or actions they perform at specific times in specific places. The macrolevel expression has been sufficiently translated into a microlevel expression that implies measures at the microlevel as well.

The second step of the translation has been anticipated. The possibility and fact of identifications whose identities are group expressions and whose measures are at the microlevel has been established. The sufficiency of many of these identifications is open to question, as will be seen in the next section. Sufficient identifications would entail the use of the ST measures or derivatives previously specified. The relevant questions here, then, is: can group terms or macrolevel identities be identified with ST measures or their derivatives? Increasingly, there is much research in disparate subspecialties of social science that answers this question affirmatively. The types of identifications available will be listed, and the sources will appear in the appropriate footnotes. This list makes no pretense at exhaustiveness.

1. People spatially arranged within architectural boundaries or "people" boundaries as an identifier of [social structure], [social position], or [group type].[47]
2. Change of position of total spatial arrangements as an identifier of [institutional or organizational or group change].[48]
3. Change of spatial position of individual within either type of boundary as an identifier of [conflict], [social interaction], [social mobility].[49]
4. Selected features of change of individual spatial position like distance, rate, and direction as identifier of [dominance], [submission], or [power].[50]
5. Selected features of change of relative spatial positions or arrangements within a group or architectural boundary as identifier of [aggregation] or [dispersal].[51]
6. Number or types of individuals (i.e., sex, age) per unit area as identifier of [social structure].[52]

7. Frequency or duration of action types as identifier of [status] and where the actions are communicative or reciprocal as an identifier of [stratification], [role sets], [institutions]. Note that duration is superior to frequency as previously noted because of the possible failure of isomorphy of the behaviors of which frequency counts are taken.[53]

8. Combinations like frequency or duration of certain action types according to spatial arrangements of the actors in groups as in the identification of [social facilitation].[54]

No attempt is made at exhaustive specification of these types of identifications, because such an exercise is insufficient proof of the empirical adequacy of the identifications. To reiterate, the crucial question is, how well do these identifications function in answering identification cycle or hypothesis cycle questions? Simply, rigorous empirical test is necessary. Short of this, such specification would be little more than an exercise. At this point it is sufficient to note that these measures have wider applicability in social science than traditionalists would allow. Even macrolevel theory is not outside the boundaries of the potential range of applicability of the measures. This is not to downgrade other measures, only to block out in broad outline the possible utility of interval and ratio ST (or derivative) scales for social science. In reality, the social scientist has little choice if he is to upgrade his identifications. To the extent that social scientists do not use these or similar high-level scales even as prerequisites for identification in the initial stages of inquiry (quadrants 1 and 2 in both cycles), they violate the demands of identification and cannot possibly develop high-level scales of whatever eventual form.

Group Terms, Data Types, and Identifications

Unless specified by the use of these interval and ratio or other ST measurements the identification of a macrolevel identity, no matter what the specific measurement-expression component, will be insufficient. In other words, minimally, macrolevel identities must be locatable, isolatable, selectable, and perceptually realizable; maximally, they must be arranged and transportable. Generally, they must be able to satisfy the demands of the identification cycle. ST specification is a necessary prerequisite. It is not the only one, as previously mentioned, but it provides the simplest rule against which to assess the effectiveness of all social science identification. Specifically, no macrolevel identity in social science satisfies the ST-rule, or for that matter, any of the other requirements of identification. It is quite obvious that group terms do not designate events that can be identified without translation, which simply rephrases the previous translation arguments into empirical necessity. Intuitive evidence makes the point a truism. [Organization] is not an analogous identity to [aggregated social amoebae]. Elsewhere, I have treated this discrepancy in detail, but with different terminology.[55] It was asserted that macrolevel identities are not observable and therefore insufficiently specified. The present statement is that these identities, even with their corresponding measurement expressions, are still deficient because they do not satisfy the demands of identification with all that it implies. The statement that they are not observable is too simplistic and must be elaborated in present terms to demonstrate the full force of the argument.

The basic argument about the failure of identification in social science can be expanded well beyond the confines of the macrolevel and microlevel distinction, and the statements about macrolevel identities can be deduced as one consequence of this broadened argument. Attention turns now to the two basic types of data that social scientists deal with, by way of broadening the argument.

There are two data types in social science that are the source of all identifications. The first type is objects, properties, or relations pertaining to human behavior. These are located by direct inspection. This data type will be called [observable human behavior] or O. The methodology most commonly employed in the formation of identifications on the basis of O is reliable observation. The second type of data are reports about human behavior or R. R are gathered by asking questions of subjects. The methodology usually employed includes use of interview schedules, questionnaires, or attitude and opinion paper-and-pencil tests.

Generally, O data more closely satisfy the demands of identification. Specifically, they are usually located in space and time and are measured by one or another of the interval and ratio scales mentioned previously: i.e., movement, duration, frequency (even though frequency is usually not a true interval scale because of lack of isomorphism of the units). This superiority of O data does not always obtain, as will be seen shortly.

R data, on the other hand, do not satisfy the ST-rule. The subject's verbal responses usually signify events that occur separately from them. The subject's reports are about events and are not the events themselves. For example, the subject may be recalling past history, describing internal states, or things he has recently experienced, or he may be speculating about future events. These indicated events are not located in space and time. Furthermore, the reports themselves are not given spatiotemporal reference. They are collected and the context of collection is not specified. These two weaknesses deserve elaboration.

In the first case, the social scientist uses the R as identifiers of identities that are inadequately specified by ST. Subjects are never asked how they earn their income or of what their education consisted. They are asked to indicate their level of income or education. The temporal or spatial context (in the formal sense) of the actions or events implicitly or explicitly designated in their verbal responses is never specified. Questions like, "Did you decide to do X at T_1 in situation Y?" or "I feel disturbed in stimulus situations X, Y, Z (yes or no)" are phrased "Did you decide (not decide) to do X?" or "I frequently feel disturbed (yes or no)." More importantly, rarely is an attempt made to independently identify the designated events. Rarely are subjects' reports about their occupation, income, or education, for example, followed up with independent identification of their occupation, income, or education. Both manifestations of the failure to specify ST context of designated events are well known by social scientists. With respect to the former, Hyman[56] notes that one consequence is the impossibility of assigning correct time order to variables, and Galtung[57] suggests that one significant problem with surveys is their attempt to synchronically measure a diachronic reality. With respect to the latter, Parry and Crossley[58] demonstrated the necessity of independently identifying such R data as age, sex, occupation, and income.

That the R themselves are not given ST reference is not so commonly recognized among practicing social scientists. Their context of recording is rarely dealt with systematically by social scientists who deal with R. The subjects' verbal responses are indicated on some form of answer sheet. Subsequently, these responses are codified as holes punched in IBM cards. Eventually, the responses are mechanically counted and transposed to printout sheets. The cards and printout sheets become the durable records of the R. These records are transported, arranged, isolated, selected, perceptually examined, and located. In other words, they are the antecedents or consequences of social scientist action. How the subjects were asked, when they were asked, and where they were asked are rarely fully identified. The ST context of collection is blurred by or substituted by the context of the scientist action with respect to the durable records of the R. This substitution transposes levels of reality for the social scientist within his domain. In effect, he is dealing with metaevents about events as if they were the events themselves. He is committing his own miniversion of the transposition of reality problem.

What is meant can be seen by examining the consequences of the requisite specification of the ST context of collection of R. There is an increasing metatheoretical literature on the varying effects of context of collection upon R data. Pittenger, *et al.*,[59] exhaustively analyze what goes on in the interview and conclude that the first five minutes can be crucial in determining the R that are gathered. Friedman and Rosen-thal[60] in a different vein review research that has to do with the effects of (mostly) actor characteristics and actions of the researcher on the subject's verbal and (less important here) nonverbal behavior. More recently, Phillips provides an extensive review of the literature in this area.[61] Yet, despite this copious literature, social scientists who use R rarely follow the implied metatheoretical precepts.

Perhaps, the most decisive illustration of the failure to specify the ST context of the collection of R is to contrast it with research in which this context is explicitly specified as part of the research rather than as part of a metatheory about the failure of such specification as in the previous examples. In other words, the R in this illustration are ST-context bound as a prerequisite to research specifically about such R, as opposed to critical metatheoretical analyses about deficiencies in use of R without ST specification. In this type of research, R is synonymous with "verbal behavior." The subjects' verbal statements are treated directly as the events to be identified and are either identified by ST and measured independently by some derivative interval or ratio scale or are measured explicitly by ST with the context of the identity being implicitly specified by ST. Examples of the former are rare, but the following will suffice: content analysis in which statements are identified by their position on a tape and have an assigned measurement consisting of judges' numerical evaluations. Examples of the latter are more extensive. Verbal behavior is certifiably categorized according to its implicit spatiotemporal context: e.g., nominals or predicates, questions or answers, and pause or continuous speech flow. The identities are then identified by ST measures or derivatives based on frequency, duration, word arrangement, or sound intensity and pattern. The degree of sophistication of the instrumentation employed is related to the measurement units and dimensions employed: the range is as wide as sonographic analysis to the use of stop watches.

The overall weakness of R data to fulfill identification demands and the ST-rule in particular is compounded by the use of aggregate data. The R data are aggregated in such a way that a statistical index of central tendency (such as mean or mode) summarizes the responses of individuals. The non-ST context of the individual responses is therefore collapsed into the non-non-ST context of the statistical index. The ultimate effect is to entirely eliminate ST context from the concerns of the social scientist. This difficulty in using aggregated data is discussed by Sidman[62] but in different terms. It should be noted, however, that social scientists who use O (as Sidman also advocates) also aggregate their data with much the same effect. Most inconsistent here are those disciples of Sidman's methodological edict who recommit the same fallacy: i.e., operant conditioners who use changes in frequency of aggregate indicators of behaviors of more than one individual as a dependent variable.[63]

The general superiority of O data with respect to the ST-rule and identification demands is not unequivocal. O and R data can be equally deficient in this respect, contingent on the conceptualizations and objectives of the particular researcher. Frequently in social science a particular identification is taken to be the identifier of an identity, thereby creating a meta-identification: e.g., [[[[status inconsistency]] is [[the discrepancy of an individual's scale value on education, income, occupation, and prestige measures]]]]]. In this example, the identity [[status inconsistency]] is identified by [[the discrepancy of an individual's scale value on education, income, occupation, and prestige measures]]; this identifier is in turn an identification consisting of the identity [discrepancy of an individual's scale value] and the identifying measurement expression [education, income, occupation, and prestige scales]. Such compound identifications will be called "indicators," a word with which most social scientists are familiar that is defined differently but synonymously by them.

To the extent that social scientists conceptualize either O or R as indicators, either one will be correspondingly deficient as identifications. The metaidentity is never specified by ST. For example, many researchers whose basic data are O establish metaidentities like [[aggression]], [[social interaction]], [[status]], [[power]], [[competition]], and [[cooperation]]. Schmitt and Marwell[64] use the metaidentification: [[[[cooperative productivity]] is [[simultaneous button-pushing by two individuals at [X frequency]]]]]. [[Cooperation]] is not locatable in space and time nor does it correspond to a particular ST context, even though in appearance it may appear to. Specifically, can mutual plunger depression within 0.5 sec. be equated with [[cooperative productivity]]? If this indicator were a true identification, the answer unequivocally would be yes, for the interdependence if not substitutivity of the meta-identity and identifying identification would establish the equivalence and result from it. However, in this case, it is possible to assert that alternative identifications $X_1 \ldots n$ are equally good identifiers of [[cooperation]] or specifically, [[cooperative productivity]]. For example, [[cooperation]] could be identified by rates of verbal exchange and [[productivity]] by rates of easily recognized everyday work behavior (like number of telephone calls or assembly line work), and the case could be made that the true indicator was being more accurately approximated. The equivocation in the identification is a direct consequence of the failure of the original metaidentity to satisfy the ST-rule. So O data, if used to form indicators, can lose their inherent superiority on this dimension over R data.

Most R data are indicators, although implicitly so. This is a paraphrase of the argument about R being metaevents confused with events. It is quite clearly illustrated by converting the argument into compatible symbolic notation. All R are metaidentities to usually implicit identifications whose identities are O. Notationally this can be represented as follows: [[[[[R]] is [[O measured by X]]]]]. Suppose the subject responds to a question about sex by checking the box for female. The $R =$ response female, the $O =$ sex of individual, and the $X =$ the measure of sex. Minimally, this measure may be the formal observation of sex characteristics. This is not so simple as it may sound, because formally it would require ST location as well as the specification of a scale of sex attributes.

In practice, of course, it is thought to be sufficient in observing sexual identification to use a binary discrimination, male or female. But practice is really scientifically unsound. How is the homosexual male or female, the sex conversionist, or the nonhomosexual transvestite to be categorized? In an urban area like New York City, these are not necessarily deviant cases. More significantly, what is the basis for the binary discrimination? Even physiological characteristics will produce great classificatory error: there are wide individual differences in secondary sexual characteristics; there are admittedly rare cases in which even primary sexual characteristics are not easily discriminable, as with hermaphrodites; and sex hormone balances show great individual variation. If sex characteristics are also "psychologically" construed—e.g., women are more "emotional" than men—the potential error in binary discrimination is enormous: witness the arguments of the women's liberationists. Perhaps, the greatest but most subtle complication for this proposed "simple" classification is the hidden "sociological" dimension conceived to be a significant associate of sex. That is, sex itself is an implicit indicator of other social events: training patterns, past histories, interactional styles, behavior repertoires, dress, occupational alternatives, and so forth. Again, the arguments of the women's liberationists are instructive. This hidden dimension also accounts for enormous error in the supposedly simple binary classification.

Sexual identification, minimally measured via the use of observation of sex characteristics, would require the use of interval or ratio scales whose dimensions would express one or another of the characteristics or implied characteristics just synoptically presented. On the other hand, such measurement maximally would possibly involve a ratio scale of hormonal differences, perhaps with units indicating the ratio of estrogen to testosterone in individuals. This measure, in turn, would be the identifier of some of the psychological or sociological sexual characteristics listed: e.g., assuming adequate ST specification, [[interaction pattern Y is measured by hormonal ratio Z]], where Y is supposed to be sex-linked.

Even the simple example of sex as an R datum demonstrates the inherent complexity of R data because they are implicit indicators. The O that are indicators have deficient identifications; and because all R are implicit indicators, they too will have deficient identifications. This problem with R is dually compounded when the R are construed as explicit indicators. This usage is most common in social science where specific forms of questionnaires are designed to indirectly measure inferred identities. In research jargon, such questionnaires are said to "tap a particular dimension." There are questionnaires that are supposed to measure [[depression]], [[anxiety]], [[internal vs. external control]], [[prejudice]], [[authoritarianism]], and so on. Notationally, the form of the indicator is the same as for R as implicit indicators: e.g., [[[[[external control]] is [[answers $U_{1 \ldots n}$ by any individual which can be mapped onto measurement scale X with unit Y and dimension Z]]]]]. $U_{1 \ldots n} =$ the particular responses of subjects to specific questions. Scale $X =$ an interval scale, and unit Y and dimension $Z =$ the response alternatives and corresponding quantification segmentation of them that are provided to the subject. It is important to note that the measurement dimension is independent of the metaidentity in explicit indicators. That is, the dimension of the response alternatives, like [favorable-unfavorable] with five demarcations quantified in some way, is different from the metaidentity. Hence, the word "indicator" for the separate measurement dimension is taken to indicate the presence of the metaidentity in varying degrees for particular respondents. R as explicit indicators are usually used to identify metaidentities that are thought to be internal states or predispositions of the individual. The measurement of attitudes is a good general example. It is well known that these internal states are problematic because they are not fully identified.[65] Carnap[66] tried to grapple with this problem years ago from a philosophy of science perspective. More recently there is a substantial body of social science research literature relevant to the problem.[67] Important here is the fact that social scientists recognize the insufficient identification of such explicit R indicators. Congruent with this analysis, this insufficiency is expressible as the nonapplication of the ST-rule to the meta-identities involved. They are even thought to be unidentifiable in this sense by many social scientists, although this fallacy is fading from the field.[68]

Because all R are implicit indicators, those R that are explicit indicators will be embedded in identifications twice removed from the ST-rule. The metaidentity will be identified by an identification whose identity is a concealed indicator because that identity will be R data that are implicit indicators themselves. The social scientist will conceive of his explicit indicator as having a metaidentity; the metatheorist recognizes that the metaidentity is actually a meta-metaidentity identified by a metaidentity (R) that is usually implicit for the social scientist. The rule is further violated by the just-noted practices of aggregation of R data and the use of statistical indices of central tendency and dispersion.

O data as explicit indicators also can have their identification problems compounded by aggregation. However, they do not involve implicit indicators. The social science data types can be partially ordinally scaled on the dimension of identification adequacy with specific reference to the satisfaction of the all-pervasive ST-rule. R-explicit indicators are least adequate; they are improved upon by O-explicit indicators and R-implicit indicators (where the subject is asked so-called "informative" or "background" direct questions), which are bettered by O nonindicators. Because O-explicit indicators and R-implicit indicators share the same scale position, this scale is a partial order.

It is important to note that the scale value of R-implicit indicators cannot be altered by providing validity checks. All these checks do is assure that the O identifiers of the R are certified and measured: i.e., such checks complete the identification process. On the other hand, the scale value of *R*-implicit indicators can be altered by converting this data type to verbal behavior. In this case, the *R*-implicit indicators would become *O* nonindicators that have to do with verbal behavior. Therefore, questions of validity are separable from questions about adequate ST specification.

This scale of data types is unidimensional. Other dimensions can be used, and this scale may become moot. For example, the dimension of [necessity] may be used. In this case *R*-implicit indicators can be shown to be necessary for some types of social-scientific research problems. Generally, when events are of rare occurrence or have occurred in the past, there may be no other way of getting information about them than asking questions. It is difficult to observe some classes of crime, for example. On the other hand, the necessity of such data should not be confused with their adequacy. It is incumbent on the social scientist to make every effort to increase the adequacy of these data, which minimally implies two things: first, validity checks and, second, possible conversion to *O* nonindicators. The first point is obvious. The second point stipulates that these data should be placed in ST-context. As previously mentioned, there is a growing body of methodological research that is doing just that. There is also increased theoretical interest in questions about such converted data. For example, person-perception theory in social psychology asks what effects labeling a person in a particular way will have on the behavior of those who receive the information.[69] Such data-conversion processes, in my opinion, hold great promise for social science, for previously inadequately researched events can thereby be adequately researched. For example, most "pain research" has faltered because "pain" as a physiological event could not be sufficiently identified. This problem tends to be less troublesome when reports about pain are studied as verbal behavior. The same is true of perception theory when reports about perception are similarly studied. Finally, many macrolevel events can be studied in much the same way: e.g., status is convertible to a labeling process, as are institutional positions generally.

It was initially stated that identification problems with group terms were a deducible consequence of these more-pervasive data-identification problems. This connection is easily demonstrated. Most macrolevel identities are embedded in identifications that are explicit indicators. Generally, these explicit indicators are *R* data. To return to the example of status inconsistency: whether or not a person is [[status inconsistent]] is determined by his questionnaire or interview responses indicating his relative ranks on several status dimensions like income, occupation, and education. These responses in turn are implicit indicators. It follows that such macro-level identities expressed by group terms and identified by *R*-explicit indicators are on the lowest scale position of identification adequacy. An increasingly popular trend among macrolevel social scientists is to identify their group terms by *O*-explicit indicators. This practice would raise the identification adequacy of group terms one scale position. The optimum would be to fully identify group terms by the use of *O* nonindicators, but unless the macrolevel fallacy is fully amended by translation and adequate identification, this improvement is clearly unachievable at present. A veritable Copernican Revolution among macrolevel theorists would be called for, because certain group terms would have to be dispensed with while others would have to undergo radical translation. One possible medium for this translation has been proposed elsewhere by this author.[70] To reiterate, group terms would be transformed into communication sequences with fully specified actor characteristics including labels assigned to actors, actions, presence of others, place, and time quantities, which, of course, corresponds to the basic paradigm of science as communication. For example, positions in organizations are equivalent to labels attached to actors, the offices they occupy, and so on, while the organizations are legal and geophysical entities.

By way of concluding this chapter and tying loose ends, the question arises, if macrolevel identities as a subset of *R*-explicit indicators are so problematic, why are they persistently used in social science? At least part of the answer relates to what was said previously about borrowed identities. There is an air of legitimacy to these indicators that presupposes their adequacy. Because they exist linguistically full-blown for the social scientist, he feels or acts bound to identify them.

5

Hypothesis Problems and Faulty Metatheory in Social Science

THE FAILURE OF THE HYPOTHESIS CYCLE

Given the interdependency between identifications and hypotheses, the deficiencies of the former result in deficiencies in the latter. Faulty identifications cannot make good hypotheses. Because social science has faulty identifications, it must have imprecise hypotheses.

This imprecision is a well-documented fact that most social scientists are aware of. Immediate evidence of it is reflected in the general form of social-scientific hypotheses: "the more (less) of X, the more (less) of Y"; "X varies directly (indirectly) with Y." Without the exact specification of the parameters of these quantifiers, as many interpretations of each prediction exist as there are possible measuring dimensions, scales, and units to interpret the quantifiers. The very statement of a hypothesis without reference to the change in measurement values that is the essence of any hypothesis must result in imprecision. Any prediction stated in general form without reference to the identifications embedded therein will have an unspecified range of translations. Of course, if the component identifications are imprecise, the hypothesis will also be imprecise whether or not the identifications are fully specified.

One manifestation of this imprecision is the equivocal falsification of many social-scientific hypotheses. That is, once falsification occurs, it rarely is believed. "The hypothesis is not false—the measures were faulty, the procedures inaccurate, the subjects uncooperative, the responses biased," and so on. Formally, the imprecision of most hypotheses is such that their falsification set offers limitless alternative hypotheses or interpretations to account for the falsification other than the fact that the hypothesis, pure and simple, is false. For this reason, social-scientific hypotheses are rarely falsified.

Another manifestation of the imprecision of hypotheses is the confusion of definitions with hypotheses. The deleterious consequence of this confusion is the failure to test some hypotheses because they are assumed to be untestable definitions. The essential interdependence between definitions and hypotheses in science has been established. Briefly, definitions in science codify well-confirmed laws and are used to establish and test relatively unconfirmed hypotheses. But in social science, definitions are conceived to be procedures of interpretation applied to identities and appended to hypotheses to make them testable. As such they, in fact, often codify untested and unconfirmed hypotheses and are used to establish and test other unconfirmed hypotheses. For example, suppose the definition is [[[hierarchy] $_{df}$ = [relationships between people characterized by increasing remoteness with each ascending step in the chain of command]]]. Even assuming adequate component identifications, this definition is a concealed hypothesis that must be tested: i.e., the hypothesis [[if [ascending positions in the chain of command], then [increasing remoteness]]] must be tested and confirmed. A good rule of thumb is that, if the supposed definition contains a quantity, it is most likely a concealed hypothesis that must be tested. The confusion of definitions and hypotheses in social science results from the overall imprecision of hypotheses because definitions must be used as prefabricated procedures even to test the hypotheses. The door is left open for definitions that are untested hypotheses. The definitional confusion and imprecision of hypotheses both spring from the common source of the failure of identification. If social-scientific identifications were adequate, all definitions would be adequate and hypotheses would be precise.

The imprecision of social-scientific hypotheses also results in the failure of social scientists to replicate or reproduce the tests of their hypotheses. A chain of interdependent antecedents is actally involved in the preceding metahypothesis. Inadequate identifications result in imprecise hypotheses. Interestingly, one manifestation of the inadequacy of the identification cycle in social science is the failure of its replication or reproduction, when and if the corresponding research occurs at all. This fact can be conceptualized as a subset of the general failure of replication and reproduction of research. Be that as it may, the use of *R*-explicit indicators, *R*-implicit indicators, and *O*-explicit indicators leads to the inadequate observance of the ST-rule, which in turn leads to identifications that are inadequate in two ways: first, the identity does not have spatiotemporal reference (with all that it implies) and, second, there usually is a failure to develop true interval or ratio scales. These identifications are imprecise, and the resulting hypotheses accordingly will be imprecise. Imprecise hypotheses are rarely amenable to replication or reproduction. Their vagueness or ambiguity interferes with their precise restatement, which is necessary for repetitive testing. In other words, if the hypotheses and identifications are indeterminant, then their statement and restatement must be indeterminant. If their statement and restatement are indeterminant, then repetitive testing is impossible.

The relationship is symmetrical. The failure of social scientists to replicate or reproduce their hypothesis cycles results in imprecise hypotheses. One necessary prerequisite to increasing the precision of any expression is its repetition. Assessment of the change in level of precision requires at least one comparison that in turn requires at least one repetition. This rule is implied by the previous general rule: assessment of change requires comparison, and comparison requires at least two "observations." The two observations, in turn, require at least two expressions of change, one prior to the observations and one subsequent to them to assess the match between the observations. Specifically, repetition of identifications is necessary to establish their stability through time, while repetition of hypotheses is necessary to assess the results of their test. If such repetition is precluded, then not only will prior imprecision be unalterable, but it will also be difficult to determine. It follows that the failure of social scientists to replicate or reproduce their identifications or hypotheses will perpetuate imprecise hypotheses and impede necessary corrective action.

Social science metatheorists of as different persuasions as Sidman, a behaviorist, and Galtung, a survey researcher,[1] have strongly emphasized the failure of replication or reproduction of research by social scientists—although the word "replicate" is usually used alone and in a more global sense. Yet, there is a general omission from consideration of this crucial symmetrical relationship between replication and imprecision. I have considered it elsewhere, but in an analysis from a different perspective.[2]

Social Science Testing: Deficiencies in Control Procedures

Several types of auxiliary hypotheses have been shown to be necessary for testing main hypotheses. The auxiliary hypotheses have basically the same form as the main hypotheses, in that changes in identifications as expressed in difference statements are predicted by changes in other identifications also expressed in difference statements. There is this difference: the auxiliary hypotheses are ancillary, or conceived to be ancillary, to the test of the main hypothesis. This means that often their test is implicit. However, auxiliary hypotheses are crucial to the cycle of inquiry, and this de-emphasis should not disguise their importance.

There is a common distinction in social science research methodology between experiment and survey. The comments to follow are more relevant to social science experimenters than to survey researchers. Specifically, an examination of auxiliary hypotheses and the logic of control will reveal several deficiencies, and these comments will be addressed more to experimentalists.

Parenthetically, however, this distinction between methodologies is not critical. The distinction is usually maintained on the basis that experimenters actively control the independent variable (antecedent identification), but survey researchers do not. Frequently appended to this is the assertion that basic to experimental methods is the control of the possible disrupting or confounding variables (control-condition identifications) while the independent variable is manipulated. If the prior definition of control is utilized, it is obvious that survey researchers and experimenters both engage in control as "planned change." The acceptance of this definition is not arbitrary, for there is no other one logically possible.[3] The initial basis of the distinction breaks down under logical scrutiny. The control of extraneous variables is really a question of the logic of control employed by the two types of researchers. Yet, this logic is invariant: it involves control by inclusion, constancy, or randomization in surveys *and* in experiments. Moreover, all three have to do with auxiliary hypotheses whose form is a constant. Therefore, the appended criterion for the distinction also does not apply.

On the other hand, as there is a difference between the activities of experimenters and survey researchers, it cannot be concluded that there is no distinction at all. The proper basis of the distinction can be culled from the mundane differences in the activities and not from any critical difference in the logic of inquiry employed. Survey researchers deal with large samples of people, emphasize elaborate sampling procedures, distribute and collect questionnaires or conduct interviews with all the accompanying procedures, code questionnaires or interviews, record the responses on (usually) IBM cards, and mechanically analyze the results. Important in all this activity is that in testing of main hypotheses and auxiliary hypotheses, and concomitantly instituting the necessary control procedures, the survey researcher deals with categories and numbers. In other words, he locates, transports, selects, isolates, observes, and arranges records of responses, often with the aid of the IBM computer and desk calculator. Experimenters, on the other hand, deal with small numbers of people, sample from known populations or randomly assign subjects to treatments or treatments to subjects and de-emphasize elaborate sampling procedures, conduct their research with a smaller N than the total N by isolating members of the smaller N in "laboratories," instruct subjects to do certain things or in some other way expose them to the "experimental manipulations," record subject responses, and tabulate results, usually with some mechanical aid. Herein lies the crucial difference between the two: the experimenter in testing the main hypotheses and auxiliary hypotheses and concomitantly instituting the necessary control procedures deals with people as well as categories and numbers. Primarily, he locates, transports, selects, isolates, observes, and arranges *subjects*, not records of subjects' responses.

This point deserves elaboration. Both experiment and survey involve planned change. In both, the researcher's behavior is antecedent in the hypotheses or plans necessary to define "control." However, in the experiment the consequence is primarily a change in the subject's behavior, while in the survey, the consequence is a change in the disposition of records of the subject's responses. Most important here is not this rather trivial difference, but the fact that the difference *is* trivial. The logic of inquiry is invariant whatever the specifics of the social scientist's actions. Therefore, the deficiencies in the auxiliary hypotheses of social science that will be discussed, specifically the subset having to do with the logic of control, have relevance for survey and experiment or, more generally, for the full range of specifiable methodologies.

Perhaps the best way of illustrating the universal relevance of the deficiencies in the auxiliary hypotheses of social science is to start with a deficiency in the area of social science methodology that is well recognized. Sidman has noted that one of the critical weaknesses of social science methodology involves a heavy reliance on randomization (i.e., random selection or assignment of subjects or treatments) as a control technique.[4] He rightly says that randomization becomes an excuse for ignorance in the sense that important contributing factors (or extraneous variables) go unexplored as randomization fulfills its role as substitute for the specification of these factors. What he fails to recognize is that randomization may be ultimately necessary, for the list of contributing factors is, in fact, open-ended. At some as yet unknown terminus, reality degenerates into a disorderly array—at least, this is the lesson of particle physics. Random models are one way of approximating this unpredictability, an admitted paradox.[5] This is an elaborate way of saying that errorless predictions are not possible because all relevant conditions or contributing factors can never be entirely controlled. Hence, randomization may be a necessary control procedure. However, Sidman's point on the whole is well taken, for randomization is relied on too heavily in social science: the specification of contributing factors terminates too early to assure minimal error in the hypotheses.

The overemphasis on randomization directly implies the failure of social scientists to rely sufficiently on control by inclusion. Sidman also argues this point extensively.[6] He is aware of the relationship between hypotheses with minimal error and the successive control of contributing factors. Although truth is ultimately an empirical question, its probabil-

ity can be maximized (and error minimized) by the inclusion
of values of relevant contributing factors into the research
design—my terminology, not his. Control by inclusion permits
more information to be gathered with each test of a hypothesis. Ultimately this assures the expression [[[X] accounted for
[Y value] of the change in [U] predicted from the change in
[V]]]. More simply, it can be ascertained how much of a difference a contributing factor has made to the results of a particular hypothesis test. The failure of social scientists to make full
use of this powerful control technique is reflected in the minimal number of variables they actually include. Studies that
employ more than a three-way analysis of variance in statistically analyzing the results are rare, which means that rarely
are even two extraneous variables incorporated in the design.

The over-use of randomization and the under-use of control
by inclusion are deficiencies common to experimental and survey research alike. More peculiar to experimental research is
the frequent failure to fully identify the control condition to
be included in the design. In terms of control hypotheses, this
failure translates into the use of inadequate identifications of
the consequence control condition, where the antecedent has
to do with scientist action necessary to produce the planned
change in the consequence identification. For example, in a
classic experiment that has led to many replications in the
social psychology of bargaining, Deutsch[7] compared different
bargaining outcomes on the basis of the predisposition or
orientation of the bargainers: whether they were cooperatively, competitively, or individualistically oriented. These
variables were included in the design by having the researcher instruct the subjects to be one or the other, with a
brief description of what this would involve. The basic
auxiliary hypothesis involved is, [[if researcher gives [instruc-
tions] to subjects to be [cooperative, competitive, or individ-
ualistic] including a [description] of what this would involve,
then subjects will be [cooperative, competitive, or individ-
ualistic]]]. Despite the differences in results according to
prediction—joint outcomes were highest with the cooperative

orientation, lowest with competitive and between the two with individualistic—the included control condition (orientation) is insufficiently identified. The measurement procedure employed was a paper-and-pencil test administered to the subjects after the experiment to assess whether they behaved appropriately. As such, it is better than no measurement, but it is still insufficient because the next-to-weakest type of data is employed, the subject's responses as R-implicit indicators. Importantly, rarely has this type of general measurement been considered formal in the sense that an attempt is made to develop interval or ratio scales of the condition.

The immediate effect of the insufficient identification is that the experimenter can never be certain of the efficacy of his actions. As the requisite feedback information is lacking, the experimenter cannot regulate his actions accordingly: e.g., he cannot certify that any two subjects will be cooperative, competitive, or individualistic to the same value on the basis of his instructions, and he cannot alter his instructions to produce this comparability. It is, in fact, open to question whether or not he has succeeded in any given case in "making" any two subjects dissimilar in the particular dimension, whether or not subject A is cooperative and subject B is competitive. The subjects may indicate that they have behaved in one way or another, but this assertion cannot be tested or falsified because of the insufficient identifications. Certainly, there is evidence for this auxiliary hypothesis because the results are according to prediction: the experimenter must have done something right because subjects instructed to have different orientations do have different bargaining outcomes as predicted. This type of indirect evidence is far removed from the demands of science, which dictate the falsifiability and confirmability of all hypotheses. The problem is even apparent if one thinks impressionistically. Just because people are instructed to behave a certain way is no guarantee of their contingent behavior, and without adequate feedback about this contingent behavior the instructor can never know the efficacy of his instructions.

The ultimate effect of this deficiency is that results from this series of experiments in bargaining cannot be nor have they ever been replicated. True, the direction of the results stays the same in the sense that an ordinal scale of outcomes is usually achievable: i.e., cooperatively oriented subjects usually receive higher joint payoffs than competitively oriented subjects. But within predictable error limits, replication is never achievable. A critical rule of science has been violated. As an addendum, the use of aggregate data in these experiments is also problematic. Such data might produce an overall result in the sense of ordinal outcomes with replication, but the individual violations of this replicated result are effectively concealed. Therefore the fact of replication is open to question: aggregate data replicated in a particular direction is quite different from individual data replicated within certain measurement values, given predictable error. It can be questioned whether the former really is "scientific" replication.

The insufficiency of social-scientific auxiliary hypotheses because of the insufficiency of the component identifications is not an isolated phenomenon. Ax, for example, in another classic experiment[8] in a quite different area does not even measure his control conditions—[fear] and [anxiety]. The point deserves evidence by counterexample. The initial Deutsch experiment would have been adequate if the following were done. First, the auxiliary hypothesis would have to be tested. This minimally implies one identity: [orientation: competitive; cooperative; individualistic]. Optimally, each orientation would be located in space and time and the appropriate interval or ratio scales supplied. It would not be necessary to explicitly identify the scientist action if this were fully standardized, hence the need *at minimum* to identify only the consequence. However, this rule clearly does not apply. It is inconceivable that one researcher could tell another precisely how to instruct a subject to act in the appropriate ways to produce the desired value of the orientation. Generally, I think there is a legitimate question about the measurement of such labels, anyway: are they shorthand notations for behaviors to be measured *qua* behaviors or are they measurable attributes? Be that as it may, because the researcher's instructional behavior is not primitive in the sense that it will be automatically standardized, it too must be fully identified. Exactly what he is to do must be given ST specification, and the instructions must be measured by interval or ratio scales. The problem becomes even more complicated because the dimension for measuring the instructions must be selected from many alternatives: pitch of voice, content of message, length of message, and so on. Presumably, content of message is most appropriate, but it is not easy to develop high-level scales for this dimension. Finally, given adequate identifications, the auxiliary hypotheses would be repetitively tested and confirmed or falsified.

This rather tongue-in-cheek revision suggests an immediate solution. Rather than instruct subjects to have a particular orientation, one should pick subjects who have that orientation, or design the experiment to constrain them by the rules of the bargaining game to have that orientation. If the orientation were adequately identified, either of these choices would be possible. The general idea is to replace the antecedent in the auxiliary hypothesis by a less problematic one; to replace behavior that requires extensive testing to be standardized by behavior that is already standardized for the social science researcher: subject sampling and game design.

The problem of the insufficiency of auxiliary hypotheses is more relevant for experimentation than survey research because in survey research control by inclusion is accomplished by rearranging categories and counting and recounting R data. The activity is highly standardized, and the values of the included conditions are implied by the act of categorization and counting. This is not to say, however, that the included conditions will be adequately specified, but quite the contrary, because of the weak form of the data. The problem is irrelevant, not solvable within the context of survey research.

In concluding this section one final problem that is relevant to both methodologies will be considered. The logic of experimentation dictates that as many relevant extraneous variables (contributing conditions) be controlled as possible while the independent variable (antecedent condition) is manipulated. Control in this sense has been taken by social scientists to mean constancy or exclusion. Sidman[9] has emphasized rightly the importance of control by inclusion (my term) for the larger process of inquiry. Even widening the methodological perspective in this way does not avoid a common fallacy which shall be called the "interaction fallacy."

No matter how liberally this assertion of experimental logic is construed, all experimental researchers are foretold to be on the watch for interaction effects. This edict is equally true of survey researchers. The experimental logic has its statistical counterpart in social science.[10] Extraneous variables are to be controlled by inclusion or constancy while the independent variable is manipulated. What differs is that the control is statistical. Again, the interaction fallacy is prevalent. The researcher is sensitized for interaction effects. His statistical techniques, most commonly analysis of variance, have a component that distinguishes main effects from interaction effects. If the latter are too sizeable, then the research is cast into doubt for the researcher.

Congruent with this analysis the hypothesis, [[Given $[C_{1,2}]$, if $[A]$ then $[B]$]], would have the following tabular representation, assuming its testability:

		B	$\sim$B
A	C_1		
	C_2		
$\sim$A	C_1		
	C_2		

If the researcher controlled by inclusion and if he had ratio measures of C_1, C_2, the table would have as many horizontal partitions as values for C_1, C_2. At one extreme, both could be held constant at the zero value and excluded from the design proper so that the table would have one horizontal partition separating A from $\sim A$. At the other extreme, both could vary freely and assume any or all values on the ratio scale; they would then be one partition for each particular value. Interaction effects occur when the values of C_1, C_2 are above the zero level and therefore two or more horizontal partitions are involved. Interaction is formally defined as the negation of additivity: assuming the cells to be filled with mean values, interaction is said to occur when the mean population difference between columns is not the same for each row, and, conversely, when the difference between rows is not the same for each column.[11] In other words, in at least one cell, the number is too large or too small to satisfy the additivity assumption. This means that one or more values of C_1 or C_2 makes a significant difference on the effect that A has on B.

The interaction fallacy in social science can now be stated more strictly. Experimenters and survey researchers are not only sensitized to interactions, they are taught that they are "bad." For one reason or another, interactions are said to decrease the inferential elegance and simplicity of a set of results, and therefore the researcher is cautioned against them in two senses. First, he is told to design the research to minimize their occurrence, which usually means to control for disruptive factors by specifying all relevant control conditions and then instituting control by constancy. Control by randomization is also emphasized in much the same vein. Second, he is told always to test for interactions and, when they occur, be forewarned that something is wrong with the research. It is usually said that the research must be redone and redesigned if interactions do occur. Simply, this most often involves an attempt to specify the "hidden" factors that are accounting for the interaction and to control for them in turn. In other words, the approximation to additivity is supposed to continue.

This approach to interaction is a fallacy in two senses. First, if the successive specification of conditions is synonymous with the search for knowledge, then interaction effects should be welcomed. Less grandiosely, control by inclusion is at the core of scientific method. If the control conditions were sufficiently identified, they would be by definition interval and ratio measures. If they are measured at this level, they could be systematically altered by scientists to assess how much of an effect they have on the antecedent's effect on the consequence. In those cases where interactions occurred, the scientist's knowledge would geometrically increase. To an extent, then, interactions should be one goal of inquiry, for when they occur, the scientist will be alerted to the fact of his increased power of prediction: if the interactions are in his favor, the error in his predictions will be decreased; if they are against his favor, the falsification of his hypotheses will come closer to being unequivocal. Without recognizing this importance of interactions, Blalock[12] notes that one possible way to cope with them is to attempt to predict their occurrence. Social scientists may be beginning the Hegelian swing back to science.

An addendum to this assertion of the importance of interactions makes this importance even more crucial for social scientists. The ultimate utility of the cycles of inquiry is in the solving of problems and answering of questions. Social scientists in increasing numbers are turning to the solution of social problems. Accordingly, their inquiries and research will have utility to the extent that these problems are solved. It is doubtful whether the problems can be solved without a consideration of interactions. The elimination or, more modestly, the management of crime, for example, will only be achievable by altering many causative factors: these inclde poverty, family background, educational level, mass media influence, influence of peers, deterioration of housing, inadequate rehabilitative facilities, and uncoordinated and inadequate criminal justice systems. This goal of problem-solving implies the search for interactions. Thus, the solution of social problems as an objective of increasing numbers of social scientists may be possible only by dealing with interactions.

The second sense in which the interaction fallacy is a fallacy is closely related to the preceding addendum. The experimental method has really been misconstrued by social scientists; it is much too strictly interpreted. Interactions may not be avoidable or deletable in the real world of science. This point differs from the statement that interactions may be desirable; it is now being asserted that they may be unavoidable. I do not wish to belabor the point because it can degenerate into the argument that social science cannot avoid interactions because of this complexity and lability. Nagel,[13] for example, argues along these lines in recommending "controlled investigation" rather than experimental methodology for social science. "Controlled investigation" is less stringent than experimentation because it utilizes interactions in much the same way as recommended here—although this is my interpretation of Nagel's comments. I have rejected the justification of social-scientific weakness on the grounds that its events are somehow different from other scientific events. I do not wish to resurrect in different form this buried corpse. Suffice it to say, interactions are not "bad things"; they are desirable and perhaps unavoidable in any science.

THE REIFICATION OF METATHEORY IN SOCIAL SCIENCE

Practically every weakness in social science noted so far has its metatheoretist-apologist. In this concluding section of the chapter, I want to examine several metatheoretical approaches to specific research problems and their interrelation to some of these problems. Basically, they will be shown to maintain the problems. This section makes no pretense at exhaustiveness, but it should be instructive.

The Maintenance of Identification-Slighting: Validity

Validity is usually defined as the ability of a measure to measure what it is supposed to measure. The question of validity of measures can be interpreted as a subset of the question of adequate definition. It has been mentioned that definition formation and use in science has been misconstrued in social science. Definition has come to be used as a substitute for identification. Dumont and Wilson's reification[14] of Hempel's concepts[15] of "meaning and empirical analysis" as components of the process of explication or redefinition is the prime example of reductio ad absurdum in this substitution process. Explication as definition or redefinition in this case is analyzed as a process whereby sociologists particularly can subject their hypotheses to precization to the point of adequate testability. As has been said, this analysis completely violates the notion of definition as the codification of well-confirmed identifications, which is how definition is utilized in science. Validity as conceived in research methodology is a subset of this misuse of definition in the sense that it is assumed to be a process whereby identities are bound to appropriate measurements. Operational definition is the subset of definition that is most relevant in questions of validity. The same fallacy of substitutability is implied, as is demonstrable with all types of validity.

Phillips[15] synoptically presents the most exhaustive list of types of validity I have ever seen:

Content validity$_{dt}$	= "the adequacy with which a domain of content is sampled" and represented by a series of test questions.
Face validity$_{dt}$	= the judgment that a measure is valid; no test implied.
Pragmatic validity$_{dt}$	= concurrent and predictive validity.
Concurrent validity$_{dt}$	= "the extent to which a measure distinguishes individuals who differ in their present status on some measure of interest to the investigation."
Predictive validity$_{dt}$	= "the adequacy of a measure in distinguishing persons who will

	differ with respect to some future criteria."
Construct validity$_{af}$	= the extent to which a measure of a variable "yields predictive and explanatory control over the phenomena under study."
Convergent validity$_{af}$	= "whether responses on a measure do or do not relate to some other variable or variables that one would, on a priori or theoretical grounds, expect it to relate to."
Discriminant validity$_{af}$	= "the ability of an instrument to distinguish one variable measured from another": e.g., can it be shown that a set of questions discriminates between subjects who respond truly and those who respond in a biased fashion?

To this list can be added two more types of validity taken from Campbell and Stanley:[17]

External validity$_{af}$	= "generalizability: to what populations, settings, treatment variables, and measurement variables can this effect (the experimental effect) be generalized?"
Internal validity$_{af}$	= "the basic minimum without which any experiment is uninterpretable: Did in fact the experimental treatments make a difference in this specific experimental instance?" Or, do the results show that the antecedent and consequence are related?

A formidable list indeed! And a prime example of the proliferation of expressions that reification leads to. Every one of these validity types is interpretable in terms of one or the other principles of research that have been presented. In spite of the special terms, the principles are primary. Questions of validity are not separable from the process of inquiry: validity is not a subdomain of research methodology, it is part of the process. If the demands of science are met, questions of validity cannot be substituted for inadequacies in the process.

Validity should be immediately suspect as a metatheoretical approach to social science problems because it deals almost exclusively with R-implicit and R-explicit indicators. That is, questions of validity usually arise with the use of these data types. It is as if weakness of the data is supposed to be compensated for by considerations of validity. This is most true of content, face, concurrent, predictive, convergent and discriminant validity and least true of construct, external, and internal validity. With O nonindicators, on the other hand, questions of validity never arise in the literature.

Content validity as defined is a subset of external validity. Both are reducible to principles of scientific inquiry as presented in the first section of this book. Both types of validity have to do with the relationship between samples and populations: i.e., are the samples representative? Content validity is more specific in that the sample is a series of test questions and the population is the entire range of questions that can be asked about a specific content area. The general relationship reduces to the following hypothesis: "if population A with an interval or ratio measure and a particular set of events matching every unit-value of the measure, then sample B with a subset of events isomorphic at every unit-value of the same measure."[18] Whether or not any sample is content or externally valid reduces to the falsifiability or nonfalsifiability of this hypothesis. The sample and population must be fully identified by the measure. In other words, this type of validity is actually a question of the sufficient identification of a population and sample such that the sample is isomorphic with the population, but contains fewer events. Thus, the identification has an identity which is numerically defined, while the identifying expression is a particular interval or ratio measure. The hypothesis asserts the isomorphy between the [population] and the [sample]. Importantly, both the sample and population must be sufficiently identified for the hypothesis to be testable. If, with repeated testing, the hypothesis is repetitively falsified, then the conclusion is that sample B is not representative of population A.

Given the specificity of content validity, an example is easy to derive. If a series of test items are supposed to represent the content of an academic course, the content of that course must be measurable on some dimension with interval or ratio scales. The dimension that comes immediately to mind is level of difficulty of the course material. It is moot here that it is difficult to develop such a measure. Selecting a *representative* sample would involve developing or borrowing at least one question for each unit-value on the dimension. Importantly, the content of the course must be known and scaled, i.e., fully identified. The prediction of representativeness must be repetitively tested and nonfalsified for each unit-value on the measure for the test to be said to be "content valid."

Generally, all questions of external validity reduce to testing hypotheses of this form. However, some subsets of these questions are more easily answerable because the researcher can rely on probability sampling. To utilize the borrowed theory of probability, the events to be chosen must be individuals or be conceptualizable as properties of individuals. On the other hand, other subsets of questions of external validity cannot be answered because this hypothesis cannot be tested. Generally, it cannot be tested when the population is not sufficiently identifiable. Most significantly, this will be the case when the population is a set of theoretical constructs or laws. In other words, whether certain constructs or laws (I am purposefully switching to more familiar terminology) are representative of a hypothetical set of constructs or laws can never be known because the hypothetical set (population) can never be identified.

The argument that experimental methodology necessarily suffers from a lack of external validity is a familiar and important variation of this fallacy. Because experiments take place in an artificial social setting, it is often asserted that it is correspondingly difficult to generalize any confirmed hypotheses to naturalistic social settings, i.e., that the hypotheses will not be externally valid. This assertion entails a paradox. The purpose of experiments *qua* research methodology is to establish and confirm hypotheses. Unless one assumes the existence of a population of discoverable hypotheses, experiments are in this sense one technique for establishing this population. Thus, the contention that experimental hypotheses may not be externally valid is tantamount to saying that they are not generalizable to themselves as one subset of discovered social scientific hypotheses.

Such logical maneuvers are unnecessary to dispute the argument. The argument against the external validity of experimental hypotheses presupposes an identified population of hypotheses that simply does not exist. I think this is what Sidman[19] is driving at when he says that the external validity of a hypothesis reduces to a question of its utility, and its utility reduces to its replicability and confirmability.

However, there are two important senses in which this argument does have merit. First, given the insufficient identification process in most social science experiments, the operational definitions that pass for identifications are indeed imprecise and open to alternative interpretations: e.g., it is indeed questionable whether [simultaneous button-pushing] is equivalent to [human cooperation]. It follows that hypotheses in which these identities are embedded can be interpreted in quite divergent ways and have no necessary logical relationship. Second, and more technically, there can be a definite discrepancy between the components of an experiment as communication sequence and the communication sequence to which it is supposed to be relevant. For example, there tends to be a definite schism between time as a component of the experiment and time as a social event: e.g., latency of response is a frequently used identification in experiments which really has no great social relevance.

Face and construct validity are also reducible within the

context of the general analysis of research and methodology. The assessment of face validity does not employ any empirical criteria for determining it. The judgment that a measure is valid is therefore predicated on logical or semantic criteria. In other words, the process for certifying face validity approximates precization. A measure will be said to have face validity when the identification in which it is embedded approximates maximum precision or unequivocal interpretability.

Construct validity is a little more complicated. The simplest reinterpretation is that a measure is said to have construct validity when the identification in which it is embedded is used in a testable and well-confirmed hypothesis. However, if this interpretation is used, construct validity and predictive validity are synonymous. This overlap is avoided with a more complicated interpretation that is congruent with a segment of this analysis that has not been greatly emphasized, i.e., the possible logical relationships between hypotheses. The interpretation hinges on the expression [explanatory control] in the definiens of [construct validity]. [Explanation] is usually defined as the deductive relationship between theoretical expressions whereby one expression is said to explain another if the latter can be deduced from the former. It follows that a variable and its measure or, in our terms, an identification will have construct validity to the extent that it is used in deductive relationships that terminate with well-confirmed hypotheses. For example, consider the deductive relationship involving the categorical syllogism:

$$A \supset B$$
$$B \supset C$$
$$A \supset C$$

where A, B, and C are identifications. Any of the identifications, A, B, or C, can be said to have construct validity. However, traditional usage is such that the significance of saying an identification has construct validity lies in the fact that that identification is not or need not be confirmed, but can still be said to be valid. In the given categorical syllogism, the B

identification need not be confirmed for the $A \supset C$ to be a testable hypothesis. Only the A and C need to be tested and adequately confirmed. B would be said to have construct validity; the significance of this statement is that B need not be tested for the deductive relationship to hold.

Concurrent, predictive, convergent, and discriminant validity are reinterpretable in much the same fashion. They all refer to the test of hypotheses as conceived in this analysis. The hypothesis corresponding to the type of validity will be placed next to it in what follows:

Concurrent: [[if [measure A with unit-value A_n] for individual [Y], then [measure A with unit-value A_{n+1}] for individual [Z]]].

Predictive: [[if [measure A with unit-value A_n] for individual [Y], at [T_n], then [measure A with unit-value A_{n+1}] for individual [Z] at [T_{n+1}]]].

Convergent: [[if [identification A] then [identification B]]].

Discriminant: [[if [identification A] then not [identification B]]].

These hypotheses are to be understood as the hypotheses that must be confirmed before a measure can be said to have one or another type of validity. Their confirmation, of course, is determined by repetitive testing. Notice that the only difference between concurrent and predictive validity is the temporal component. The difference between convergent and discriminant validity is more categorical. An identification will be said to have convergent validity to the extent that the criterial hypothesis relating it to another identification is derived extraneous to the cycle necessary to test it, i.e., to the extent that it is "based on a priori or theoretical grounds". On the other hand, an identification will be said to have discriminant validity to the extent that the criterial hypothetical relationship is one of difference: i.e., "the ability of an instrument to distinguish one variable measured from another."

These are several possible interpretations of a "difference relationship." The simplest is that two identifications are in fact different. Of itself this is trivial, but it is not trivial if the identifications were considered to be identical prior to the statement of the difference hypothesis, i.e., if at T_1, identification [A] was thought to be identification [B], then the assertion at T_2 that this is not the case has added significance. To give a specific example, suppose a questionnaire were being used by social scientists to "measure" subject [depression]. Further, suppose it were discovered that some depressed subjects responded consistently on the questionnaire in a socially desirable fashion so that they "registered" as not depressed. The dilemma is clear: some subjects may be depressed but are measured as not depressed because of a social desirability response set. It is indeed significant if the questionnaire can be redesigned to discriminate true responders from biased responders. This relationship is essentially that expressed by the criterial hypothesis: if subjects respond in such a way as to have unit-value X on lie scale A, then they are not [not depressed]. If this hypothesis were not falsified, then the questionnaire would be said to have discriminant validity.

The reinterpretation of internal validity is not as simple as with the given set, because internal validity has to do specifically with the interrelationships between alternative hypotheses. Campbell and Stanley broadly view the question of internal validity as a question of the number of permissible alternative interpretations of a main hypothesis, assuming the nonfalsification of that hypothesis.[20] The permissible alternative interpretations will have the same consequence but different antecedents. They list eight possible antecedents, including "'history,' the specific events occurring between the first and second measurement in addition to the experimental variable"; "'maturation,' processes within the respondents operating as a function of the passage of time per se (not specific to the particular events), including growing older, growing hungrier, growing more tired, and the like"; and "'testing,' the effects of taking a test upon the scores of a second testing." These factors severally or in concert may account for the nonfalsification of the hypothesis: i.e., as the test of the main hypothesis may actually be a test of one of these alternative hypotheses, even if the hypothesis is not falsified, the researcher cannot be sure whether this result is due to the hypothesis or to one of the alternatives.

Internal validity is slightly more complicated than in this analysis. Campbell and Stanley say that they are dealing with "classes of extraneous variables." Congruent with the terminology herein, this statement means they are concerned with contributing factors expressed as control conditions rather than antecedents. However, these conditions are substitutable for the antecedent. Rather than positing that the control conditions are supplemental to the antecedent as would normally be the case, Campbell and Stanley assert that these control conditions may become antecedents in alternative or, in their terms, "rival" hypotheses. A more important qualification is that these alternative hypotheses are formulatable on the basis of the nonfalsification of the main hypothesis. This, of course, assumes a test of the hypotheses. The results of the test may be interpreted as confirmatory of a rival hypothesis if the main hypothesis is lacking in internal validity.

A subtle distinction is apparent with respect to the logic of proof as embodied in the notion of internal validity as opposed to that presented earlier. The sequence of events implied by Campbell and Stanley involves presentation of the hypothesis, the test of the hypothesis, the nonfalsification of the hypothesis, and the possible "eruption" of rival hypotheses to account for the nonfalsification in the sense that the confirmation can be said to be of the rival hypotheses and not the initial main hypothesis. They propose maximizing internal validity (or, conversely, minimizing the number of plausible rival hypotheses) by design considerations. That is, internal validity can be maximized by using certain numbers of control groups and sequences of tests. I shall return to this shortly. This general sequence contrasts with the sequence proposed here as part of the logic of proof: i.e., a hypothesis is presented for test; it is tested; the hypothesis is falsified or not falsified; if it is falsified and if it is not maximally precise, then there will be as many interpretations of the falsification as there are interpretations of the initial hypothesis. The ultimate objective then is to approximate unequivocal falsification. This is accomplished via the adequacy of identification and the hypothesis cycle with all that it entails.

Campbell and Stanley's version of the logic of proof reinforces several of the weaknesses of social science by misrepresenting what science is about. In science, the idea of alternative interpretations of a nonfalsified hypothesis is an absurdity. The direction of science is the falsification of hypotheses or, more correctly, the maximization of the unequivocal falsification of hypotheses. All necessary precautions and actions are taken to achieve this end, using the components of the identification and hypothesis cycles. The end result is that when a hypothesis is falsified, *it is falsified*: i.e., the negation of the hypothesis is tautological. Because of the necessary precautions and activities, when the hypothesis is not falsified, it will be maximally precise anyway: there will be a minimum of alternative interpretations. Hence, science proceeds in the opposite direction from Campbell and Stanley's model. What is a consequence of good science—i.e., unequivocal nonfalsifiability of hypotheses—is given antecedent status.

Their reversal of the logic of proof has three deleterious consequences for social science. First, emphasis is placed on nonfalsification rather than falsification. One of the most glaring deficiencies of social science is the failure to falsify hypotheses. If Campbell and Stanley cannot be blamed for this, they can be blamed for not providing a metatheory to correct it. Second, social scientists trained under their tutelage (most social scientists have been exposed to their logic) have the mistaken impression that there is a limited set of extraneous variables that, once controlled for, will satisfy the requirements of internal validity. There is no such limited set despite the specification of C_8 by these authors. In fact, the list has boundaries contingent on theoretical and empirical exigencies, which means the list will be potentially infinite. The specification of an artificially limited list, in turn, imposes an artificial limited conception of research design on the social scientist. The process of inquiry must proceed on the basis of creativity in the sense that research designs are constructed according to inquiry and not vice versa.

The second point merges with the third to be mentioned, which is more specific and technical. Campbell and Stanley's conception of research design is a static one. Control groups are juxtaposed in certain configurations and measurements and scientist actions are serially ordered in differing ways, producing sixteen suggested research designs. Not only does this conception impose premature metatheoretical closure on the social scientist, but more importantly, it disguises the overwhelming importance of replication and reproduction in the logic of proof. In the most complicated design there are twelve repetitions of the measure of the hypothetical anteced- ent.[21] The word "measure" with respect to the antecedent should be interpreted with caution because for Campbell and Stanley the antecedent can include any planned change of events by social scientists. Their upper limit on replications is twelve, according to the rule that each measurement of the consequence equals one replication. A measurement of the consequence without the antecedent can be interpreted as a test of the converse of the hypothesis, i.e., the measurement should record as "$\sim B$" when associated with no antecedent, "$\sim A$," according to the hypothetical pair, $[[\text{if } [A] \text{ then } [B]]]$ and $[[\text{if } [\sim A] \text{ then } [\sim B]]]$. Their conception of research design is static in the sense that it imposes a limitation on repli- cation or reproduction. Twelve repetitions is not the limit; there is no limit that can be statically predefined.[22] Replica- tion or reproduction are necessary principles to the process of inquiry. They should be emphasized as such. The crucial shortcoming of social science in the failure of replication or reproduction cannot but be reinforced by Campbell and Stan- ley's artificial limits, given their static conception of research design.

MEASUREMENT THEORY IN
SOCIAL SCIENCE

Several types of metatheoretical inquiry can be classified as measurement theory in social science. Closest to considerations of validity in the sense of being conceptualized as subsets of the general problem are Lazarsfeld's latent structure analysis,[23] Coombs' theory of scaling,[24] and the analysis of multiple measures. The latter is represented in the work of Webb, *et al.*,[25] and more formally in that of Costner[26] and Blalock.[27] There might be some reservation in classifying this body of work as measurement theory. "True" measurement theory can be taken as referring to studies that deal with the development and use of different measurement scales and procedures. Representative of this domain is the work of S. S. Stevens and associates,[28] the work on "conjoint measurement" and "functional measurement" in psychology,[29] and Hamblin's attempts to introduce ratio scales into sociology.[30] In this section I will consider measurement theory within the broader interpretation, including latent structure analysis and the like as well as true measurement theory. There is good analytic reason for lumping these divergent areas of metatheoretical inquiry into one section. Despite their divergence, they contribute to social-scientific inadequacy in much the same way.

Both Coombs and Lazarsfeld, from differing perspectives, are concerned with the problem of identification in social science. Their techniques specifically have to do with this problem as it applies to indicators or identities whose identifiers are indentifications. For both of them the identity exists separately from its identifier and is legitimate in and of itself. In large part their metatheories are concerned with matching identifying identifications with their identities. Generally, in order to do this, they must assume certain things about the identity, specify certain things about the identifying identification, and use mathematical operations to map the latter onto the former. Specifically, the identification-identifier is empirically accessible: it is constructed according to whatever empirical contingencies hold for the data in question. On the other hand, the identity is latent (Lazarsfeld's term) or not empirically accessible. It is taken to exist, but its parameters and mathematical properties are assumed. In other words, given that it exists separately from its identifier, it is assumed to have an independent identification that is implicit. This implicit identification is constructed on the basis of assumed mathematical properties. The bulk of the metatheory involves the matching of the implicit and explicit identification, by calculating how well the explicit identification satisfies the mathematical properties of the implicit identification on the basis of the mathematical operations that would apply to the explicit identification if it had the mathematical properties of the implicit identification. If the operations can be performed successfully, then it is inferred that the explicit identification is an adequate indicator of the implicit identification.

This mathematical and logical approach to the problem of identification and indicators is also reflected with different emphasis in the inquiry into conjoint and functional measurement in psychology. Again, although the specifics differ, the rationale is the same. First, a composition rule (Krantz and Tversky)[31] or law of science (Anderson)[32] must be known. Essentially these are synonymous with equations that express relationships between identifications whose identities are measurement dimensions. Thus Krantz and Tversky[33] give the example of Hull's equation: $R = H (D + K)$, where R is [response strength], H is [habit strength], D is [drive], and K is [incentive]. These laws or composition rules are analogous to the most advanced laws of science. Second, certain mathematical relationships are specified that are implied by the law and by the level of scale desired. Krantz and Tversky, for example, ask the question: "What are the ordinal conditions that data must satisfy in order to be compatible with the composition rules . . . ?" Third, the data are analyzed to see if they satisfy these mathematical relationships: scales are constructed on the basis of the data and rejected or not rejected depending on their not satisfying or satisfying the requisite mathematical relationships.

Essentially the purpose of the "measurement theory" is the same as the inquiry into the status of indicators. In this case, the "law" is treated as an indicator. The identity is the equation, the identifier is the scale constructed using the data, and the relationship between the two consists of certain mathematical conditions and operations that must be satisfied by the identifier before it can be mapped onto the identity. This is no didactic analogy. It expresses the fundamental similarity between the diverse subdomains of measurement theory. The task is viewed as measuring something, which in turn is conceptualized as a problem of linking unmeasured, not empirically accessible identities with measured, empirically accessible identifications, usually via advanced mathematics.

The logico-mathematical metatheory of multiple measures parallels these other approaches in intent but adds a new solution. The intent is clearly stated: unmeasured, unempirically accessible identities are to be sufficiently identified by being matched with sufficient identifications. In other words, the unmeasured but measurable is to be measured via association with an adequate identification, a problem of the adequacy of indicators. The element that differs here is that little emphasis is placed on mathematical relationships between the identity and identifier, while maximum emphasis is placed on the relationship between identifiers. The multiple measures provide the inferential base for asserting that the indicator is adequate: if certain relationships hold between the measures, then it is asserted that the empirically inaccessible and unmeasured identity is sufficiently identified. This formal approach to multiple measures has its empiricial counterpart in the previously discussed concept of multiple operationism of Webb *et al.* The basic logic is the same.

Measurement theory, whatever its manifestations, owes much to the pioneering work of S. S. Stevens. This work has a logico-mathematical and an empirical component. With respect to the former, he has specified the different scale types as defined according to mathematical criteria. With respect to the latter, his experiments in psychophysics have resulted in the development of one of the few ratio scales in social science and one of the few laws in the form of the equivalence relationship between measurement dimensions.

His work has been influential beyond the area of psychophysics. Hamblin sees measurement procedures as the key to developing true ratio scales in sociology. According to Hamblin, this could be done via "cross-modality matching." In cross-modality matching, subjects are trained to approximate a ratio scale in their reported perceptions on a given stimulus dimension. They are then asked to map a different dimension onto this constructed ratio scale, thereby measuring this different dimension with a ratio scale. Hamblin forsees this technique as having great utility in sociology: e.g., in one study he cites, a ratio scale of differential "utility" values is constructed on the basis of this technique.

Importantly, in one respect the empirical aspect of Steven's work and of Hamblin's research as an extension of it is an analog of the logico-mathematical approach to measurement theory. In both the unmeasured is being measured. In other words, this empirical manifestation of measurement theory is concerned with the formation of indicators—albeit the empirically based formation of them. Steven's psychophysical law evidences this. His law purportedly provides the transformation of [sensation] into measurements with dimensions that are the differing stimuli continua (acoustic, visual, etc.) and with ratio scales. The law may appear to be analogous to the laws of science relating measurement dimensions as identities, but it is markedly different, because it is an indicator in equation form. [[Sensation]] is a metaidentity that is purportedly being identified by an identification. As an indicator, this "law" is problematic because [[sensation]] is unempirically accessible and unmeasured but still has an implicit independent identification. That is, this "law" as an indicator suffers the problems of indicators. Savage[34] repeatedly and exhaustively criticizes Steven's empirical and logico-mathematical work on the basis of this confusion of law and indicator, although in different terms. His essential point is the same: sensation is not being measured because sensation is not measurable; it is an expression, not an event.

It is in the underlying theme of the legitimacy of indicators that measurement theory is faulty. Essentially, the difficulty is the same as that encountered with definition and validity: the essence of science is being violated and logical considerations and techniques are being mistaken for fact. Indicators have no legitimate status in science. The demands of identification are ubiquitous. Equivalence between spatiotemporarally referenced identities and their measures is the goal of the identification cycle; in no specific science has this process been terminated at the level of indicators.

Identities are never twice-removed from their measures in science as they are with indicators. The reason is that indicators are too flexible as components of the communication sequence. The metaidentity can be identified with alternative identifications because it is conceived of as separable from its identifier. In this sense, it is interpreted as a set that can have alternative members. As a set, it cannot be a member of itself; therefore the metaidentity has a quality of primacy above and beyond its identifiers. Sequentially, the researcher is forced to commit the fallacy of working from the top down, as mentioned previously with respect to the concept of definition and specifically operational definition. He has a metaidentity and tries to identify it. This, of course, is in violation of the identification process in science whereby identities and identifiers (measurement expressions plus any necessary action object expressions) are formed as a gestalt. The identity may be separable linguistically from its identifier, but in no other sense is it separable. Furthermore, the equivalence of the identity and the identifier and the gestalt of the identification gives such separability the status of convention or notational convenience: the essential bind is understood or implicit. On the other hand, the metaidentity because of its primacy is interpreted as empirically separable from its identifier. It is as if a range of potential identifiers that need to be discovered was bound to it. Unfortunately, because these are potential, there are no limits to this range, and researchers fish around for identifiers and tag them onto metaidentities. Therefore, indicators are too flexible as components of the communication process because the researcher's actions are equivocal. The constraints of the identification process are missing.

This pervasive difficulty is manifested by the misconception of measurement in measurement theory. Measurement is divorced from its theoretical significance. "Measurement for what?" is the question that is never properly answered or is never even addressed. Anderson[35] provides an answer that is representative: "Paper theories of measurement can be constructed without end, but one should expect a real measurement theory to really measure something." It is indeed true that "paper theories can be constructed without end," and one reason they have been is the inherent freedom that the indicator bias assures. But the objective of "really measuring something" is not much of a restraint. Measurement exists in science to identify and to relate identifications. It is the cornerstone of science because it provides an invariant communicative base that permits the formation and transmission of the expression of relationships, which is the essence of scientific information. The significance of any measurement is not in its relation with that which it is supposed to measure, but in the relation of it *qua* identification component with other measures *qua* identification component. Simply, no measure has significance apart from its contextual relation with other communicative elements of the scientific cycles of inquiry. In either cycle, this relation permits scientists to do and say certain things. The fallacy of isolating measurement is analogous to the previously cited fallacy of considering definitions in isolation from the theoretical expressions and context in which they are embedded.

Each instance of measurement theory can be faulted according to the commission of this fallacy. The highly mathematical measurement theories Lazarsfeld and Coombs have developed occupy their own theoretical subdomain and generate no substantive hypotheses. Further, as they are little used in practical application by the social researcher, they are not even operative as catalysts to the generation of substantive hypotheses. Conjoint and functional measurement are relatively new developments in psychology, but much the same statements can be made about them. They generate no substantive hypotheses, nor do they have such practical applicability that these hypotheses can be generated. Krantz and Tversky, in fact, make the explicit statement that they are not interested in functional relations between variables, which is equivalent to the denial of the objective of the development of hypotheses and identifications. It might well be asked what their highly mathematicized theory is good for, if it is not good for facilitating social-scientific inquiry. Interestingly, even within the context of their isolation they espouse a limited objective by concentrating on the evaluation of how well data accommodates ordinal scaling, the weakest form of measurement, assuming nominal scales not to be an instance of measurement. Of what utility can such a metatheory of measurement be, given its restricted isolation?

The domain of multiple measures has a partial corrective for this overly narrow scope in its emphasis on the relations among the multiple measures. These relations can be phrased as hypotheses, and in a sense those social scientists concerned with multiple measures are very much concerned with hypothesis formation. For example, if the compound identification is [[[A] is [X]; [Y]]], where X *and* Y are independent measures of A, then [X] should be related to [Y], and this relation can be expressed as a hypothesis: [[if [X] then [Y]]]. It is understood of course that the hypothesis expresses the expected relation between the measures, nothing more or less. If A = prejudice, X = a semantic differential to measure prejudice, and Y = the Bogardus social distance scale, then X and Y should correlate positively according to degree of prejudice. So multiple measures cannot totally be faulted according to the standard of theoretical significance because they do generate hypotheses. On the other hand, the hypotheses tend to suffer isolation in two senses. First, in the domain of metatheory they go untested: multiple-measurement metatheorists and advocates do not test the derivative hypotheses that they propose. Blalock and Costner never descend from the logico-mathematical plane; and Webb, *et al.* offer suggestive, impressionistic evidence at best. Second, the class of hypotheses is so restricted in content and scope that it cannot function as the derivative base of theoretically significant social science hypotheses. This point may be more understandable if phrased differently: this class of hypotheses has to do with a subject matter that is unbounded by the demands of scientific inquiry, which makes its hypothesized relations trivial. Perhaps the most glaring manifestation of the unbounded nature of multiple-measure theory is the presumed legitimacy of identities specified by multiple equivalent independent measures. Such compound identifications are problematic and unpermissible in science because of their imprecision and the consequences of their imprecision. The hypotheses stating relations between multiple measures represent an attempt to confer legitimacy upon this type of illegitimate compound identification, and hence their triviality. In effect, the social scientist can posit multiple measures and test hypothetical relations between them ad infinitum.

Finally, Steven's psychophysical experiments and mathematical theory of measurement are also divorced from theoretical significance. First, and most obvious, is his unequivocal acceptance of the legitimacy of nominal and ordinal scales. Had he considered measurement relative to its scientific utility, he would have recognized that these scales are mathematical entities that have no or limited scientific significance: i.e., nominal scales are more correctly interpreted as identities and not as measures and as such must be and are identified by interval and ratio scales, and ordinal scales are usable under very special empirical contingencies. Second, Steven's psychophysical experiments have had tremendous success, but it is disputable what this success consists of. He has demonstrated that subjects can be trained to scale certain classes of physical stimuli on ratio scales. He has not demonstrated that these ratio scales have any application whatever in specifying relations between different classes of human behavior at the physiological, individual, or social levels of analysis. Thus, his empirical studies have led to a psychophysical theory of measurement of the narrowest sort. It is no accident that Hamblin's attempted extrapolation of Steven's work to sociological inquiry offers synoptic examples of terribly restricted scope. This is not poor scholarship; it is a meta-example of the limited utility of such a metatheory of measurement because of the inherent narrow conceptualization of measurement.

The misconception of measurement and science in these so-called measurement theories has deleterious consequences for social science. Important weaknesses are reinforced rather than ameliorated. The identification cycle is completely bypassed, and the indicator bias supplants it. Even more important are the consequences entailed for the logic of proof. Falsification is de-emphasized. Neither Lazarsfeld nor Coombs makes provision for falsification. The theory of multiple measures entails falsifiable hypothetical relations, but the compound identification cannot be falsified via these potential falsifications. With conjoint and functional measurement, data can be rejected as not fitting the mathematical properties of particular scales, but the data cannot be falsified and neither can the scales. Both data and scales would be falsifiable if embedded in hypotheses relating them as compound identifications to scientist action in an analogous fashion to what was done with social science data types in this chapter and measurement scales in Chapters 2 and 3. Finally, Steven's logico-mathematical metatheory is not empirically falsifiable because it is based on mathematical axioms. Also, there is good reason to question whether his psychophysical law is falsifiable in the sense that a person can be said to have no sensations or no sensations of a particular type. Hamblin's extrapolation of Steven's technique of cross-modality matching would be non-falsifiable in the same sense. Derived ratio scales will not be falsifiable of themselves: subjects may be said to be incapable of being trained to scale certain nonphysical stimuli according to ratio-scaled physical stimuli, but the ratio scales are nonfalsifiable. Further the derived ratio scales will have nonfalsifiable utility because they are not juxtaposed with scientists action; conversely, "what can they be used for?" is unanswerable.

The quality of nonfalsifiability of these aspects of measurement theory derives from the nonfalsifiability inherent in the indicator bias to which all of them are subject. As long as the task is defined as matching identifications with metaidentities and as long as there are no constraints on this task, every metaidentity will be taken to be the source of an unbounded range of identifications. Because every falsification will be equivocal it will not be strictly a falsification of the metaidentity. The identifying identifications can be falsified, but their falsification is not sufficient to falsify the metaidentity. In the event of falsification of the identification, the identification will be said to be inapplicable to the metaidentity, but the indicator still pertains. The search for alternative identifying identifications and their successive rejection or acceptance continues. The metaidentity has legitimacy beyond its assumed range of identifiers; if some are falsified, others will be found that will not be falsified. So this faulty process of inquiry continues unabated by the constraints of falsification. It is in this sense that latent strcture analysis must yield indicators, that Coombs' theory of scaling must produce scaled data, that multiple measures can be "discovered" for social science variables, that Steven's work can unfailingly result in subjects trained to produce ratio scales, and that these constructed ratio scales can be extrapolated to sociology by training subjects to match them to other prefabricated stimulus dimensions.

CONCLUSION 1: MATHEMATICS IN SOCIAL SCIENCE

The misuse of mathematics in social science is well known.[36] Rather than reproduce old arguments, in this section I want to bring a previous critique of social science mathematics presented elsewhere into conformity with the present analysis. There were two components in my previous critique. First, the heavy reliance of social scientists (with emphasis on sociologists) on inductive statistics has led to a de-emphasis of replication (and reproduction). Second, mathematical model builders have reified their symbols without due consideration for the designative relation between these symbols and the events in the social science domain: the symbols have become inadequate substitutes for problematic identifications and metaexpressions. Both of these criticisms are reducible to elements of the present analysis.

Mathematics is a full-blown theory that is borrowed by science for various reasons that generally have to do with the facilitation of inquiry. As a theory, the component expressions of mathematics satisfy the demands of precision. Thus, when sciences borrow mathematical theory, they are borrowing precision. However, this precision is never a substitute for theoretical precision but is a complementary technique permitting and facilitating the increased precision of science as communication. When inductive statistics are used in science (except social science), they are used after the expressions of that science have satisfied the demands of rigorous test and proof. This means that replication and reproduction of identifications and hypotheses have preceded the reliance on inductive statistics. In this sense, inductive statistics function to increase the power of inference from each additional replication or reproduction. In social science, inductive statistics are used in lieu of replication or reproduction. They are used prematurely and thereby supplant the logic of proof as predicated on reproduction or replication. Simply, in social science inductive statistics perpetuate a crucial weakness because of premature use.

The same can be said of mathematical model-building. The symbols of mathematics are precise: in fact, they are maximally precise because the boundary of mathematics is tautology. In social-scientific mathematical model-building the symbols are substituted for identifications that are not well confirmed. The precision of the symbols is substituted for the precision of the identifications. The precision of the mathematical relationships between symbols is substituted for the precision of the hypothetical relationships between identifications. The mathematics is used prematurely because the precision is borrowed and not derivative of the process of inquiry. In effect, the mathematics is used to superimpose maximal precision by having its symbols and equations substitute for identifications and hypothetical relationships. Thus, to say $X =$ "people do something" is to convey illegitimate precision on a vague expression.[37]

CONCLUSION 2: AN APOLOGIA FOR NO CONCLUSION

Any critique can be damned for being inadequate if it does not provide constructive alternatives. Optimally, I would conclude this book with a chapter outlining a redesign of social science *qua* science. I will not do so for two reasons. First, the model of science presented in Section I has clear implications for the conduct of social research. Burdensome redundancy would result from repeating these implications. Also, Section II has falsified certain trends in social science in such a way that what not to do or what to avoid is implied.

However, there is a second more important reason. Any solution of the problems of social science research is contingent on doing, and "it ain't been done yet." I have several leads and several principles that I follow in my own research. For example, an emphasis on ethological studies of human behavior via observation and experimentation (in the loosest sense) seems to be an appropriate path to take. Also, moving beyond the confines of academe and dealing with social problems expressed in precise questions seems to be one way of focusing the endeavor. And there are other more technical components to the hodge-podge. But there is no ultimate solution to be had at this time. To write as if there were would be deluding and transparent.

Therefore, I can conclude with little more than a reaffirmation of faith in the ultimate utility of social science in solving the problems of human existence. However, this is no trivial statement, for it is ultimately this faith that drives all social scientists on. I hope this book forwards the advance.

Endnotes

The citation in parentheses following "op. cit." tells where the reference is located in these endnotes. "Op. cit." with no parentheses following means that the reference is within the same chapter.

Introduction

1. KERLINGER, F. N., *Foundations of Behavioral Research*. New York: Holt, Rinehart and Winston, Inc., 1965.

    PHILLIPS, B. S., *Social Research, Strategy and Tactics*, second edition. New York: The Macmillan Company, 1971.

    SIMON, J. S., *Basic Research Methods in Social Science*. New York: Random House, 1969.

2. PITTINGER, R. E., HOCKETT, C. F., and DANEHY, J. J., *The First Five Minutes: A Sample of Microscopic Interview Analysis*. Ithaca, N.Y.: Martineau, 1960.

3. See PHILLIPS, D. L., *Knowledge from What?* Chicago: Rand McNally and Company, 1971, pp. 12–49, 50–98.

4. ROSENTHAL, R., *Experimenter Effects in Behavioral Research*. New York: Appleton-Century-Crofts, 1966.

5. FRIEDMAN, N., *The Social Nature of Psychological Research*. New York: Basic Books, 1967.

6. HEMPEL, C. G., *Foundations of Concept Formation in Empirical Science*. Chicago: University of Chicago Press, 1952.

    KAPLAN, A., *The Conduct of Inquiry*. San Francisco: Chandler, 1964.

    KEMENY, J. G., *A Philosopher Looks at Science*. New York: Van Nostrand, 1959.

KUHN, T. S., *The Structure of Scientific Revolution*. Chicago: University of Chicago Press, 1971.

NAGEL, E., *The Structure of Science*. New York: Harcourt Brace Jovanovich, 1961.

POPPER, K., *The Logic of Scientific Discovery*. New York: Basic Books, 1959.

7. POPPER, *op. cit.*

8. HEMPEL, *op. cit.*

9. DUMONT, R. G., and W. J. WILSON, "Aspects of concept formation, explication, and theory construction in sociology," *American Sociological Review*, 1967, **32**, 985–995.

10. KAPLAN, KEMENY, and NAGEL, *op. cit.*

11. SIDMAN, M., *Tactics of Scientific Research*. New York: Basic Books, 1960.

12. Given the diversity of work in the area of animal and human communication, it is perhaps a mistake to use a global expression like "communication theory." The following are some representative sources.

CHERRY, C., *On Human Communication*. Cambridge: M.I.T. Press, 1957.

DUNCAN, S., "Nonverbal communication," *Psychological Bulletin*, 1969, **72**, 118–137.

NAESS, A., *Interpretation and Preciseness: A Contribution to the Theory of Communication*. Oslo: Gondahl & Sons, 1953.

PARRY, J., *The Psychology of Human Communication*. New York: American Elsevier, 1968.

SEBEOK, T. A., Animal Communication. Bloomingdale: Indiana University Press, 1968.

WATZLAWICK, P., BEAVIN, J., and JACKSON, D. D., *Pragmatics of Human Communication*. New York: W. W. Norton & Co., 1967.

13. BATESON, G., JACKSON, D. D., HALEY, J., and WEAKLAND, J., "Toward a theory of schizophrenia," *Behavioral Scence*, 1956, **1**, 251–264.

WATZLAWICK *et al.*, *op. cit.*

14. SEBEOK, *op. cit.*

15. KUHN, *op. cit.*

16. WATSON, J. D., *The Double Helix*. New York: Atheneum, 1968.

17. SHAPERE, D., Review of Kuhn, *op. cit.*, *Science*, 1971, **172**, 706–709.

18. FRIEDRICHS, R. W., *A Sociology of Sociology.* New York: The Free Press, 1970.

19. GOULDNER, A. W., *The Coming Crisis of Western Sociology.* New York: Basic Books, 1970.

20. HENSHEL, R. L., "Sociology and prediction," *American Sociologist,* 1971, 6, 213–220.

21. For a nonsocial-scientific analysis of science based on many of the communication components of science, although not stated as such, see: JORAVAK, D., *The Lysenko Affair.* Cambridge, Mass.: Harvard University Press, 1970.

22. BLALOCK, H. M., *Causal Inferences in Nonexperimental Research.* Chapel Hill: University of North Carolina Press, 1964.

Chapter 1

1. KATZ, J. J., "Semi-sentences." In J. A. Fodor and J. J. Katz, eds., *The Structure of Language: Readings in the Philosophy of Language.* Englewood Cliffs, N.J.: Prentice-Hall, 1964.

2. DUNCAN, *op. cit.* (note 12, Intro.)

3. LACHENMEYER, C. W., "The language of literature: a conceptual reanalysis," *Linguistics,* 1969, 55, 32–47.

4. TARSKI, A., "The semantic conception of truth." In L. Linski, *Semantics and the Philosophy of Language.* Champagne-Urbana: University of Illinois Press, 1952.
    ———, *Introduction to Logic and to the Methodology of Deductive Sciences.* Oxford University Press, 1965.

5. NAGEL, *op. cit.* (note 6, Intro.)

6. TARSKI, *op. cit.*

7. CHASE, S., *The Tyranny of Words.* New York: Harcourt Brace Jovanovich, 1938.

8. [Power] *is* definable by use of disposition concepts in which the actions of certain actors are contingent on the actions of other actors; see:
    KADUSHIN, C., "Power, influence and social circles," *American Sociological Review,* 1968, 33, 685–699;
    LACHENMEYER, C., *The Language of Sociology.* New York: Columbia University Press, 1971.

9. a. CARNAP, R., "Testability and meaning." In N. Feigl and May Brodbeck, eds., *Readings in the Philosophy of Science.* New York: Appleton-Century-Crofts, 1953.
    b. ———, "The methodological character of theoretical con-

cepts." In H. Feigl and M. Scriven, eds., *Minnesota Studies in the Philosophy of Science*, vol. I. Minneapolis: University of Minnesota Press, 1956.

10. WITTGENSTEIN, L., *Philosophical Investigations*. New York: Macmillan, 1971.

11. *Ibid.*

12. HANSON, N. R., *Patterns of Discovery*. Cambridge: Cambridge University Press, 1958.

13. KUHN, *op. cit.* (note 6, Intro.)

14. POPPER, *op. cit.* (note 6, Intro.)

15. KAPLAN, *op. cit.* (note 6, Intro.)

16. KESSEL, F. S., "The philosophy of science as proclaimed and science as practiced: identity or dualism," *American Psychologist*, 1969, **24**, 999–1005.

    SKINNER, B. F., "Are theories of learning necessary?" *Psychological Review*, 1950, **57**, 193–216.

17. NAESS, A., *Communication and Argument—Elements of Applied Semantics*. London: Allen & Unwin, Ltd., 1966.

18. SCRIVEN, M. S., "Definitions, explanations and theories." In H. Feigl, M. Scriven, and G. Maxwell, eds., *Minnesota Studies in the Philosophy of Science*, vol. II. Minneapolis: University of Minnesota Press, 1958.

19. QUINE, W. V., *Mathematical Logic*. New York: Harper & Row, 1951.

20. TARSKI, *op. cit.*

21. WITTGENSTEIN, *op. cit.*

22. CHOMSKY, N., *Aspects of the Theory of Syntax*. Cambridge, Mass.: M.I.T. Press, 1965.

    LOUNSBURY, F. G., "Linguistics and psychology." In S. Koch, ed., *Psychology, A Study in Science*, vol. 6. New York: McGraw-Hill, 1963.

23. EPSTEIN, W., "Influence of syntactical structure on learning," *American Journal of Psychology*, 1961, **74**, 80–85.

24. NAESS, A., *op. cit.* (note 12, Intro.)

25. LACHENMEYER, *op. cit.* (note 8, Ch. 1)

26. POPPER, *op. cit.* (note 6, Intro.); TARSKI, *op. cit.*

27. a. ULLMAN, S., *Semantics, an Introduction to the Science of Meaning*. New York: Barnes & Noble, 1962.

    b. LACHENMEYER, C. W., "An experimental test of the double-bind phenomena." Unpublished Ph.D. dissertation, University of North Carolina: Chapel Hill, 1969.

C. LACHENMEYER, C. W., "An experimental technique for testing certain linguistic and psycholinguistic phenomena," *Language and Speech*, June, 1972.

d. SCRIVEN, *op. cit.*

28. LACHENMEYER, *op. cit.*, note 27b.
29. LACHENMEYER, *op. cit.*, note 27c.
30. SIDMAN, *op. cit.* (note 11, Intro.)
31. GALTUNG, J., *Theory and Methods of Social Research.* New York: Columbia University Press, 1967.

Chapter 2

1. NATSOULAS, T., "What are perceptual reports about?" *Psychological Bulletin*, 1967, **67**, 249–272.

   LACHENMEYER, C. W., "The reduction of psychology to physiology," *Journal of General Psychology*, 1972, **86**, 39–53.

2. BERLYNE, D. E., "Curiosity and exploration," *Science*, 1966, **153**, 25–33.

3. RESCHER, N., (*The Logic of Commands.* New York: Dover Publications, 1966) suggests termination as the criterion for evaluating the efficacy of commands.

4. BUNGE, M., *Causality.* Cambridge: Harvard University Press, 1959.

5. HEMPEL, C. G., *Aspects of Scientific Explanation.* New York: The Free Press, 1965.

6. GALTUNG, *op. cit.* (note 31, Ch. 1), makes a similar point.

7. COHEN, M. R., and E. NAGEL, *An Introduction to Logic and Scientific Method.* New York: Harcourt Brace Jovanovich, 1934.

8. *Science Journal*, 1970, **6** (#7), p. 11.

   Science Journal, 1970, **6**, p. 15.

9. YANG, C. N., *Elementary Particles: A Short History of Some Discoveries in Atomic Physics.* Princeton, N.J.: Princeton University Press, 1962.

10. CARNAP, *op. cit.* (note 9b, Ch. 1)

    NORTHROP, R., *The Logic of the Sciences and Humanities.* New York: Macmillan, 1947.

11. BLALOCK, H. M., "The measurement problem: A gap between the language of theory and research." In H. M. Blalock and A. B. Blalock, eds., *Methodology in Social Research.* New York: McGraw-Hill, 1968.

12. WITTGENSTEIN, *op. cit.* (note 10, Ch. 1)
13. CARNAP, *op. cit.* (note 9b, Ch. 1)
    NAGEL, *op. cit.* (note 6, Intro.)
14. TARSKI, *op. cit.* (note 4, Ch. 1)
15. WITTGENSTEIN, *op. cit.* (note 10, Ch. 1)
16. CARNAP, *op. cit.* (note 9a, Ch. 1)
17. HEMPEL, *op. cit.* (note 6, Intro.)
18. POPPER, *op. cit* (note 6, Intro.)
19. ANDERSON, M. H., "Functional measurement and psychophysical judgment," *Psychological Review*, 1970, **77**, 1953–170.
    KRANTZ, D. N., and TVERSKY, A., "Conjoint measurement analysis of composition rules in psychology," *Psychological Review*, 1971, **78**, 151–169.
20. GOODMAN, M. and QUINE, W. V., "Steps toward a constructive nominalism," *Journal of Symbolic Logic*, 1947, **12**, 105–122.
    HEMPEL, C. G., "The theoretician's dilemma: a study in the logic of theory construction." In H. Feigl, M. Scriven, and G. Maxwell, eds., *Minnesota Studies in the Philosophy of Science*, vol. II. Minneapolis: University of Minnesota Press, 1958.
21. An excellent source for all these examples in *The Way Things Work*, vol. 2. New York: Simon & Schuster, 1971.
22. JOHNSTON, J. W., MOULTON, D. G., and TURK, A., eds., *Communication by Chemical Signals*. New York: Appleton-Century-Crofts, 1971.
23. BONNER, J. T., "Hormones in social amoebae and mammals," *Scientific American*, 1969, **220**, 78–91.
24. POPPER, *op. cit.* (note 6, Intro.)
25. See SCRIVEN, M. S., "Definitions, explanations, and theories." In H. Feigl, M. Scriven, and G. Maxwell, eds., *Minnesota Studies in the Philosophy of Science*, vol. II. Minneapolis: University of Minnesota Press, 1958.
26. POPPER, *op. cit.* (note 6, Intro.).
27. The original and classic formulation of Steven's concept of measurement appears in STEVENS, S. S., "On the theory of scales of measurement," *Science*, 1946, **103**, 677–680. That his ideas have remained relatively invariant over the years can be seen in one of his most recent formulations of the concept of measurement: STEVENS, S. S., "Measurement, statistics, and the schemaperic view," *Science*, 1968, **161**, 849–856.

28. SAVAGE, C. W., *The Measurement of Sensation.* Berkeley: University of California Press, 1970.

29. LUCE, R. D., Review of S. W. SAVAGE, "The Measurement of Sensation," *Science*, 1971, **171**, 165–166.

30. KAPLAN, *op. cit.* (note 6, Intro.)

31. See ADAMS, E. W., "On the nature and purpose of measurement," *Synthese*, 1966, **16**, 125–169.

32. KAPLAN, *op. cit.* (note 6, Intro., p. 187)

33. For a review of the measurement literature including Campbell's original formulations see ADAMS, *ibid.*, and KRANTZ, D. H., "A survey of measurement theory." In G. B. Dantzig and A. F. Veinott, Jr., eds, *Mathematics of the Decision Sciences, Part 2.* Providence, R. I.: American Mathematical Society.

34. *Op. cit.*, note 33.

35. SAVAGE, *op. cit.*

36. TAYLOR, J. G., "Particles faster than light," *Science Journal*, 1969, 5A; 42–47.

37. INKELES, A., *What is Sociology?* Englewood Cliffs, N.J.: Prentice-Hall, 1964.

    OSGOOD, C. E., SUCI, G. J., and TANNENBAUM, P. H., *The Measurement of Meaning.* Urbana: University of Illinois Press, 1957.

    WITTGENSTEIN, L., *Tractatus Logico-Philosophicus.* Trans. by D. F. Pears and B. F. McGuiness. London: Routledge and Kegan Paul, 1961.

38. OSGOOD, *et al.*, *ibid.*

39. SAVAGE, *op. cit.*

40. OLDSTONE, M. B. A., and DIXON, F. J., "Inhibition of antibodies to nuclear antigen and to DNA in New Zealand mice infected with lactate dehydrogenase virus," *Science*, 1972, **175**, 784–785.

41. GREEN, T. R., and RYAN, C. A., "Wound-induced proteinase inhibitor in plant leaves: A possible defense mechanism against insects," *Science*, 1972, **175**, 776–778.

42. KERLINGER, *op. cit.* (note 1, Intro., p. 191)

43. *Ibid.*, p. 422.

44. SIMON, *op. cit.* (note 1, Intro., p. 301)

45. *Ibid.*, p. 301.

46. SCRIVEN, *op. cit.* (note 18, Ch. 1)

47. CARDWELL, D. S. L., *From Watt to Clausius*. Ithaca, N.Y.: Cornell University Press, 1971.
48. BASTIAN, T., ed., *Quantum Theory and Beyond*. New York: Cambridge University Press. 1971.
49. KEMENY, *op. cit.* (note 6, Intro.)
50. WHITEHEAD, A. N., and RUSSELL, B., *Principia Mathematica*. Cambridge University Press, 1925.
51. The distinction between measurement as feedback and as a new class of information is not hard and fast. The criterial distinguishing attribute is that as feedback the action contingent on the measurement is the same at T_1 and T_2, while as new information the action at T_2 is different. Note, however, that the basic sequence of measurement-action-measurement-action is the same in both cases. As it is a truism that no action can be repeated without error, in practice there should be instances when it would be hard to distinguish measurement as feedback and as new class of information: i.e., as the action at T_1 cannot be repeated perfectly at T_2, the basis of the distinction becomes blurred.
52. PHILLIPS, *op. cit.* (note 1, Intro., pp. 204–205)
53. LACHENMEYER, C. W., "The subject matter of social science," *Journal of General Psychology*, 1972 (in press).
———, "A critique of social science measurement." Unpublished manuscript.
54. *Science Journal*, 1969, 5A, 16.

Chapter 3

1. BUNGE, *op. cit.* (note 4, Ch. 2)
2. BUNGE, *ibid.*
3. TARSKI, *op. cit.* (note 4, Ch. 1)
4. GALTUNG, *op. cit.* (note 31, Ch. 1, p. 310)
5. POPPER, *op. cit.* (note 6, Intro.)
6. GALTUNG, *op. cit.* (note 31, Ch. 1, pp. 451–458)
7. HEMPEL, *op. cit.* (note 20, Ch. 2)
8. See ADDINGTON, A. S., *The Nature of the Physical World*. New York: The Macmillan Co., 1929, Chapter X.
9. See HENDRY, D., *Conditioned Reinforcement*. Homewood, Illinois: Dorsey Press, 1969.

10. LOUNASMAO, O. U., "New methods for approaching absolute zero," *Scientific American*, 1969, **221**, 26–35.

11. MILLER, G. E., *et al.*, "Mercury concentrations in museum specimens of tuna and swordfish, *Science*, 1972, **175**, 731–734.

12. WEBB, E. J., CAMPBELL, D. T., SCHWARTZ, R. D., and SECHREST, L., *Unobtrusive Measures: Nonreactive Research in The Social Sciences*. Chicago: Rand McNally & Co., 1971.

13. *Ibid.*, p. 3.

14. *Ibid.*, p. 3.

15. *Ibid.*, p. 4.

16. See LACHENMEYER, *op. cit.* (note 8, Ch. 1)

17. Kaplan makes this point quite elegantly: KAPLAN, *op. cit.* (note 6, Intro., pp. 72–73)

18. WITTGENSTEIN, *op. cit.* (note 10, Ch. 1)

19. KAPLAN, *op. cit.* (note 6, Intro.)

20. See KINCHLA, R. A., and ALLAN, L. G., "A theory of visual movement perception," *Psychological Review*, 1969, **76**, 537–558.

21. MORISON, R. S., "Death: process or event," *Science*, 1971, **173**, 694–697.

    KASS, L. R., "Death as an event," *ibid.*, 698–702.

22. CARNAP, *op. cit.* (note 9a, Ch. 1)

23. LACHENMEYER, C. W., "The relation of investigation to measurement, *Dialectica*, in press.

24. LANE, H. L., "A behavioral basis for the polarity principle in linguistics." In K. Salzinger and S. Salzinger, eds., *Research in Verbal Behavior and Some Neurophysiological Implications*. New York: Academic Press, 1967.

25. See FRANCIS, R. G., *The Rhetoric of Science*. Minneapolis, Minn.: University of Minnesota Press, 1961; KANG, T. S., "Linking form of hypothesis to type of statistic: an application of Goodman's Z"; NOWAK, S., "Some problems of causal interpretation of statistical relationships." *Philosophy of Science*, 1960, **27**, 23–28. The statement that causal relationships can be expressed by frequency distributions of test outcomes in the $A \supset B$ and $\sim A \supset \sim B$ categories, given that A always temporally precedes B, is a simplification that is open to question. In greater agreement with the above references would be the statement that the equivalence relation can be expressed by such a distribution of outcomes. As noted

previously, the concept of "cause" is a problematic one. However, the stipulation of time order in addition to the specified distribution is a close enough approximation for the purposes of empirical research.

It should also be noted that there are other types of relationships that can be expressed by varying the number of cells according to level of scale of measurement of the antecedent and consequent conditions and by specifying different distributions of outcomes. These, however, are simple extensions of this mode of presentation, and the implication statement remains the preferred mode of expression of hypotheses. Interestingly, Kang's example (p. 361) of the use of the equivalence relation reinforces this preference by demonstrating how an otherwise viable sociological hypothesis is transformed into an absurdity by forcing it into the equivalence relation: i.e., [[[high fertility rate] if and only if [rural area]]]. There are no logical or linguistic constraints on the expression of this relationship in this way. However, by so doing, it would certainly be proven false a large proportion of the time. The dilemma which would then confront the sociological researcher is how to evaluate the original hypothesis in light of the results.

26. In *A System of Logic*, vol. I (New York: Harper, 1891), John Stuart Mill first presented his experimental methods, the methods of agreement and difference, the joint method, and the method of residues. These methods have become the base of modern logic: see COHEN, M. R., and NAGEL, E., *An Introduction to Logic and the Scientific Method.* New York: Harcourt Brace Jovanovich, 1934. These methods can be restated according to the present logic of proof and falsification. In the method of agreement the inference that A causes P is justified if P occurs under conditions A, B, and C, and P occurs under conditions A, not-B, and not-C. This means that A will be said to cause P; if A, then P. It is now well recognized that Mill was wrong in this assertion. In the method of difference, the inference that A causes P is justified if P occurs under conditions A, B, and C and, if $\sim A$, B, C, then $\sim P$; if $\sim A$, $\sim B$, C, then $\sim P$; if $\sim A$, B, $\sim C$, then $\sim P$; if $\sim A$, $\sim B$, $\sim C$, then $\sim P$. This translates, A will be said to cause P, if A, then P, and if $\sim A$, then $\sim P$. In the joint method, A will

be said to cause *P* if the following hold: *A, B, C* ⊃ *P*; *A*, ∼ *B*, ∼ *C* ⊃ *P*; ∼ *A, B, C* ⊃ ∼ *P*. This translates into the pair *A* ⊃ *P* and ∼ *A* ⊃ *P* with the added condition of replication. Finally, in the method of residues, the scientist can be said to discover *X* under the following conditions: *A, B, C* ⊃ *X*; *A*, ∼ *B*, ∼ *C* ⊃ *X*; and *X* is not immediately known. This translates into if *A* ⊃ *X* where *X* is not known. The important point is that Mill's methods translate into the crucial comparisons plus replication. His emphasis is different in that he has postulated a series of conditions entailing irrelevant and relevant comparisons.

27. POPPER, *op. cit.* (note 6, Intro.)
28. LACHENMEYER, *op. cit.* (note 8, Ch. 1)
29. LACHENMEYER, C. W., "Literary, conventional, and scientific language systems," *Journal of Literary Semantics*, in press.
30. Randomization as a concept has extensive utility throughout all of science [see POPPER, *op. cit.* (note 6, Intro.)]. In this extensive sense, it is a key component of scientific theorizing and mathematics. However, as a control procedure, it is almost exclusively used in sciences whose events are organisms. (There are important exceptions to this rule.) In this intensive sense, randomization is used as a rule for sorting and selecting individuals for study. It is in this sense that randomization is being dealt with in the text. This, of course, is most relevant to the concerns of social science.
31. TVERSKY, A. T., and KAHNENNAN, D., "Belief in the law of small numbers," *Psychological Bulletin*, 1971, **76**, 105–110.

Chapter 4

1. LACHENMEYER, *op. cit.* (note 8, Ch. 1)
2. LACHENMEYER, C. W., Status inconsistency as a subset of behavioral conflict, *Pacific Sociological Review*, 1968, **13**, 81–94.
3. LACHENMEYER; KADUSHIN, *op. cit.* (note 8, Ch. 1)
4. KROEBER, A. L., and KLUCKHON, C., *Culture: A Critical Review of Concepts and Definitions*. Cambridge, Mass.: The Museum, 1952.
5. MANDLER, G., and KESSEN, W., *The Language of Psychology*. New York: John Wiley & Sons, Inc., 1959.

6. MACHLUP, F., *Essays in Economic Semantics*. New York: W. W. Norton and Co., Inc., 1967.

7. BERELSON, B., and STEINER, G. A., *Human Behavior: An Inventory of Scientific Findings*. New York: Harcourt Brace Jovanovich, 1964.

8. SKINNER; KESSEL, *op. cit.* (note 16, Ch. 1)

9. For example, see, ZIMBARDO, P., and EBBESEN, E. B., *Influencing Attitudes and Changing Behavior*. Reading, Mass.: Addison-Wesley Publishing Co., 1970, pp. 114–121.

10. AYLLON, T., and AZRIN, N., *The Token Economy*. New York: Appleton-Century-Crofts, 1968.

11. DEUTSCH, M., "The effect of motivational orientation upon trust and suspicion," *Human Relations*, **13**, 123–139, 1960.

12. BERELSON and STEINER, *op. cit.*

13. PREMACK, D., "Language in Chimpanzee," *Science*, 1971, **172**, 808–822.

14. LACHENMEYER, C. W., "The effectiveness of a 'recreational' and 'therapeutic' encounter with psychiatric patients," *The Journal of Psychology*, 1971, **79**, 295–297.

15. SZASZ, T. S., *The Manufacture of Madness: A Comparative Study of the Inquisition and the Mental Health Movement*. New York: Harper & Row, 1970.

16. *1972 Criminal Justice Plan: The City of New York*. Executive Committee, Criminal Justice Coordinating Council.

17. STEVENS, *op. cit.* (note 27, Ch. 2)

18. *Op cit.* (note 12, Intro.)

19. BIRDWHISTELL, R., *Kinesics and Context*. Philadelphia: University of Pennsylvania Press, 1970.

20. SOMMER, R., "Small group ecology," *Psychological Bulletin*, 1967, **67**, 145–152.

———, *Personal Space: The Behavioral Basic of Design*. Englewood Cliffs, N.J.: Prentice-Hall, 1969.

21. BARKER, R., *Ecological Psychology*. Stanford: Stanford University Press, 1968.

22. WEBB *et al.*, *op. cit.* (note 12, Ch. 3)

23. GLASER, B. G., and STRAUSS, A. L., *The Discovery of Grounded Theory*. Chicago: Aldine, 1967.

24. BERELSON and STEINER, *op. cit.*, p. 453.

25. *Ibid.*

26. WEBB *et al.*, *op. cit.* (note 13, Ch. 3, p. 2)

27. BLALOCK, *op. cit.* (note 22, Intro., and note 11, Ch. 2)

28. WEBB *et al.*, *op. cit.* (note 12, Ch. 3, p. 39)
29. *Ibid.*, p. 57
30. BLALOCK, H. M., "Status inconsistency and interaction: some alternative models," *American Journal of Sociology*, 1967, **72**, 305–315.
31. DUNCAN, *op. cit.* (note 12, Intro.)
32. LABOVITZ, S., "The assignment of numbers to rank order categories," *American Sociological Review*, 1970, **35**, 515–524.
33. BURGESS, R. L., and BUSHELL, D., *Behavioral Sociology*. New York: Columbia University Press, 1969.
34. MILBY, J. B., "Modification of extreme social isolation by contingent social reinforcement," *Journal of Applied Behavior Analysis*, 1970, **3**, 149–152.
35. STEVENS, *op. cit.* (note 27, Ch. 2)
36. DUNCAN, *op. cit.* (note 12, Intro.)
37. SOMMER, *op. cit.*
38. HOMANS, G. C., *The Elementary Forms of Social Behavior*. New York: Harcourt Brace Jovanovich, 1961.
39. BURGESS and BUSHELL, *op. cit.*
40. COTTRELL, L., "The analysis of situational field in social psychology." *American Sociological Review*, 1942, **7**, 370–382.
————, "The adjustment of an individual to his age and sex role," *American Sociological Review*, **7**, 617–620.
41. CHOMSKY, N., "Verbal behavior (a review)," *Language*, 1959, **35**, 26–58.
42. LACHENMEYER, C. W., "A technique for the codification of common-sense predictions," *Psychological Reports*, 1971, **29**, 545–546.
LACHENMEYER, *op. cit.*, note 14.
43. BRODBECK, M., "Methodological individualism: definition and reduction," *Philosophy of Science*, 1958, **25**, 9–17.
LAZARSFELD, P. F., "Evidence and inference in social research," *Daedalus*, 1958, **87**, 99–129.
WISDOM, J. O., "Situational individualism and the emergent group properties." In Borger, R., and Cioffi, F., eds., *Explanation in the Behavioral Sciences*. Cambridge University Press, 1970.
44. BRODBECK; WISDOM, *ibid.*
45. LACHENMEYER, C. W., "The subject matter of social science," *Journal of General Psychology* (in press).
46. BRODBECK; WISDOM, *op. cit.*

47. SOMMER, *op. cit.*
48. CROOK, J. H., *Social Behavior in Birds and Mammals.* New York and London: Academic Press, 1970.
    SEBEOK, *op. cit.* (note 12, Intro.)
49. *Ibid.*
50. *Ibid.*
51. *Ibid.*
52. *Ibid.*
53. BURGESS and BUSHELL, *op. cit.*
54. WEISS, R. F., and MILLER, F. G., "The drive theory of social facilitation," *Psychological Review,* 1971, **78,** 44–57.
55. LACHENMEYER, C. W., "Reduction in sociology: A pseudo-problem," *Pacific Sociological Review,* Fall 1970, 211–217.
56. HYMAN, H., *Survey Design and Analysis.* Glencoe, Illinois: Free Press, 1955.
57. GALTUNG, *op. cit.* (note 31, Ch. 1)
58. PARRY, H. J., and CROSSLEY, H. M., "Validity of responses to survey questions," *Public Opinion Quarterly,* 1950, **14,** 61–80.
59. PITTENGER *et al., op. cit.* (note 2, Intro.)
60. FRIEDMAN, *op. cit.* (note 5, Intro.)
    ROSENTHAL, *op. cit.* (note 4, Intro.)
61. PHILLIPS, *op. cit.* (note 3, Intro.)
62. SIDMAN, *op. cit.* (note 11, Intro.)
63. See BURGESS and BUSHELL, *op. cit.*
64. SCHMITT, D. P., and MARWELL, G., "Reward and punishment as influence techniques for the achievement of cooperation under inequity," *Human Relations,* 1970, **23,** 37–46.
65. MC GUIRE, W. J., The nature of attitudes and attitude change. In G. Lindzey and E. Aronson, eds., *Handbook of Social Psychology,* vol. III, Reading, Mass.: Addison-Wesley, 1969, 136–314.
66. CARNAP, *op. cit.* (note 9b, Ch. 1)
67. See MC GUIRE, *op. cit.*
68. ZIMBARDO and EBBESEN, *op. cit.*
69. TAGUIRI, R., "Person perception." In G. Lindzey and E. Aronson, eds., *Handbook of Social Psychology,* vol. III. Reading, Mass.: Addison-Wesley, 1969.
70. LACHENMEYER, *op. cit.* (note 45)

Chapter 5

1. GALTUNG, *op. cit.* (note 31, Ch. 1)
   SIDMAN, *op. cit.* (note 11, Intro.)
2. LACHENMEYER, *op. cit.* (note 8, Ch. 1)
3. The definition of "control" is analogous to the definition of "cause." As Hume has shown, there are no empirical correlates of "cause" in the sense that a relation exists that can be labeled unequivocally as "causal." "Cause," then, is a label for an inference based on certain empirical conditions. The same can be said of "control." Therefore, the only logically possible definition must be one that has a component referring to inferential thought processes (i.e., hypothesis formation).
4. SIDMAN, *op. cit.* (note 11, Intro.)
5. POPPER, *op. cit.* (note 6, Intro.)
6. SIDMAN, *op. cit.* (note 11, Intro.)
7. DEUTSCH, *op. cit.* (note 11, Ch. 4)
8. AX, A. F., "The physiological differentiation between fear and anger in humans," *Psychosomatic Medicine*, 1953, **15**, 433–442.
9. SIDMAN, *op. cit.* (note 11, Intro.)
10. BLALOCK, *op. cit.* (note 22, Intro.)
11. BLALOCK, H. M., *Social Statistics*. New York: McGraw-Hill, 1961.
12. BLALOCK, *op. cit.* (note 20, Ch. 4)
13. NAGEL, *op. cit.* (note 6, Intro.)
14. DUMONT and WILSON, *op. cit.* (note 9, Intro.)
15. HEMPEL, *op. cit.* (note 6, Intro.)
16. PHILLIPS, *op. cit.* (note 3, Intro., p. 16)
17. CAMPBELL, D. T., and STANLEY, J. C., *Experimental and Quasi-Experimental Designs for Research*. Chicago: Rand McNally, 1963, p. 5.
18. Brackets have been deleted in this example.
19. SIDMAN, *op. cit.* (note 11, Intro.)
20. CAMPBELL and STANLEY, *op. cit.*, p. 5.
21. *Ibid.*, p. 56: "design" 13a.
22. SELIGMAN, M. E. P., "Control group and conditioning," *Psychological Review*, 1969, **76**, 484–491. Seligman concludes similarly that there are no a priori rules for control group formation.

23. LAZARSFELD, P. F., "Latent structure analysis." In S. Koch, ed., *Psychology: A Study of a Science*, vol. 3. New York: McGraw-Hill, 1959.

24. COOMBS, C. H., *A Theory of Data*. New York: John Wiley & Sons, 1964.

25. WEBB *et al.*, *op. cit.* (note 12, Ch. 3)

26. COSTNER, H. L., "Theory, deduction, and rules of correspondence," *American Journal of Sociology*, 1969, **75**, 245–263.

27. BLALOCK, H. M., "Multiple indicators and the causal approach to measurement error," *American Journal of Sociology*, 1969, **75**, 264–272.

28. STEVENS, *op. cit.* (note 27, Ch. 2)

29. KRANTZ and TVERSKY; ANDERSON, *op. cit.* (note 19, Ch. 2)

30. HAMBLIN, R. L., "Ratio measurement for the social sciences," *Social Forces*, 1971, **50**, 191–206.

31. KRANTZ and TVERSKY, *op. cit.* (note 19, Ch. 2)

32. ANDERSON, *op. cit.* (note 19, Ch. 2)

33. KRANTZ and TVERSKY, *op. cit.* (note 19, Ch. 2)

34. SAVAGE, *op. cit.* (note 28, Ch. 2)

35. ANDERSON, *op. cit.* (note 19, Ch. 2)

36. JOHNSON, H. M., "Pseudo- mathematics in the mental and social sciences," *American Journal of Psychology*, 1936, **48**, 342–351.

LACHENMEYER, *op. cit.* (note 8, Ch. 1), Ch. 4.

LONDON, I. D., "Psychologists' misuse of the auxiliary concepts of physics and mathematics," *Psychological Review*, 1944, **51**, 266–291.

37. CRISWELL, J. H., SOLOMON, H., and SUPPES, P., *Mathematical Methods in Small Group Processes*. Stanford: Stanford University Press, 1962.

INDEX